Brown Sugar

ALSO BY JOYCE WHITE

Soul Food: Recipes and Reflections from African-American Churches

Brown Sugar

Soul Food Desserts from Family and Friends

JOYCE WHITE

HarperCollins*Publishers*

HarperCollins books may be purchased for educational, business, or sales promotional use. For information, please write: Special Markets Department, HarperCollins Publishers Inc., 10 East 53rd Street, New York, NY 10022.

FIRST EDITION

Designed by Jessica Shatan

Photographs on pages iv, 6, 108, and 238 © Laura Straus, NY; pages 156 and 184, courtesy Austin Hansen Collection, Photographs and Prints Division, Schomburg Center for Research in Black Culture, The New York Public Library, Astor, Lenox and Tilden Foundations; pages 50 and 208, courtesy of Photographs and Prints Division, Schomburg Center for Research in Black Culture, The New York Public Library, Astor, Lenox and Tilden Foundations.

Printed on acid-free paper

Library of Congress Cataloging-in-Publication Data
White, Joyce (Joyce Adams)
    Brown sugar / Joyce White.—1st ed.
        p. cm.
    ISBN 0-06-620973-0 (hardcover)
    1. Desserts. 2. African American cookery. I. Title.

TX773.W488 2003
641.8'6—dc21   2002068478

03   04   05   06   07   ❖/RRD   10 9 8 7 6 5 4 3 2 1

To Mama, Aunt Mary,

Aunt Agnes, Grandma Addie,

and my sister, Helen

For your tough hands and tender love

Contents

Preface

I just couldn't wait any longer. Mama and I had picked the blackberries early that morning in the woods surrounding our house in the Alabama county of my childhood, and now the fruit was piled high in an old enamel pan, as plump and tempting as jewels.

Gripped with excitement, I scattered 4 cups of blackberries into a pie pan and sprinkled on a couple handfuls of sugar, a dab of butter, and a pinch of cinnamon. I didn't yet know how to mix and roll out a piecrust, but there were a few biscuits left over from breakfast and I sliced the bread and arranged the pieces over the berries, making a kind of crust.

Pretty soon the kitchen was filled with the tart, sweet aroma of the berries, which, when I impatiently peeked into the oven, were edging the crusty biscuits with a thick, purplish-pink juice. Later when Mama returned home from visiting Aunt Agnes she said that I could have added a drop or two of vanilla extract but other than that my first-ever baked dessert was just fine.

And so began my informal training in the art of making desserts, which were always the crown jewels at our soul food table.

Over the following summers I watched and helped the women in my family pick blackberries, huckleberries, peaches, strawberries, muscadine grapes, figs, and several varieties of plums, which they turned into pies, cobblers, cakes, puddings, and fruit sauces that made hand-cranked vanilla ice cream even more delicious. We greeted numerous relatives and friends from up North at church revivals and family gatherings with our desserts, but we also thought of the winter ahead. And in doing so, we canned fruits and put up jars of jellies, jams, and preserves, so that we could enjoy our summer bounty at our winter table.

The fall of the year eased the intensity of the Alabama heat and ushered in the harvest of apples, pears, pecans, peanuts, sweet potatoes, and sugarcane, which became the new star ingredients at our table. Cinnamon-laced apple and sweet potato pies and pones edged out the peach and berry cobblers and pies of the summer. Pecans were baked in pies or sugared and turned into candy and pralines. Peanuts or goobers—the African word for peanuts—were roasted and eaten out of hand, stirred into cookie batter, or boiled with syrup for delectable peanut brittle. The juice from sugarcane was caramelized into molasses, which the improvisational women in the county used to flavor cakes and cookies. Pears were put into a brown bag, ripened to perfection, and then sugared, topped with allspice and nuts, and baked for a scrumptious dessert that was heavenly with ice cream or custard.

The year-end holidays brought on a frenzy of baking. The week after Thanksgiving Mama would make two or three fruitcakes, which she would wrap in a square of white cloth soaked in a little of the peach brandy she had made in the summer, and then wrapped again in foil, and stored to age in the old Empire credenza that still stands in our family home. A few days before Christmas our holiday baking would begin in earnest, as we began baking five or six more pies and cakes. All day long we would candy fruit peel, crack nuts, measure out spices, roll out pastry crusts, stir up cake batters. As the desserts baked, a heady, soul-satisfying aroma floated through our house as the busy pace of our lives halted for the holidays. On Christmas Day and for the next few days, Mama would bring out all of the desserts, and expected and unexpected guests alike would be offered a "slice of pie," or "a piece of cake." That was tradition.

I vividly remember—perhaps because these became my favorites over the years—a tart but sweet Pineapple Iced Cake (page 98), a thick and rich Spicy Molasses Pecan Pie (page 148), a light and ephemeral Lemon Meringue Pie (page 111), and a luscious Coconut- Peach Cake (page 85), which I have since learned goes back to our plantation days.

That information came from the late Velma Mosley, who showered me with recipes and family and church history for my first cookbook, *Soul Food: Recipes and Reflections from African-American Churches*. So much so that once I half-jokingly said to her, "I have to feature somebody else in this book other than your family and friends."

But there was no deterring Mrs. Mosley, who was a generous and spirited woman, and the day the Federal Express deliveryman handed me a package mailed from her home in Tyler, Texas, I was expecting another batch of recipes. But the package held photographs, and there she was, wearing an ankle-length dress, waist cinched, holding a little parasol jauntily over her head, dancing down an aisle at a social gathering.

Mrs. Mosley, a registered nurse and community activist, was meticulous about details and the photograph was captioned: CAKEWALK CONTEST, 1980, TYLER, TEXAS.

"I took the cake," she said to me excitedly over the phone when I called a few minutes later. "I won the cakewalk."

This conversation drove me straight to the Schomburg Center for Research in Black Culture in Harlem, where I learned that the cakewalk, a high-stepping dance, began on Southern plantations in the 1840s. Initially our ancestors probably performed the walk to provide physical and emotional release from the toil and backbreaking labor of the fields, or maybe just to make fun of the master's stilted waltz. But soon the plantation owners got in on the act, and often they would venture down to the clearing in the piney woods behind their carriage houses and watch the slaves couple-off and perform the dance. Prize for the couple executing the most intricate steps was a towering, extra-sweet coconut cake, which remains popular in the South to this day.

By the 1890s the cakewalk was performed at many African-American social gatherings and eventually at white political rallies, barbecues, and parties throughout the South, where it remained a popular pastime until the 1920s. The expressions "to take the cake," meaning first rate or first prize, and "piece of cake," meaning easy to do, grew out of this dance and moved into common usage. And again, this shows just how virtually every aspect of our life in this country—from our speech pattern to our inventive soul food—has influenced and shaped mainstream culture.

Truthfully, I can't think of anything I would rather do in the kitchen than make desserts. I enjoy the alchemy of taking the simplest ingredients: butter, sugar, flour, eggs, milk, flavorings, nuts, spices, fruits, jellies and jams, and transforming them into delectable creations. In an hour or two you can have crisp homemade cookies, beautiful tender cakes, aromatic pies, satiny puddings and custards, and home-churned ice cream that will have your guests vying for the pleasure of scrapping the dasher, just like I did when I was a child.

These are desserts for Sunday dinners, for special occasions, holidays, rituals, and celebrations. But when you think about it, a homemade dessert such as an apple tart made with honey, or a peach cobbler made with fresh ingredients, is far more nourishing than most fast food or store-bought junk. And is there anything more delicious and simple than a dessert bowl of watermelon chunks topped with a few sweetened berries?

This book, *Brown Sugar: Soul Food Desserts from Family and Friends,* features cookies, cakes, pies, custards and puddings, candies, ice cream, and simply delicious fruit desserts. The recipes come from family and friends across the country, and I thank all of you.

Jacqueline Corr of Detroit, a professional chef whose passion is making ice cream, sent me recipes for twenty of her delectable crank-churned concoctions, and then challenged me to pick the six I liked best! Another friend, Florida Ingram Brown, who grew up near Columbus, Georgia, but now lives in Altadena, California, sent me a stack of family recipes, including one for the beautiful bronze Caramel Cake (page 94), along with a rather terse note: "Nobody in L.A. knows how to make this cake anymore."

Thank you; they will now.

Friends from the Caribbean shared recipes for coconut pie, Jamaican-style spice cookies, plus several delectable tropical fruit desserts that brim with sunshine and goodness. Chloe McKoy, who hails from the beautiful island of Nevis, came to my apartment and walked me through the steps of the rum-infused West Indian Christmas Cake (page 103). I literally had to barricade my front door to keep out neighbors.

Most of the recipes featured in this book are straightforward and easy to do, not bogged down by hard-to-find ingredients and numerous steps. And in that vein, I share with you simple techniques for how to frost a cake without spending hours with a pastry bag forming elaborate rosettes and swirls, as well as how to flute and crimp picture-pretty piecrusts.

There are numerous how-to tips and background information on leavening agents, types of sugars, flours, chocolates, spices, and flavorings. I also share with you notes on equipment, which includes mixers, pie and cake plates, and measuring utensils.

The idea with desserts is to eliminate as much guesswork as possible, so that you can then let your creativity flow, our soul food signature. Enjoy.

Love and peace,
Joyce White

Thanks

So many people helped me with this book so I will express my thanks in no particular order, but simply by putting down the names as they come to mind. So profound thanks to:

Lynn Wilcox, head of the Literary Club at St. Albans Congregational Church in Queens, New York, who not only supported my first cookbook *Soul Food,* with zeal, but encouraged friends at the church to put their recipes on paper and contribute to this book. Thank you, Lyn; you are a grand and elegant woman, and often I wish I was back in school, so that I could sit in one of your classrooms and learn the wisdom of your teaching.

Special thanks also to my dear friend Shirley Brown of Farmington Hills, Michigan, who chides me constantly for not visiting often enough, as if New York is closer

to Detroit, than vice versa. Several years ago Shirley introduced me to her friend, Jacqueline Corr, who became my friend too. Jackie is an expert ice cream maker, and enthusiastically shared many of her recipes and techniques with me for this book. Thank you, dear Jackie.

My friend, and neighbors, Brenda and Mark Richardson are a joy. Not only did they set aside their busy schedules and taste recipe after recipe with me, but during the holiday season when I was closing out the book, rescued me from the demands of entertaining at home as I normally do. They simply invited me and several of my close friends to their home for holiday meals! Don't we love friends like that?

Special thanks also to my neighbor and friend Edith Collins. At the drop of a telephone call she would whisk over to my apartment—every hair in place, makeup perfect, clothes crisp and sparkling—and sit and taste desserts with me. Love you Edith.

My old college friend, Florida Ingram Brown, is as steady as the Rock of Gibraltar. We are both from the Deep South and share many of the same memories. Besides that, Florida is a real foodie, and her knowledge and expertise were just a phone call away.

My beloved brother, John, who has been leading me by the hand since I was 12 years old, went about in his deliberate way, prodding and gently cajoling, and collected a batch of recipes from family and friends on the Gulf Coast, where he lives. Thank you John, you are not only a cool brother but an extraordinary man. I love you.

Brian Maynard of KitchenAid sent equipment, and I thank you. My agents, Barbara Lowenstein and Madeleine Morel,

suggested this book, and what a wonderful idea. I thank you.

And the book was brought to fruition by the remarkable staff at HarperCollins, the publisher. My editor, Susan Friedland, always challenges me to do better, and usually I get mad and show her I can. Thank you Susan, for your guidance, patience, and most of all, for your confidence in me.

I also thank Monica Meline, assistant editor at HarperCollins, who graciously moved things along, as well as Estelle Laurence, the fine copy editor who checked the manuscript with a keen eye and judicious pen, and Jessica Shatan, the talented designer.

Finally, I thank all of my friends and family, especially nephews and nieces, who contributed to this book. And I relay my deep love in these pages to my wonderful son, Roy B. White, who helps me stay connected to both the past and the future.

Brown Sugar

INTRODUCTION

Sweet Talk: Kitchen Encounter

The kitchenware saleswoman looked at me with disbelief.

"You mean you are still making cakes and pies with those old portable beaters!" she exclaimed. "You better get modern and cut your mixing time in half. These stand mixers are for real. They do everything!"

I had just baked a dozen sweet potato pies for holiday gifts and my right elbow was aching from the whipping and stirring. I had been putting off buying a heavy-duty standing electric mixer for years, telling myself that the oversized gadget would take up the little counter space I had left in my kitchen. But as I stood telling all of this to the sister, I knew it was time to throw in the towel. So I took her advice, bought one of the miracle workers, and hurried home and looked around in my kitchen to see what else I had been "making do" with over the years.

I was about to make 115 desserts for this cookbook and knew that cakes, pies, cookies, puddings, and candy require more precision than stirring up a pot of stew or greens. Timing is critical, pan sizes are important, and you need sturdy and heavy saucepans that will stand up to scalding caramel sauce without buckling, or hold enough heat to thicken a custard without scorching.

I also needed a variety of mixing bowls, spoons, spatulas, ladles, thermometers, timers, and baking dishes, plus cutting boards, measuring equipment, and pastry utensils, all of which make easier and faster work.

I went shopping. Of course I overlooked

specialized designer equipment that only a restaurant pastry chef needs. I bought basic, durable cookware and equipment made by companies such as Revereware, Farberware, Ekco, Wearever, and Wilton. I found much of the equipment at discount outlets and at professional restaurant supply stores at bargain prices.

Once my kitchen was fully equipped, making the desserts for this book turned out to be "a piece of cake."

Here are suggestions for equipping your kitchen:

BEATERS: I kissed good-bye to a lot of old kitsch and found a permanent home for my new standing mixer on a countertop. The saleslady was right. My robot-like companion creams butter and sugar for cake batter, kneads dough for breads, whips heavy cream and egg whites, and does so with amazing efficiency and ease. And never complains about an aching arm.

I still use a hand mixer for making boiled frosting and candy, but I decided that my old model had seen its best day. I traded up to a new KitchenAid model, which is not as powerful as the standing mixer, but it is a pretty good pinch hitter. Trust me.

For years the blender was my primary workhorse. I used it to puree fruits, to whirl coconut milk, to whip up ice cream shakes, and to fluff up frozen sherbet.

Recently a well-intentioned friend sent me a food processor, along with a chiding note about how it makes perfect piecrusts, rambling on about labor-saving devices. Never mind. I am still making piecrusts by hand, but that food processor is slowly moving my blender to the side. It does all the above, plus chops nuts and citrus peels and grates coconut.

Tip: When chopping nuts or grating peel in the processor, add a few tablespoons of the sugar or flour called for in the recipe to the nuts or peel. The dry ingredients will prevent the nuts or peel from sticking and the processor can do its job better.

POTS AND PANS: Standard 8- or 9-inch round cake pans, $1^1/_2$ inches deep, are recommended for layer cake recipes in this book, all of which are multilayered and best baked in shallow pans.

Most of the other cakes in this book are baked in one pan, and the key concern is that the batter should reach about two-thirds full. Less than that and the cake will not rise or brown properly and will end up dry and crusty; if you add more than two-thirds batter, it is likely to spill over during the baking and make a mess. If your cake pan is not big enough, simply fill it two-thirds the way and bake the remaining batter as cupcakes for about 20 minutes at 350 degrees.

But the nice thing about cake pans is that they really aren't all that expensive and you can buy an array without going broke.

I particularly like Wilton's 8 × 3-inch round pan, 9 × 2-inch round pan, and the company's 9 × 3-inch contour pan, which has a graceful sloped bottom. For a little more dramatic presentation, consider at least one 7- or 8-cup fluted kugelhopf or fluted mold or ring pan.

A 9 × 5 × 3-inch loaf pan is nice for baking small fruitcakes and banana cake, and springform pans can be used for both batter cakes and cheesecakes. I have an 8$^1/_2$ × 2$^1/_2$-inch and a 9 × 3-inch springform pan and get plenty of use from both. Add an 8- or 9-inch square pan and use it for brownies, fudge, and other candy.

All of these cake pans should be made of heavy-gauge aluminum or tinned steel, which is a good conductor of heat, and should be bright and shiny. Dull, dark pans cause cake layers to brown fast and unevenly, and for that reason, I am not crazy about nonstick pans for layer cakes.

When making cookies, it is a good idea to use two or three baking sheets, so that you can assemble one pan of cookies while the other one is baking in the oven. And have ready at least two large wire racks for cooling the cookies (see Cookie Points, page 32).

Reminder: Look for a baking sheet that has only one or two turned-up or lipped sides, which allow the cookies to brown evenly. Don't confuse this type of baking sheet with an old-fashioned jelly-roll pan, which must have four sides to contain a batter. The jelly-roll pan is used to make sponge cakes for those luscious pinwheels filled with whipped cream, and with jelly and jam.

As for pies, ovenproof glass (Pyrex) allows you to look at the crust and determine when it is brown enough. Glass pie pans also hold heat better than aluminum, resulting in a crisper crust. You can use the 9- or 10-inch pie pan for recipes in this book.

Many pies look fabulous made in the two-piece tinned pan with the removable bottom that the French use for fruit tarts and the savory custard pie known as quiche. I often use a 10-inch tart pan to bake chess pies or for cream pies, and it is a perfect fit.

Most of the custard and bread pudding recipes in this book call for a 1$^1/_2$- to 2-quart baking dish, which can go from the oven to the table and make a nice appearance. Pyrex, Corning, and Anchor Hocking offer a wide variety. Le Creuset also makes attractive enameled cast-iron baking dishes that are fine for puddings, custards, and fruit cobblers.

A large roasting pan or a 12-inch cast-iron skillet can hold a water bath for custards and puddings, and a double boiler comes in handy for melting chocolate and for cooking delicate custards, especially for ice cream. Candy making requires a heavy saucepan or deep skillet that holds at least 4 quarts, such as the enameled cast iron made by Le Creuset. All-Clad also makes excellent cookware.

THE HEAT: Ovens can be real temperamental, so check the temperature with an oven thermometer every few months to determine if yours has "gone off." Any fluctuation of more than twenty degrees should be dealt with immediately; have the thermostat calibrated by a professional.

You'll also need a candy thermometer, preferably a glass metal-backed clip-on variety, which is both durable and accurate. Have at least two on hand in case you break one during a fast-paced candy-making session.

Taylor makes a deep fry thermometer that can pinch hit for a candy thermometer. And remember that all-glass thermometers are real accurate but they are fragile and break quite easily.

MEASURING UP: A while back I spent a few weeks with my sister, Helen, and every time she got ready to bake one of her delicious cakes, I would grab measuring cups, spoons, and a notepad and jot down just what she meant by a "teacup" of this and a "pinch" of that.

One day a neighbor was visiting, and finding herself fully amused by my antics, said: "You mean after all these years you still have to measure what goes in a cake?"

Most times. I use heatproof glass measuring cups for liquids, such as milk, water, and juice. The 2- and 4-cup size are more practical than the 1-cup, since they hold more and can serve as a mixing utensil for hot custards and sauces. All of these have a rim above the top cup line so as to prevent spillage. Set the cup at eye level and fill to desired mark; never to the rim of the cup.

Dry ingredients such as flour and sugar should be measured in graduated nesting cups, not in glass measuring cups with a rim. Fill the cup to heaping full and then level off the excess with the edge of a knife or metal spatula so that the measurement is accurate. Remember to measure flour by spooning it into the cup rather than scooping with the cup.

Also use graduated measuring spoons for baking powder, baking soda, and spices. Dip the correct spoon size into the box or can or bag of each ingredient, fill, lift out, and level off with the edge of a knife or metal spatula.

Measuring cups for dry ingredients run from $1/4$ to 1 cup, and the measuring spoons from $1/8$ teaspoon to 1 tablespoon. These are made in stainless steel and heavy-duty plastic. Keep several sets on hand so you don't have to stop and wash when you are cooking.

A kitchen scale is indispensable. I use it to weigh sweet potatoes, apples, peaches, plums, pears, and other produce, especially when making fillings for pies or canning preserves. I have a Hanson model that is as old as my grown son, but it still serves me well. Many other fancy models are on the market today.

The majority of the cakes in this book were made with either all-purpose or cake flour and the exact type of flour is specified in each recipe. Self-rising flour, which is all-purpose or cake flour already mixed with baking powder and salt, won't work in the recipes, and is not used.

Unbleached all-purpose flour is increasingly popular; it has a higher protein (gluten) content than either cake or bleached all-purpose flour and yields a product with soft but firm crumbs and texture. It is fine for rustic one-pan cakes, such as the Honey Carrot Cake (page 61).

And yes, one capful of vanilla extract does equal 1 teaspoon.

STIR IT UP: Stainless steel bowls are light to handle, nestle easily, don't take up much space or break, but they aren't nearly as pretty as glass or ceramic bowls. I use a variety of bowls, including tinted Pyrex from the 1950s, and several old earthenware bowls that my sister gave me, plus small heatproof custard cups for melting chocolate or holding an egg yolk, and I also have a nest of stainless steel bowls.

Whatever bowls you choose, buy as many as you can store, in different sizes. They'll get plenty of use.

You also need a dozen or so stirrers, such as a couple wire whisks for making custards and sauces, wooden spoons to stir hot syrup for candy, rubber spatulas for scraping the cake or cookie batter bowl, and several large stainless steel spoons—including the slotted type—for mixing berries and other fruits.

A metal spatula can be used to transfer cookies to a cooling rack, to spread on cake frosting, and to scrape dough from the pastry cloth or kitchen counter. They come in several sizes and widths.

THE CUT: A chopping board and a set of high-quality knives will allow you to chop nuts and cut citrus peel into exactly the size you want. For health reasons, if you use wood chopping boards, buy at least two. Reserve one for fish, chicken, and meat, and the other for fruits, vegetables, and nuts. Wash and scald both boards after every use.

Make sure that one knife has a serrated blade, and use it to cut a cake into serving wedges, or to cut a cake layer horizontally in half so you can double the number of layers. The serrated edge prevents the cake from becoming mushy and heavy when you press down and cut.

The peels of lemons, limes, oranges, tangerines, and grapefruit are full of natural oils and flavoring; I use them often in desserts. For strips, cut away the peel with a vegetable peeler, making sure you avoid the white pith, which is bitter.

Use a food processor or a four-sided box grater—the second smallest holes— to grate both nutmeg and citrus peel for zest. When using freshly grated zest or spices in cake batters, cream the flavoring with the butter and sugar, since this abrasive action releases the essential oil and aroma.

A juicer, either a glass or aluminum or ceramic reamer, is indispensable for juicing lemons, limes, and oranges. My vintage Foley squeezer gets a lot of use when I make desserts.

I grind spices such as cardamom and coriander seeds and allspice and juniper berries in an inexpensive coffee grinder, which does an excellent job. A small mortar and pestle, in marble, is also handy.

DESSERT PRATTLE: I often have two timers going at the same time when I make desserts; one in the kitchen and the other in my apartment office, in case I check the computer and get carried away and forget I have a cake going in the oven.

There are many reliable, inexpensive windup timers for ten dollars or less, so don't stint on these. Digital timers cost a few dollars more but are handy and accurate. Timing is critical when baking cakes and cookies.

A few years ago I got fed up with skimpy store-bought pastry cloths, which seem to shrink an inch after every laundering. I bought two yards of heavy, natural-colored canvas at a fabric shop, cut the fabric into generous squares, and now I have the best pastry cloths ever.

A rolling pin is needed for making piecrusts and for rolled cookies. If you cover the rolling pin with a cotton sleeve or stocking, it keeps the dough from sticking and absorbing excess flour, which can make it leather-like and tough.

A set of cookie cutters will help you cut fancy shapes during holiday baking. Pastry brushes can be used to apply glaze to cakes and cookies, and to wipe away sugar crystals when you make candy.

You'll need a sifter—for aerating flour for a cake batter or cookies. If you sift the flour onto a square of wax paper or parchment paper, you'll have one less bowl to wash later. A sieve is also fine.

A large stainless strainer is necessary for straining custards, and a small tea strainer is ideal for dusting cookies or candy with sugar or cocoa.

Other essential kitchenware includes pastry bags and several tubes for decorating cakes, and parchment paper and wax paper for lining cake and cookie pans. Glass jars in various sizes with tight-fitting lids are perfect for storing spiced sugar, cookies, candies, spices, candied citrus peel, and chopped nuts.

If you decide to give candy and cookies, or cakes and pies for gifts, cardboard boxes, crepe and wrapping paper, decorative tin cans, tiny foil cups, and colorful ribbons make a bold statement.

DEEP FREEZE: There are many ice cream freezers on the market that don't require ice, most in the 1- to 2-quart range, and these technological genies make excellent ice cream. Top-rated brands are Krups, Cuisinart, and Donvier. A couple of spiffy imported models from Italy by two prominent ice cream makers, Musso and Simac, cost as much as a color TV or a used car.

White Mountain makes both hand-turn and electric crank ice cream freezers, and those old churners bring joy and ritual to homemade ice cream.

My childhood memories are still keen: a sweaty, wooden bucket ice cream freezer groaning under a shady tree on a hot Sunday afternoon, teasing us with its promise.

Go burn!

ONE

Some

Cookies

The Traveling Book Club certainly isn't a gathering of galloping gourmets—and that was never the intention—but when girlfriends meet food is usually served and good presentation does count and please. This is a home-based club, so the host spruces up the apartment or house, sets the table, and often a member or two arrives bearing a special dish—a boon to the presiding host.

Tina Callender is club president, and for dessert she often serves a platter piled with an assortment of cookies, so that the members can select their favorite kind. This seems to work out well, but occasionally somebody decides that a certain variety is just sublime, and all hands reach for that one.

She just shrugs at the odds, and reminds herself to bake a larger assortment the next time, since cookies can be made in so many ways. The dough can be dropped from a spoon or rolled out and cut into stars, half-moons, circles, triangles, squares, houses, trees. You can add nuts, spices, honey, molasses, chocolate chips, or finely minced dried fruits to the batter; scatter on bits of candied fruit or peel before baking, or fancy up with icing or a glaze.

And a frozen batch of cookie dough can be popped into the oven for both impromptu gatherings and expected guests, producing a delectable treat in no time. When time is tight, this is exactly what Tina does.

"We are all real busy," says Tina, a school librarian in New York City. "We try to prepare something quick and easy to do."

The Traveling Book Club was formed several years ago when Tina, her friend Jo-Ann Estella, a school principal, and several other sisters noticed that at social gatherings their conversations often turned to books. Not just man-bashing tomes about no-good brothers, but books on various subjects: finances, politics, travel, food, art and photography, other cultures.

So somebody hit upon the idea to start a book club and soon a format was set: every third Sunday from 2 P.M. to 5 P.M., with the venue (or household) changing every month, hence the name, Traveling Book Club. A preselected book would be discussed at each gathering, and when possible, a local author would be invited to the session, and the presiding host would serve food. The first meeting was at Tina's charming Brooklyn apartment, and after that at the homes of the other members, who are scattered about: some in upstate New York, others in New Jersey, one or two in Long Island.

All are longtime friends, and most of them met more than 20 years ago when they began working together as city schoolteachers or at the Board of Education. New members are always old friends of old members.

"We have mentored each other and cried together over the years," says Tina.

And shared cookies. Here's a recipe for an easy-to-do drop cookie:

Brown Sugar Cookies

1¾ cups all-purpose flour
½ teaspoon baking soda
Pinch of salt
1 teaspoon ground cinnamon, more if desired
½ teaspoon ground or finely crushed whole cloves
1 cup nuts, such as pecans or walnuts or blanched almonds

8 tablespoons (1 stick) unsalted butter, softened
1 cup light brown sugar, firmly packed
1 large egg, at room temperature
2 tablespoons dark rum or 1 teaspoon rum extract
1 to 2 tablespoons milk or plain yogurt
3 or 4 tablespoons brown sugar, preferably brown crystallized sugar (See Dark and Sweet, page 25)

Sift together the flour, baking soda, salt, cinnamon, and cloves. Coarsely chop the nuts. Set aside.

Combine the butter and sugar in a large mixing bowl. Using a handheld electric mixer set at medium-high or creaming speed, beat until light and fluffy, about 2 minutes, scraping the bowl with a rubber spatula once or twice. Add the egg and rum or rum extract and beat until well blended.

Using a wooden spoon, stir in the chopped nuts. Add the flour mixture a cup at a time, alternately with the milk or yogurt, mixing only until blended.

Cover the bowl and refrigerate the batter for at least an hour, or longer if desired.

Preheat the oven to 350 degrees. Lightly butter a baking sheet. Remove the cookie batter from the refrigerator and if it is stiff, knead with your fingers for a minute or so to warm it.

Using a heaping teaspoon of dough for each cookie, push the batter onto the baking sheet with a rubber spatula, placing the cookies 2 inches apart. Sprinkle the top of the cookies liberally with some of the sugar.

Set the pan of cookies in the center of the preheated oven on the middle shelf. Bake the cookies for 9 to 11 minutes, or until they are pale brown and firm, and lightly browned on the bottom, turning the pan front to back in the oven midway through the baking.

Remove the pan from the oven and let the cookies set for a minute or two on a wire rack. Then, remove the cookies from the pan with a metal spatula and cool completely on the rack.

Bake the remaining batter in batches, one pan at a time, in the same way.

Makes about 48 cookies

Sometime in the early 1900s, my maternal grandmother and my great-aunt settled in the southern tip of Choctaw County in Alabama, bringing a "funny" Geechee talk that had a different syncopation and rhythm than the local speech. Exactly where Grandma Addie and Aunt Agnes—sisters—came from was a matter of debate, but stories were rife with imagination.

Some said they left South Carolina in the company or perhaps employ—or both—of a rice planter; others said they were following brothers who walked with a determined gait. Or maybe, as my niece Pat says, they simply got their directions confused and thought they were following the North Star, when actually they were moving deeper southward.

But anyway, their speech pattern was passed on to Mama, and so was their determination. Shotgun houses were spotlessly kept, beautified with calendar pictures and church fans, ringed with plants and flowers, and fenced with "drink" bottles stuck in the loamy soil, neck upside down at a jazzy angle. Quilts patched with intricate Cubist-like designs, stitched together from colorful flour sacks and scraps of dress fabric bought at the local store, still remain in our family. Plain tables were set with scrumptious rice dishes, a Carolina specialty, and desserts, especially cakes and cookies, were often flavored with molasses and sesame seeds, two evocative ingredients.

My niece Pat is less than a half-decade younger than me and we both grew up with Aunt Agnes. But we have fewer memories of Grandma Addie, the mother of three mulatto children and no husband, who lost her memory and died during our early childhood.

Aunt Agnes, like Grandma Addie, was small in stature with high cheekbones, sloping forehead, and satiny skin the color of strong brewed coffee. She was slightly reserved, had a singsong voice, and carried a certain melancholy air, as if she was either trying to remember or forget something.

But what Pat and I remember most are Aunt Agnes's cookies: crunchy sesame wafers, aromatic but lacy molasses cookies, pale and tender wafers that were delightful with peach ice cream.

All were quick-and-easy drop cookies; no rolling required. The drop cookies included here span generations and geography, gathered from friends and family members far and near. All are delectable, fanciful, and memorable.

Sesame or Benne Wafers

Sesame seeds are indigenous to tropical Africa, and archaeological diggings and ancient scrolls indicate that the aromatic condiment was cultivated in the motherland as long ago as 1600 B.C.

Sesame is actually an herb, prized for its tiny seeds, which contain about 50 percent oil, although its leaves have long flavored food in Africa and India.

By the seventeenth and eighteenth centuries, sesame seeds, known as benne, were in widespread use in Africa and were brought to the Americas during the slave trade. South Carolina was a primary port of entry, and African-American cooks in and around Charleston made delectable confections, cookies, and cakes with the seeds.

This delicious recipe has been in our family almost a hundred years.

5 tablespoons unsalted butter, softened	¾ cup light or dark brown sugar, firmly packed
½ cup untoasted sesame seeds	
½ cup unbleached all-purpose flour	1 large egg, at room temperature
Pinch of salt	1 teaspoon vanilla extract

Melt 1 tablespoon butter in a heavy small skillet over low heat. Stir in the seeds and heat over medium-low heat, stirring frequently, for about 5 minutes, or until the seeds are very lightly toasted. Watch carefully and don't let the seeds burn.

Remove the pan from the heat and set aside. Sift together the flour and salt and set aside. Combine the remaining butter and sugar in a medium-size bowl.

Using a handheld electric mixer set at medium-high or creaming speed, beat until light and fluffy, about 2 minutes, scraping the sides of the bowl at least once with a rubber spatula. Add the egg and vanilla extract and beat until smooth.

Using a wooden spoon, stir in the sesame seeds, mix well, then stir in the flour, mixing only until blended. Cover the bowl with plastic wrap and chill the dough for 30 minutes to an hour.

Preheat the oven to 350 degrees. Line a baking sheet with parchment paper (see Note, page 12).

Using a rounded teaspoon of dough for each wafer, push the dough onto the baking sheet with a rubber spatula, placing the cookies about 3 inches apart.

Set the pan of cookies in the center of the preheated oven on the middle shelf. Bake the cookies for 10 to 12 minutes, or until the edges are lightly browned, turning the pan front to back in the oven midway through the baking.

Remove the cookies from the oven and set the pan on a wire rack. Using a metal spatula, immediately remove the cookies from the pan and cool on the rack.

Bake the remaining batter in batches, one pan at a time, in the same way.

Makes about 48 cookies

Note: If you don't have parchment paper, generously butter the baking sheets and dust lightly with flour. Bake the cookies and remove immediately from the pan after taking out of the oven, using a metal spatula to pry the cookies gently from the pan. The cookies don't stick to the parchment, but will stick to the pan and you have to remove them quickly and carefully.

Lemon Vanilla Wafers

My niece Pat is the only family member I have in New York other than my son, Roy. She and an African sister, Maria, who hails from Guinea, own a shop in the Riverdale section of the Bronx called Masidi's Urban African Store. The store, located on the busy Broadway thoroughfare, offers dazzling African fabrics, clothes, art, and crafts for sale. Masidi's is also a gathering place for book signings, fashion shows, music events, and after-church socials.

I baked a box of these cookies for a recent event at the store, using the recipe that Pat's mother, my sister, Helen, passed on to me from Aunt Agnes. These wafers are pale, elegant, and delicious.

1 cup unbleached all-purpose flour
Pinch of salt
10 tablespoons (1¼ sticks) unsalted butter, softened
1 cup confectioners' sugar, firmly packed

2 to 3 teaspoons grated lemon peel
2 medium egg whites, at room temperature
1 teaspoon vanilla extract, or more if desired
2 tablespoons lemon juice

Sift together the flour and salt and set aside.

Combine the butter, sugar, and lemon peel in a large mixing bowl. Using a handheld electric mixer set at medium-high or creaming speed, beat until light and fluffy for 2 or 3 minutes, scraping the bowl once or twice with a rubber spatula.

Add the egg whites and beat 1 minute longer, scraping the bowl as needed. Stir in the vanilla extract and lemon juice and mix well.

Using a wooden spoon, stir in the flour, mixing only until blended. Gather the dough into a ball in the center of the bowl. Cover the bowl with plastic wrap and chill for 30 minutes to an hour.

Preheat the oven to 375 degrees. Lightly butter a baking sheet and dust lightly with flour, inverting to shake off any excess flour.

Using a rounded teaspoon of dough for each wafer, push the dough onto the baking sheet with a rubber spatula, placing the cookies 2 inches apart. (Or, fit a pastry bag with a ½-inch tube. Fill about half full with the dough. Press out the strips of dough about 1½ inches long for each cookie, spacing 2 inches apart.)

Set the pan of cookies in the center of the hot oven on the middle shelf. Bake the wafers for 11 to 13 minutes, or until the edges are golden brown and crispy and the centers are puffy and firm, turning the pan from front to back in the oven midway through the baking. The center of the cookies will not brown during the baking.

Remove the pan from the oven and set on a wire rack; cool the cookies for a few minutes, and then remove from the pan with a metal spatula. Cool the cookies completely on a wire rack.

Bake the remaining batter in batches, one pan at a time, in the same way.

Makes 35 to 40 wafers

Drop and Bake

The best way to drop cookie batter is to scoop the batter with a teaspoon or tablespoon and then push the dough off the spoon with a rubber spatula onto the baking sheet, dropping about 2 inches apart. This way you get even-size cookies that look as though they have been rolled and cut.

If you prefer flat and crispy cookies (I do), gently flatten the mounds with your fingertips or a metal spatula. On the other hand, if a round and soft cookie is desired, like Tina's Brown Sugar Cookies (page 8), just drop and bake.

If I am making oblong cookies, such as Lemon Vanilla Wafers (page 13), I transfer the batter to a pastry bag and pipe out a 2-inch strip, since the shape holds better this way. Otherwise, it's back to the spoon and spatula, and no pastry bag to wash later.

All cookies though, whether drop or rolled, hold their shape better if the dough is chilled for at least 30 minutes; an hour is better. The chilling develops elasticity, yielding a smooth, glossy cookie. ❊

Molasses Lace Cookies

One day, when my son, Roy, was about ten years old, I made a batch of lace cookies that spread into thin wafers with a crinkled or webbed surface.

As soon as I pulled the pan out of the oven, I rolled each cookie around a buttered wooden spoon handle, and made a little tube for a rolled or curled effect. These are ideal for dipping into ice cream or filling with whipped cream.

Roy grabbed one of the rolled cookies and immediately exclaimed, "Mom, I love these candy-cookies."

There are many types of lace cookies, but I especially like the aromatic, crispy, and candylike cookies that Aunt Agnes made.

They are pretty and dressy and will please children and adults alike.

1 cup unbleached all-purpose flour
2 teaspoons ground ginger
Pinch of salt
8 tablespoons (1 stick) unsalted butter
$\frac{1}{2}$ cup light brown sugar, firmly packed

$\frac{1}{2}$ cup light molasses or dark corn
   syrup
$\frac{1}{2}$ teaspoon lemon juice or cider
   vinegar
$\frac{1}{4}$ teaspoon baking soda

Sift together the flour, ginger, and salt and set aside. Combine in a medium heavy saucepan the butter, sugar, molasses or syrup, and lemon juice or vinegar. Place on medium heat and cook, stirring for 4 or 5 minutes, just until the butter melts, the sugar dissolves, and the molasses or syrup is bubbling but not quite boiling.

Remove the pan from the heat and stir in the baking soda and mix well. Stir in the flour and mix only until just blended. Cool the batter and then chill for at least 30 minutes or longer.

Preheat the oven to 375 degrees. Lightly butter a baking sheet and dust lightly with flour, inverting to shake out any excess flour. Butter the handle of a wooden spoon and set aside.

Using a rounded teaspoon for each cookie, push the batter onto the baking sheet with a rubber spatula, placing at least 3 inches apart. The cookies will spread into lacelike rounds during baking. (Or, fill a pastry bag fitted with a $\frac{1}{2}$-inch tube with dough. Press out a quarter-size mound of dough for each cookie, spacing at least 3 inches apart.)

Set the pan of cookies in the center of the preheated oven on the middle shelf. Bake for 10 to 12 minutes, or until the cookies are crispy and brown around edges, turning the pan front to back in the oven midway through the baking.

Remove the sheet of cookies from the oven and set on a wire rack. Let cool for 2 to 3 minutes.

While still warm, lift the cookies from the pan with a metal spatula and quickly roll around the wooden spoon, forming tubes.

(If the cookies become too stiff to roll, set the pan of cookies back in the hot oven for a minute or two to soften.)

Cool the rolled cookies on a wire rack.

Bake the remaining cookies in batches, one pan at a time, in the same way.

Makes about 36 cookies

Note: If desired, omit the rolling and serve the cookies as flat, lacy wafers.

Rum Raisin Oatmeal Cookies

A few years ago when I was teaching a soul food class at the Hudson Guild, a local community center in my neighborhood, we decided to have an end of summer party in the center's beautiful rear garden.

We set up a barbecue grill, covered tables with pretty cloths, decorated the trees with balloons, and every class member brought a dish, or two.

Rita Reid graced the day with these wholesome oatmeal cookies, which none of us could stop eating.

Rita hails from St. Croix in the U.S. Virgin Islands, and I am sure it was the rum accent that made these cookies so popular.

½ cup dark raisins	8 tablespoons (1 stick) unsalted butter, softened
2 tablespoons dark rum	
¾ cup all-purpose flour	¾ cup dark brown sugar, firmly packed
½ teaspoon baking soda	1 large egg, at room temperature
½ teaspoon ground cinnamon	1 cup old-fashioned rolled oats, uncooked
Pinch of salt	

If the raisins are plump and large, chop coarsely. Combine the raisins in a cup or small bowl with the rum and toss well. Set aside.

Sift together the flour, baking soda, cinnamon, and salt and set aside.

Combine the butter and sugar in a large mixing bowl. Using a handheld electric mixer set at medium-high or creaming speed, cream the mixture for 2 minutes, scraping the bowl once or twice with a rubber spatula.

Add the egg and beat 1 minute longer.

Using a wooden spoon, stir in the oats and the raisins and rum. Add the flour mixture and beat the batter with the spoon until it is smooth and combined.

Cover the bowl and chill the dough for at least 30 minutes or longer.

Preheat the oven to 350 degrees. Lightly butter a baking sheet.

Using a rounded tablespoon of dough for each cookie, push the batter onto the baking sheet with a rubber spatula, placing at least 2 inches apart.

Set the pan of cookies in the center of the preheated oven on the middle shelf. Bake the cookies for 12 to 15 minutes or until they are just lightly brown and crispy, turning the pan from front to back in the oven midway through the baking.

Remove the pan from the oven and cool the cookies 2 to 3 minutes on the pan and then transfer to a wire rack with a metal spatula and cool completely.

Bake the remaining cookies in batches, one pan at a time, in the same way.

Makes about 24 cookies

Note: If desired, substitute 1 teaspoon rum extract for the dark rum. Mix the extract with a couple tablespoons of apple juice and stir into the batter.

Kwanza Peanut-Chocolate Cookies

Peanuts are not tree nuts, but are actually members of the bean and legume or pea family, and they grow beneath the ground under leafy plants. When I was a child my family called peanuts goobers, possibly after the African word *nguba*.

The peanut is a native of South America, probably of the country known now as Brazil. Slave traders carried the plant to Africa, and it was brought to the United States and the Southern states during the torturous slave trade.

Peanuts are full of nutrients, and they are wonderful in cookies made with chocolate and scented with coriander, such as this best-ever chocolate chip recipe.

The inspiration for this recipe comes from my friend Johanna Anguilé, who lives in Paris and hails from Gabon in West Africa, where dishes flavored with coriander are often topped with roasted peanuts.

I make these cookies for our annual Kwanza celebration, but they are good and evocative any time of year, for any occasion.

1½ cups all-purpose flour
Pinch of salt
¾ teaspoon baking soda
2 teaspoons coriander seeds
1¼ cups lightly toasted peanuts
8 ounces good-quality bittersweet or
   semisweet chocolate

12 tablespoons (1½ sticks) unsalted
   butter, softened
½ cup granulated sugar
¾ cup dark brown sugar, firmly packed
2 medium eggs, at room temperature
1 teaspoon vanilla extract

Sift together the flour, salt, and baking soda. Scatter the coriander seeds over the bottom of a small skillet. Set over low heat and toast for 4 or 5 minutes, swirling the pan a couple of times. Remove from the heat, crush the seeds in a coffee grinder or with a mortar and pestle or with a rolling pin, and combine with the flour mixture, mixing well. Set aside.

Chop the peanuts coarsely; if very small, leave whole. Chop or cut the chocolate coarsely into ¼-inch pieces. Set aside the peanuts and the chocolate.

Combine the butter and both sugars in a large mixing bowl. Using a handheld electric mixer set at medium-high or creaming speed, beat until light and fluffy, about 2 minutes, scraping the bowl with a rubber spatula once or twice. Add the eggs and vanilla extract and beat until well blended.

Using a wooden spoon, stir in the peanuts and chocolate. Add the flour and spice mixture, about $^1/_2$ cup at a time, mixing only until blended.

Cover the bowl with plastic wrap or wax paper and chill the dough for 1 hour.

Preheat the oven to 375 degrees. Lightly butter a baking sheet.

Scoop a rounded tablespoon of dough for each cookie, push the batter onto the baking sheet with a rubber spatula, placing about 2 inches apart. Lightly dampen your finger tips with cold water, form each mound of dough into a ball, and then press lightly and flatten to about $^1/_2$-inch thickness.

Set the pan of cookies in the center of the preheated oven on the middle shelf. Bake the cookies for 11 to 13 minutes, or until they are pale golden and firm on the top and the bottoms are lightly browned and crispy, turning the pan from front to back in the oven halfway through the baking.

Remove the cookies from the oven, cool on a wire rack for 1 to 2 minutes. Using a metal spatula, transfer the cookies to a wire rack and cool completely.

Bake the remaining batter in batches, one pan at a time, in the same way.

Makes about 48 cookies

Cinnamon Nut Cookies

It was hard for me to resist the urge to take one of the Scarf Lady's beautiful squares and use it as a tablecloth. But I didn't. This was when the owner of this charming boutique, Paulette Gay, invited me to set up a table and sign copies of *Soul Food* during a Saturday afternoon workshop at the shop, which is located on Lenox Avenue in Harlem.

My offering for the occasion was a large platter of cinnamon cookies, which my son, Roy, enjoyed as a child with a big mug of hot cocoa. And so did I—and still do.

They are aromatic and festive, and perfect to box and give as a gift during the Christmas holidays, along with one of Paulette's beautiful scarves. In fact, these tasty cookies are a thoughtful gift year-round, and so is a Scarf Lady scarf.

2¼ cups all-purpose flour
1 teaspoon ground cinnamon plus 2 to 3 teaspoons
Pinch of salt
8 tablespoons (1 stick) unsalted butter, softened

1 cup granulated sugar
2 medium eggs
½ teaspoon vanilla or almond extract
1 cup nuts, either pecans, walnuts, unsalted pistachios, or blanched almonds

Sift together the flour, 1 teaspoon of the cinnamon and the salt. Set aside.

Combine the butter and sugar in a large bowl. Using a handheld electric mixer set at medium-high speed, beat until light and fluffy, for about 2 minutes, scraping the bowl once or twice with a rubber spatula. Add the eggs and vanilla or almond extract and beat again.

Using a wooden spoon, stir in the flour mixture a cup at a time, mixing with a large spoon only until just combined. Shape the dough into a ball, dusting lightly with flour if it is sticky.

Wrap the dough in plastic wrap or wax paper, and chill for 1 hour, or until easy to handle.

Finely chop the nuts. (You can also pulse these nuts in a food processor. To do so, add 2 tablespoons of sugar to the nuts and pulse only until they are finely chopped, taking care not to grind into a paste.)

Combine the remaining cinnamon with the nuts and spread on a plate or in a shallow pan.

Preheat the oven to 350 degrees. Lightly butter a baking sheet. Remove the dough from the refrigerator.

Dampen your fingertips with cold water. Using a level tablespoon of dough for each cookie, shape the dough into tiny balls with your fingers or roll in the palm of your hands. Roll the balls in to the nut-cinnamon mixture, pressing firmly to cover all over.

Place the cookies on a baking sheet about 2 inches apart. Press down each cookie gently with your fingers to flatten slightly.

Set the pan of cookies in the center of the preheated oven on the middle shelf. Bake the cookies for about 12 minutes or until they are firm and set and the bottoms are lightly browned, turning the pan from front to back midway through the baking.

Cool on a wire rack for 2 minutes and then remove the cookies from the pan with a metal spatula and cool completely.

Bake the remaining batter in batches, one pan at a time, in the same way.

Makes about 36 cookies

Variation: Substitute 2 teaspoons finely grated orange peel or ground ginger for the cinnamon for an equally delicious flavor.

Jamaican Spice Cookies

Almost two decades ago Ernest McCaleb arranged for me to meet his friend Norma Boucher, thinking that since we were both sports fanatics, we could fight it out on the basketball or tennis court. We did. But Norma and I also became best friends.

Norma, a tennis player and coach, lives in Rochdale Village in Queens, New York. Besides being a superb sportswoman, she is an elegant hostess and fine cook.

Her specialty is her native cuisine, the spicy and succulent food of Jamaica, in the West Indies. These cookies are made with fresh ginger, and they are fragrant and delicious.

1 2-inch piece fresh ginger
1 cup granulated sugar
2 cups unbleached all-purpose flour
$\frac{1}{8}$ teaspoon salt
$\frac{1}{2}$ teaspoon baking soda
$1\frac{1}{2}$ teaspoons ground allspice
$\frac{1}{2}$ teaspoon grated nutmeg, mace, or ground cloves

12 tablespoons ($1\frac{1}{2}$ sticks) unsalted butter, softened
1 egg, at room temperature
2 or 3 tablespoons brown sugar, preferably brown crystallized sugar (see Dark and Sweet, page 25)

Peel the ginger and grate or chop finely. You should have 3 tablespoons. Combine the ginger and granulated sugar in a food processor and pulse until well combined, about 30 seconds. Set aside.

Sift together the flour, salt, baking soda, allspice, and nutmeg, mace, or cloves and set aside.

Combine the sugar-and-ginger mixture and butter in a large bowl. Using a handheld electric mixer set on medium-high or creaming speed, beat the mixture until it is light and fluffy, 2 to 3 minutes, scraping the bowl with a rubber spatula as needed. Stir in the egg and beat until well blended.

Using a wooden spoon, add the flour-and-spice mixture to the creamed mixture 1 cup at a time, mixing only until blended. Form the dough into a ball in the center of the bowl, cover, and chill for at least 2 hours.

Preheat the oven to 375 degrees. Lightly butter a baking sheet.

Scatter a tablespoon at a time of the brown sugar on the work surface.

Dampen the tip of your fingers with cold water. Using a level tablespoon of dough for each cookie, form the dough into balls with your fingers or roll in the palm of your hand.

Roll the balls of dough lightly in the sugar, and then place on the baking sheet about 2 inches apart. Lightly flatten the balls with a spatula or pat with your fingers to $1/2$-inch thickness.

Set the pan of cookies in the center of the hot oven on the middle shelf. Bake the cookies for 12 to 14 minutes, or until the bottoms are brown and the tops are lightly brown and firm, turning the pan from front to back in the oven midway through the baking.

Remove the pan from the oven and set on a wire rack. Let the cookies remain in the pan for 2 or 3 minutes; then remove the cookies with a metal spatula and cool completely on the rack.

Bake the remaining batter in batches, one pan at a time, in the same way, coating the cookies with the remaining brown sugar.

Makes about 30 cookies

Dark and Sweet Brown sugars with names such as muscovado, Demerara, golden baker's, golden caster, and amber crystals are bubbling hot.

These beauties come from the island of Mauritius off Africa in the Indian Ocean, and the sugars are totally different from the little boxes of supermarket brown sugar that we have been using for years. The new arrivals are made from the initial pressing of sugarcane grown in volcanic soil, and therefore retain much of their natural molasses, color, crystals, and distinctive burnished flavor.

No bad rap here on commercially boxed light and dark brown sugar. It adds a nice caramel flavor to desserts, but truth be told, this is actually white refined sugar that is coated with molasses.

But you'll be pleased with the robust flavor of the untamed "brownies." Most can replace light or dark commercial brown sugar in recipes, and are real showstoppers.

Muscovado comes in a light and dark variety, just like the regular supermarket light and dark brown sugar, but has much more flavor and complexity. Dark muscovado is delicious in hot cocoa on winter nights, adding a rumlike flavor and aroma. I also sprinkle it on apples for pies, and add to fudge sauce for a real bracing flavor. Light muscovado is nice in carrot cakes, peach cobbler, sweet potatoes pies, fruit batter cakes, and pecan pies.

Demerara is pale golden crystallized sugar and is similar in texture to turbinado, which is sold in health food stores and supermarkets as Sugar in the Raw. Both of these are great for sprinkling on cookies before baking, and for ice cream and custards.

Two other deep-flavored granulated sugars from Mauritius are golden caster and amber crystal, packaged by Simpson & Vail, which also makes excellent Dutch-process cocoa. Golden caster is a fine granulated sugar with tiny crystals. Amber crystal sugar has large crystals. Both sugars are light tan in color and add crunch to cookies, piecrust, or pudding.

Golden baker's sugar is more finely granulated than golden caster. It is soft, pale beige in color, and generally can be substituted for regular white granulated sugar in baking.

Golden baker's is especially lovely in meringue; it adds a nice tawny color, reminding me of the brown sugar meringue of the Old South. ❀

Years ago Camille Peoples spent weeks shopping for colorful tin cans and boxes to pack the twenty dozen cookies she bakes for her family's annual Christmas dinner in Queens, New York. But then she finally hit upon a novel idea that lifts recycling to artful practicality. She passed out tins of cookies at the end of the feast, and promptly told every recipient to save the container and bring it back the next year for a refill.

Some thirty family members and friends attend this gathering at her parents' home, and nobody balked. And that's because few people can resist a gift of home-baked cookies, and when the selection is as varied and lovingly tended as Camille's, it is eagerly awaited.

She makes at least eight or nine different types of cookies, including coconut macaroons, peanut butter and chocolate kisses, butterscotch bar cookies, oatmeal cookies, brandy rolls, rum balls, and my favorite, Aunt Ella's Butter Cookies (page 27), which are rich and tender.

Camille, a registered nurse, started her holiday baking more than fifteen years ago when she decided she was going to stop wasting time buying Christmas presents, realizing she could create more personal gifts in her kitchen. So three or four weeks before Christmas Day she assembles the ingredients. Soon afterward she makes and freezes the cookie batters. And then, three or four days before Christmas, she goes into a marathon mode and bakes around the clock, sending drive-you-crazy aromas from her brownstone apartment in Fort Greene, Brooklyn.

Her first baking project wasn't quite so sought after. That was almost four decades ago when, at the tender age of seven or eight, she decided to bake up a batch of cookies on the spur of the moment, and understandably, had a little trouble with the recipe.

"I put in a pinch of sugar and at least a half-cup of salt," she recalls, laughing. "My two younger brothers ate the salty cookies but they never stop letting me hear about it. But I've gotten better over the years."

And Aunt Ella's Butter Cookies (page 27), a recipe passed on by her father's sister, Aunt Ella, is a perfect and delicious example of her expertise.

Aunt Ella's Butter Cookies

Ideally, the standard or classic butter cookie recipe calls for an equal weight of butter and flour, and this translates into 1 cup or 2 sticks of butter and 2 cups of flour, both weighing about 8 ounces—the same. The sugar is to taste, but you can improvise and vary the basic recipe. Increase the flour and the cookies resemble a cake in texture; add more butter and they are delicate and feathery. Borrowing from a trick I learned from my own Aunt Mary, I usually mix in a little cornstarch with the flour, which adds a delightful silky texture to the cookies.

This is a rich dough, and when well chilled, it can be rolled and cut into fancy shapes, such as stars, trees, leaves, houses, half-moons, rounds, triangles, and bars.

However, many other cookie batters, such as gingersnaps, cocoa cookies, and sand tarts, are just as versatile, and in some cases, just as rich as butter cookie batter. Just roll out these cookie batters and reach for the cookie cutter.

I like butter cookies tinged with brown edges rather than soft and pale. And since these cookies have such a high butter content, they can change color and texture quite quickly. So begin checking the cookies for doneness after 9 minutes have passed, noting the time required for doneness to your liking. A longer baking time produces crisp but drier cookies.

1¾ cups all-purpose flour	1 cup granulated sugar
½ cup cornstarch	1 large egg, at room
¼ teaspoon salt	temperature
½ pound (2 sticks) unsalted butter, softened	1 teaspoon vanilla extract

Sift together the flour, cornstarch, and salt and set aside.

Combine the butter and sugar in a large bowl. Using a handheld electric mixer, beat the mixture at medium-high or creaming speed until it is light and fluffy, about 2 minutes, scraping the bowl once or twice with a rubber spatula. Add the egg and vanilla extract and cream 30 seconds longer.

Using a wooden spoon, add the flour mixture to the creamed mixture 1 cup at a time, stirring until just blended.

Shape the dough into a ball, dusting with a little flour if sticky. Cover the bowl with plastic wrap or wax paper, and chill the dough for 3 or 4 hours.

Preheat the oven to 375 degrees. Lightly butter a baking sheet and then dust with flour, shaking off the excess.

Remove the dough from the refrigerator and cut into four pieces. Using one piece of dough at a time (return the other three pieces of dough to the refrigerator while you form and cut the cookies), dampen your fingertips with cold water and shape into a log, about $1^1/2$ inches in diameter and about $3^1/2$ inches long.

Place the log on a chopping board lightly dusted with flour and cut crosswise into $^1/4$-inch slices.

Place the cookies an inch or so apart on the baking sheet. Shape another piece of dough in the same way, cut into cookies, and place on the baking sheet. Pat the scraps together and return to the refrigerator.

Set the pan of cookies in the center of the hot oven on the middle shelf. Bake the cookies for 11 minutes or until the edges are lightly browned and the centers are pale but firm, turning the pan from front to back in the oven midway through the baking.

Cool the cookies on a wire rack for 2 minutes, and then remove from the pan with a metal spatula and cool completely on the wire rack.

Form it into a log and bake the remaining dough in the same way, one pan at a time. Reshape the scraps when well chilled and bake as directed above.

Makes about 48 cookies

Variation: This dough can also be cut with a cookie cutter. Place each piece of dough on a very lightly floured work surface, top with a sheet of wax paper, and lightly roll or pat out into a 10-inch circle, about $^1/4$-inch thick. Remove the wax paper. Dip a 2-inch cookie cutter into flour, shake off the excess, and cut out the cookies, coating the cutter with flour as needed.

Cookie Cutters

Cookie Cutters Butter cookie dough is rich, tender, and plain, the perfect foil for adding spices and flavoring. Bake these variations and you end up with a half-dozen different cookies from one basic dough. Remember, this batter works best when well chilled.

Brown and Bold: Substitute 1 cup light brown sugar for the granulated sugar. Stir into the cookie batter 1 cup chopped assertively flavored nuts such as black walnuts or Brazil nuts, my childhood favorite.

Candied: Toss $1/4$ cup finely chopped candied lemon or orange peel or citron into the cookie batter (see Candied Citrus Peel, page 124).

Coffee Kick: Mix 1 to 2 tablespoons instant coffee powder with 1 tablespoon hot water, cool, and add to the creamed butter and sugar.

Fruity: Add $1/2$ cup chopped dried fruit such as cherries, peaches, pineapples, or apples or $1/2$ cup raisins or currants to the cookie batter.

Nutty: Add to the cookie batter a generous $1/2$ cup of coarsely chopped unsalted skinned pistachio nuts, chopped pecans, walnuts, or blanched almonds.

Spiced: Mix 2 teaspoons grated orange rind, 1 teaspoon ground cinnamon, and 3 to 4 tablespoons granulated sugar and sprinkle a little over each cookie before baking (see Sugar and Spices, page 45).

Sugar-Crusted Cocoa Cookies

This is an updated version of the rich and succulent chocolate cookies that Mama and my sister, Helen, made during the Christmas holidays.

All of the ingredients were on hand: fresh coconut, a box of cocoa, a few bars of chocolate, and locally grown pecans.

I have modified the recipes over the years, substituting powdered sugar for some of the granulated sugar, and topping the cookie with ginger sugar. Dutch-process cocoa gives an extra-deep chocolate flavor, and often I top each cookie with a blanched almond or walnut half, replacing the traditional pecan.

These are delightful double-chocolate cookies, and when you set them out on a platter, they go real fast.

2 cups all-purpose flour
¼ cup unsweetened cocoa, preferably
    Dutch-process
½ teaspoon baking powder
⅛ teaspoon salt
4 ounces semisweet chocolate
½ pound (2 sticks) unsalted butter,
    softened
1¼ cups confectioners' sugar
½ cup granulated sugar plus 3 or 4
    tablespoons granulated sugar or

brown crystallized sugar (see Dark
    and Sweet, page 25)
1 large egg, at room temperature
1 teaspoon vanilla or almond extract
1 cup grated coconut, canned or fresh
    (see Cracking Coconuts, page 245)
1 egg white
1 scant cup blanched almond or pecan
    or walnut halves
1 teaspoon ground ginger

Sift together the flour, cocoa, baking powder, and salt and set aside.

Cut or break the chocolate into ½-inch-size pieces—or smaller—and set aside.

Combine the butter, confectioners' sugar, and ½ cup granulated sugar in a large mixing bowl. Using a handheld electric mixer set at medium-high or creaming speed, beat the mixture until light and fluffy, for about 2 minutes, scraping the sides of the bowl with a rubber spatula once or twice.

Add the egg and the vanilla or almond extract and cream until well blended.

Using a wooden spoon, stir in the coconut and reserved chocolate, mixing well. Add the flour and cocoa mixture 1 cup at a time, mixing only until blended.

Form the dough into a large ball, dusting lightly with flour if the dough is sticky. Cover the dough with plastic wrap or wax paper and chill until firm, about $1^1/_2$ hours.

Preheat the oven to 350 degrees. Lightly butter a baking sheet.

Place the dough on a very lightly floured board or cloth and cut into four pieces. Lightly roll or pat out one piece of dough at a time until it is about $^1/_4$ to $^1/_3$ inch thick. (Return the other pieces of dough to the refrigerator while you roll and shape the cookies.)

Using a $2^1/_2$-inch cookie cutter, cut the cookies into rounds. Place the cookies an inch or more apart on the baking sheet.

Lightly brush the top of each cookie with a little egg white. Press two almonds or a pecan or walnut half in the center of each cookie and brush the nuts lightly with a little more egg white.

Combine the remaining granulated sugar and ginger. Sprinkle the top of the cookies with a generous half-teaspoon of the aromatic sugar.

Set the pan of cookies in the center of the preheated oven on the middle shelf and bake for 13 to 15 minutes or until they are firm and the sugar topping is crusted and tinged with brown, turning the pan from front to back in the oven midway through the baking.

The tops may crack, which is common and a characteristic of this cookie.

Cool the pan of cookies on a wire rack for 2 or 3 minutes, and then remove the cookies from the pan with a metal spatula and cool completely on a wire rack.

Roll out and bake the remaining dough in the same way, one pan at a time. Reroll the scraps, chill well, and bake.

Makes about 24 large cookies

Note: If using unprocessed cocoa, such as Nestlé or Hershey's, omit the baking powder and use $1/2$ teaspoon baking soda instead. Cookies or cakes made with ingredients high in acid such as cocoa, molasses, and buttermilk rise best when baking soda is used for leavening. Dutch-process cocoa, such as Droste, is manufactured with a substance similar to baking soda and doesn't require additional baking soda for rising.

Cookie Points

Even children make cookies but they really require just as much attention as cakes. Here are pointers:

- Invest in a good oven thermometer, such as Taylor's, and check your oven for accuracy. If the oven temperature is off, have it professionally serviced and calibrated.

- Cookies bake fast, usually in 8 to 12 minutes in a 350-degree oven. To test for doneness, lift up the bottom with a metal spatula, and if it is lightly brown, the cookie is done. Perfect cookies are moist—not dried out—with crispy bottoms. Many cookies never turn golden brown on the top, and if they do, they are probably overbaked.

- Cream the butter and sugar for cookie batter thoroughly, for about 2 minutes—about half the time for a cake batter. Too little creaming results in flat cookies, while excessive creaming causes the cookies to spread during the baking.

- Don't beat the batter once the flour is added; this causes tough cookies. Add the flour to the creamed mixture and stir only until just blended.

- Cookies bake best on baking sheets without sides or with one or two turned-up or lipped sides or ends. Pans with high sides prevent the cookies from browning evenly.

- Heavy-gauge aluminum pans and tinned steel pans are best for baking cookies. Avoid industrial-weight pans and dark nonstick pans; they cause cookies to brown too quickly.

- Grease the baking sheet with butter; it imparts a nice flavor to cookies and doesn't burn as easily as margarine. Cookies made with thin batter, such as lace and wafers, don't spread so much if you lightly butter the baking sheet and then dust with flour.

- A pan of cookies needs a good circulation of heat during baking, so bake only one pan at a time. Set the pan on the middle oven rack and turn the pan around in the oven halfway through the baking so that the cookies can brown evenly.

- If you place unbaked cookies on a hot baking sheet the batter will spread out of shape before the cookies are done. So have at least two baking sheets available when you bake cookies; that way one pan will always be at room temperature and you can work faster. And when baking cookies in batches, keep the dough in the refrigerator until ready to use and bake.

- Unless otherwise specified, cool just baked cookies on the baking sheet for no more than 1 or 2 minutes, and then transfer to a wire rack with a metal spatula and cool completely.

- Airtight cookie jars or flat containers like those made by Rubbermaid or Tupperware, or tight tin boxes, will keep cookies fresh and crisp for about two weeks. Store flat cookies, wafers, and bars in single layers, between sheets of waxed paper. Store glazed cookies, such as brownies or sand tarts, in a single layer, bottoms down.

- Cookie batter can be frozen for at least 3 months; a boon for holiday baking. ❀

Pecan Sand Tarts

These sand tart cookies are a dream, and actually are the best version I have had of this popular Southern cookie.

Aunt Mary made her cookies with ground pecans added to the batter. Halfway through the baking she sprinkled on grated chocolate.

These cookies have a seductive "gritty" texture, and are perfect with ice cream, fresh fruit, a cup of coffee or tea, or simply to satisfy a longing sweet tooth.

1 cup pecans
1½ cups all-purpose flour
1 teaspoon ground cinnamon
½ teaspoon baking powder
Pinch of salt
8 tablespoons (1 stick) unsalted butter, softened
¾ cup confectioners' sugar

¼ cup dark brown sugar, firmly packed and free of lumps
1½ teaspoons vanilla extract
1 large egg, at room temperature
½ cup coarsely grated bittersweet or semisweet chocolate (about 2 ounces)
2 tablespoons granulated sugar

Chop the pecans rather finely but don't pulverize into a powder. Set aside. Sift together the flour, cinnamon, baking powder, and salt and set aside.

Combine the butter and both sugars in a large mixing bowl. Using a handheld electric mixer set at medium-high or creaming speed, beat until light and fluffy for 2 to 3 minutes, scraping the bowl once or twice with rubber spatula.

Add the vanilla extract and egg and beat 30 seconds longer.

Remove the bowl from the mixer. Stir in the chopped pecans and mix well. Stir in the flour and mix only until blended.

Gather the dough into a ball in the center of the bowl. Cover the bowl with plastic wrap and chill for 1½ hours.

When ready to bake, combine the grated chocolate and the granulated sugar and set aside.

Preheat the oven to 375 degrees. Lightly butter a baking sheet.

Dampen your fingertips with cold water. Using level tablespoons of batter for each cookie, shape the dough into bars about $^3/_4$ to 1 inch wide and $2^1/_2$ inches long, patting into shape with your fingers.

Place the bars on the baking sheet, about 2 inches apart.

Set the pan of cookies in the center of the preheated oven on the middle shelf and bake the cookies for 8 minutes.

Remove the pan from the oven and sprinkle the cookie tops with some of the chocolate-sugar mixture, using about 1 teaspoon per cookie. Return the cookies to the oven, reverse pan from front to back, and bake for 5 to 7 minutes longer, or until lightly browned and the topping is melted.

Remove the cookies from the oven and set the pan on a wire rack. Let the cookies cool on the pan for 2 or 3 minutes, and then remove from the pan with a metal spatula and cool completely on the rack.

Bake the remaining cookies, one pan at a time, in the same way.

Makes about 30 cookies

Gingersnaps

Patricia Stinson sent me the recipe for these spicy, crispy cookies, along with a note relating that the recipe was passed on by her father's mother, the late Isabella Woodward of Edgewater, New Jersey.

Patricia is a writer and editor, and since she is erudite on such matters, she said that years ago the cookies were made with lard or bacon drippings, and sweetened with molasses, but no sugar.

Right on, girlfriend!

But I don't always listen. For a modern-day flavor, I replaced the lard with butter and added just a little sugar to please the real sweet tooth.

These cookies are delightful, and although Patricia says that they "keep forever," don't bet on that. It's hard to have one or two of these old-fashioned goodies and stop.

2¼ cups unbleached all-purpose flour

2 to 3 teaspoons ground ginger

⅛ teaspoon salt

10 tablespoons (1¼ sticks) unsalted butter, softened

½ teaspoon baking soda

½ cup dark molasses

½ cup light brown sugar, firmly packed

1 large egg

½ teaspoon lemon extract or 1 tablespoon lemon juice

¼ cup brown crystallized sugar or turbinado sugar, such as Sugar in the Raw (see Dark and Sweet, page 25).

Sift together the flour, ginger, and salt and set aside.

Place the butter in a small saucepan and melt over low heat. Remove the pan immediately from the heat and pour the butter into a large mixing bowl. Stir in the baking soda.

Let the mixture cool for a few minutes, and then stir in the molasses, sugar, egg, and lemon extract or lemon juice.

Using a handheld electric mixer set at medium speed, beat until well blended, for at least 1 minute.

Using a wooden spoon, add the flour and spices, a cup at a time, to the molasses mixture and stir until just blended.

Form the dough into a ball, using a little more flour if it is sticky, but don't work in too much flour; the batter will become streaky.

Wrap the dough in plastic wrap or wax paper and chill for at least 2 hours, or until firm enough to roll.

Preheat the oven to 375 degrees. Lightly butter a baking sheet.

Remove the dough from the refrigerator and cut into four pieces or quarters. Roll out one piece of dough at a time on a lightly floured surface, into $1/4$-inch thickness. (Return the remaining pieces of dough to the refrigerator while you roll and cut the cookies.)

Using a 2-inch cookie cutter, cut the dough into rounds. Scatter the sugar on a plate. Dip both sides of the cookies in the sugar.

Place the cookie rounds on the baking sheet at least 1 inch apart. Roll out and cut another piece of dough the same way and place the cookies on the pan. Sprinkle the tops with a little more sugar.

Set the baking sheet in the center of the hot oven on the middle shelf. Bake the cookies 10 to 12 minutes, or until they are lightly browned, turning the pan from front to back in the oven midway through the baking for even browning.

Remove the pan of cookies from the oven and set on a wire rack. Cool for 1 minute, remove the cookies from the pan with a metal spatula, and cool completely on the rack.

Bake the remaining cookies in the same way, one pan at a time, rerolling the scraps.

Makes about 40 cookies

Lemon Coriander Tea Cakes

Eva Petty wears many hats, but before you snatch one of her lovely creations off her head, just go to the boutique she owns in Harlem. Her shop is called Harlem's Heaven Boutique, and it is located on busy Seventh Avenue, and yes her shop is heavenly.

A registered nurse by profession, Eva decided to go into business for herself more than two decades ago when people started inquiring about the fabulous clothes she was designing and wearing. She opened up a clothing store and put her talents to work. A high-end designer shoe store and a vintage collectible clothing shop followed.

At Harlem's Heaven Boutique, girlfriend makes all kinds of hats, ranging in price from fifty to five hundred dollars: all-lace, handmade with beads or sequins, trimmed in rhinestones or fur; made from felt, leather, grosgrain ribbon, and imported Italian straw. All of Eva's hats are one of a kind, and her customers range from local church sisters to Westchester and downtown matrons, to mail orders to the Caribbean.

Eva is a real sister and a while back on a Saturday afternoon she made space in her boutique, set up a table with several dishes cooked from my first book, *Soul Food,* and invited me to come out and sign the book for her customers.

I did, and my offering was a platter of old-fashioned tea cakes from an updated family recipe.

These crisp cookies are infused with coriander and lemon and are perfect with a hot cup of tea. Coriander has a flavor similar to lemon and sage, and it works beautifully in these tea cakes, which folklore says came out of the Southern plantation kitchens.

⅓ cup golden raisins
2 tablespoons lemon juice
2¼ cups all-purpose flour
¼ teaspoon baking soda
Pinch of salt
1 tablespoon coriander seeds, crushed (see Got a Crush, page 60)

12 tablespoons (1½ sticks) unsalted butter, softened
1 cup light brown sugar, firmly packed (see Dark and Sweet, page 25)
1 large egg, at room temperature
1 teaspoon vanilla extract
2 tablespoons brown sugar for sprinkling

Chop the raisins finely and mix in a glass bowl or cup with the lemon juice. Sift together the flour, baking soda, and salt. Set aside.

Set aside 1 teaspoon of the crushed coriander seeds to use as a topping. Combine the remaining seeds, butter, and sugar in a large mixing bowl.

Using a handheld electric mixer set at medium-high or creaming speed, beat until light and fluffy, for about 2 minutes, scraping the sides of the bowl with a rubber spatula once or twice. Add the egg and vanilla extract and beat until well blended.

Using a large spoon, stir in the raisins. Add the flour and mix only until blended. Form the dough into a ball, dusting lightly with flour if sticky.

Wrap the dough in wax paper or plastic wrap and chill in the refrigerator for about 2 hours or until the dough is firm and easy to handle.

Preheat the oven to 375 degrees. Lightly butter a baking sheet.

Divide the dough in half, and return one piece to the refrigerator.

Lightly flour a work surface. Roll out the dough into a circle about $^1/_4$ inch thick and about 8 inches in diameter.

Using a $2^1/_2$-inch cookie cutter, cut the dough into rounds. Place the cookies about 2 inches apart on the baking sheet.

Combine the remaining teaspoon of coriander seeds with the sugar and sprinkle each cookie with about $^1/_2$ teaspoon of the sugar-spice mixture. Gently press the topping with your fingers so that it sticks.

Set the pan of cookies in the center of the hot oven on the middle shelf. Bake for 11 to 14 minutes or until the bottoms are just lightly brown and the cookies are pale golden around the edges, turning the pan from front to back in the oven halfway through the baking.

Remove the cookies from the oven and set the pan on a wire rack. Cool the cookies for 5 minutes on the pan and then remove from the baking sheet with a metal spatula. Cool on a wire rack.

Bake the remaining dough in the same way, one pan at a time, rerolling the scraps.

Makes about 24 cookies

Short'nin' Bread Cookies

Anna Vernell Coaxum said that she hadn't eaten these cookies in years when I delivered her a box as a gift.

Dear Anna heads the nursing unit at Metropolitan A.M.E. Church in Harlem, and after all, she did invite me to several book signings when I was on the road with *Soul Food*. And I know how friends appreciate home-baked cookies and candies. Better than an old store-bought gift any day.

But Anna particularly liked the story I told her about baking these cookies during my childhood, where nobody ever called them "short-bread." So Scottish. She couldn't remember what they called these rich and buttery cookies down in McClellanville, South Carolina, where she grew up.

So when I broke out in the little song I sang as a child: "Mama's little baby loves short'nin', short'nin' . . ." she started laughing like crazy.

But she really keeled over when I added: "These scrumptious cookies belong to us; right out of those plantation kitchens."

2 cups unbleached all-purpose flour
1 teaspoon ground cinnamon
$\frac{1}{4}$ teaspoon baking soda
Pinch of salt
1 cup walnuts or pecans

$\frac{1}{2}$ pound (2 sticks) unsalted butter, softened
1 cup light brown sugar, firmly packed
1 teaspoon vanilla extract

GLAZE:
4 ounces semisweet or bittersweet chocolate

2 tablespoons unsalted butter

Sift together the flour, cinnamon, baking soda, and salt, and set aside. Chop the nuts coarsely.

Combine the butter and sugar in a large mixing bowl. Using a handheld electric mixer set at medium-high or creaming speed, beat until light and fluffy, for about 2 minutes, scraping the sides of the bowl with a rubber spatula once or twice. Stir in the vanilla extract and the nuts, mixing well.

Using a large spoon, stir in the flour, mixing only until blended. Form the dough into a ball, dusting lightly with flour if sticky.

Wrap the dough in wax paper or plastic wrap and chill in the refrigerator for about $1^1/_2$ hours or until the dough is firm and easy to handle.

Preheat the oven to 350 degrees. Have available a baking sheet but don't butter or grease it.

Divide the dough in half, and return one piece to the refrigerator. Lightly flour a work surface. Roll out the dough into a 6×7-inch rectangle, about $^1/_2$ inch thick.

Using a sharp, damp knife, cut the dough in half lengthwise. Cut crosswise into 1-inch-wide strips.. Then cut the dough strips into $1 \times 1^1/_2$-inch pieces for each cookie.

Place the cookies at least 1-inch apart on the ungreased baking sheet. Set the pan of cookies in the center of the hot oven on the middle shelf. Bake for 15 to 18 minutes or until bottoms are just lightly brown, turning the pan from front to back in the oven midway through the baking.

Remove the cookies from the oven and remove from the pan with a metal spatula. Cool on a wire rack. Bake the remaining dough in the same way, one pan at a time.

Prepare the glaze. Cut the chocolate into small pieces. Melt the butter in a small skillet over low heat. Add the chocolate and stir briskly with a whisk until melted and smooth.

Remove the pan from the heat and cool the glaze for a few minutes.

Place a sheet of wax paper or foil under a wire rack. Dip half of the cookie into the glaze or drizzle the chocolate over the top of the cookies. Let the cookies set until the glaze hardens.

These cookies keep superbly in an airtight container, in one layer.

Makes about 48 cookies

Variation: I also like these cookies dipped into or coated with an exquisite brown sugar glaze made with buttermilk. See Nut Brown Glaze, page 70.

Rita Reid steadfastly refused to turn over the recipe for her American Best Chocolate Chip Cookies for this book, but I was able to coax a brownie recipe out of her. And since both cookies are delicious and passionately loaded with chocolate, all transgressions are now forgiven and our little contretemps is settled.

But a word about those chocolate chip cookies. She and her daughter, Sharon, plan to go into business and sell them at any moment, hence the secret recipe. In the meantime we'll just have to wait until they hit the market.

I don't mind too much. I already have a to-die-for recipe for Kwanza Peanut-Chocolate Cookies (page 19), and Rita did give me a yummy recipe for Rum Raisin Oatmeal Cookies (page 17), and friendship is more precious than business, reason enough to close the subject.

And I certainly realize that Rita's life is chock-full of activities and new ventures. A few years ago she took early retirement from the Metropolitan Life Insurance company, where she had worked for years, and today is as busy as a bee taking quilting classes, beading classes, jewelry making, computer classes.

She also teaches an arts and crafts class at the Hudson Guild, a community center in New York City, where she is president of a members' group. And since she is almost fluent in Spanish, she often pitches in and teaches that class, too.

Rita is a loving and supportive sister, so when I asked her again just when she was going to start marketing those chocolate chip cookies, I really wasn't trying to dis her or anything. Nevertheless, she gave me a deadpan look and replied:

"You aren't getting that recipe for that book."

Never mind. Right now I am enjoying a pan of crunchy, dense, fudgelike brownies that are a delectable treat, made from her Double Fudge Brownies (page 43) recipe.

And who can resist brownies? They come in so many guises: full of nuts and chewy, as thick and creamy as chocolate mousse, as velvety and rich as fudge candy, and sometimes as crumbly as a fine layer cake.

Granted, I am partial to cookies that you bake and cut, such as brownies. They are easy to do; no dropping mound after mound of cookie dough on baking sheets, no rolling and cutting into myriad shapes. You just bake and cut.

And since almost everybody loves brownies, they make delicious gifts. And if you send them by mail, don't forget to include the recipe—another gift. I share my recipes.

Double Fudge Brownies

¾ cup all-purpose flour

3 tablespoons unsweetened cocoa, not
    Dutch-process

¼ teaspoon baking soda

⅛ teaspoon salt

½ cup pecans, or more if desired

6 ounces semisweet or bittersweet
    chocolate

6 tablespoons unsalted butter

1 cup granulated sugar

1 teaspoon vanilla extract

2 large eggs, at room temperature

Preheat the oven to 350 degrees. Butter an 8- or 9-inch square baking or cake pan and dust lightly with flour, shaking out any excess.

Sift together the flour, cocoa, baking soda, and salt. Coarsely chop the pecans. Set aside. Coarsely chop the chocolate into 1-inch pieces.

Melt the butter in a medium saucepan over low heat. Add the chocolate and heat, stirring, until the chocolate melts. Remove the pan from the heat right away.

Stir in the sugar and vanilla and mix well. Cool the mixture for about 10 minutes, or until just lukewarm. Whisk in the eggs one at a time, and beat the batter until it is smooth and glossy.

Stir in the flour mixture and then the nuts, and mix only until the batter is just blended.

Spread the batter evenly in the prepared pan. Set the pan on the middle oven rack and bake the brownies for 20 to 25 minutes, or until a tester inserted in the center comes out moist but clean.

Remove the pan from the oven and set on a wire rack. Allow the brownies to remain in the pan for at least 3 hours or longer.

When thoroughly cooled, using a serrated knife, cut the brownies in the pan into 2 × 2-inch square pieces. Run a metal spatula around the edge of the brownies and remove the pieces from the pan.

Makes 24 brownies

Coconut Almond Brownies

My late sister-in-law, Marie, sent me this recipe years ago, saying that the topping turns down-home brownies into a fancy cake.

She was right. These are elegant brownies, slightly gooey, but cake-like at the same time, sporting a sugared top hat of shredded coconut and almond.

Chocolate lovers will lust after these brownies, and I understand why. They are seductive and delicious.

TOPPING:

3 tablespoons unsalted butter

1 cup slivered almonds, untoasted

1 cup finely shredded fresh coconut
(see Cracking Coconuts, page 245)

or sweetened flaked coconut

¼ to ⅓ cup dark brown sugar, firmly packed

½ teaspoon vanilla extract

BROWNIE LAYER:

¾ cup all-purpose flour

½ cup unsweetened cocoa, preferably Dutch-process

½ teaspoon baking powder

Pinch of salt

½ cup granulated sugar

½ cup dark brown sugar, firmly packed

8 tablespoons (1 stick) unsalted butter, softened

2 large eggs, at room temperature

1 teaspoon vanilla extract

Melt the butter in a small saucepan over low heat. Immediately remove from the heat and stir in the almonds, coconut, sugar, and vanilla. Mix well and set aside. (If using fresh coconut, you may need the larger amount of sugar.)

Preheat the oven to 350 degrees. Butter an 8- or 9-inch square baking or cake pan and dust lightly with flour, shaking out any excess flour. Set aside.

Sift together the flour, cocoa, baking powder, and salt.

Combine both sugars and the butter in a large mixing bowl. Using a handheld electric mixer set at medium-high or creaming speed, beat until light and fluffy, for 3 to 4 minutes, scraping down the bowl with a rubber spatula once or twice.

Add the eggs and vanilla and beat 30 seconds more.

Remove the bowl from the mixer. Add the flour-cocoa mixture and beat the batter briskly with a wooden spoon for a few seconds.

Pour the batter into the prepared pan, and spread evenly with a spatula. Shake the pan gently to level the batter. Spoon on the topping and spread evenly with a metal spatula.

Set the pan on the middle oven rack and bake the brownies for 25 to 30 minutes, or until a tester inserted in the center comes out moist but almost clean, and the topping is crusted and lightly brown.

Remove the pan from the oven and set on a wire rack. Allow the brownies to remain in the pan for at least 3 hours.

When thoroughly cooled, using a serrated knife, cut the brownies in the pan into 2 × 2-inch square pieces. Run a metal spatula around the edge of the brownies and remove the pieces from the pan.

Makes 24 brownies

Sugar and Spices

Sprinkle a few tablespoons of aromatic sugar on a batch of cookies and you transform it to a special treat. Some scented sugars go on before you stick the pan of cookies in the oven; others add a decorative but flavorful note to a freshly baked batch.

No matter. Any cookie baker worth his or her salt always has a jar or two of sprinkling sugar on hand. They are easy to make and smell real sweet.

Aromatic: Grind or pulverize a cinnamon stick or piece of cinnamon bark in a coffee grinder. Combine with 1 cup granulated sugar, mix well and store in a covered jar. For another flavor, crush 1 tablespoon allspice berries in a coffee grinder or with a mortar and pestle. Combine in a food processor with 1 cup sugar and pulse until the mixture is well blended, about 3 minutes.

Oreo: Cut 2 vanilla beans into small pieces. Grind into tiny bits in a coffee grinder. Then, place in the small bowl of a food processor with 1 cup granulated or golden baker's sugar (see Dark and Sweet, page 25). Pulse for 3 minutes or until the mixture is well combined.

Place the sugar in a jar with a tight-fitting lid and store at room temperature. It can keep for months.

Seed-y: Lightly toast 2 to 3 tablespoons of cardamom or coriander seeds or star anise pieces in a small skillet over medium heat for 4 or 5 minutes. Remove from the heat and crush the seeds with a mortar and pestle or in a coffee grinder.

Place the seeds in the small bowl of a food processor with 1 cup granulated sugar. Pulse until the mixture is well combined, 3 to 4 minutes.

Transfer the spiced sugar to a jar, cover tightly, and store at room temperature.

Sweet Crystals: Just before sticking a batch of cookies in the oven, sprinkle the tops with a few tablespoons of minimally refined brown crystallized sugars such as turbinado or Sugar in the Raw, or with crystallized Demerara sugar, or granulated brown sugar (see Dark and Sweet, page 25). The sugar caramelizes into a toothsome crunchy icing. So quick and sweet.

Tangy: Using a vegetable peeler, lightly cut the peel from 3 or 4 lemons, oranges, or tangerines in strips, avoiding the bitter white pith. Place the peel in the small bowl of a food processor and chop roughly. Add 1 cup granulated sugar and pulse until the zest is finely ground, for about 3 minutes.

Remove the bowl from the processor and stir in ½ cup more sugar, mixing well. Spread the lemon sugar on a baking pan and let sit at room temperature, preferably in a warm sunny spot, for several hours to dry. Transfer to an airtight container and keep refrigerated.

This sugar will also keep at room temperature for about 1 month. ❀

Coffee Brownies

The late Velma Mosley could sometimes overwhelm even me with her zeal, and I really was surprised the day the UPS deliveryman handed me a box and said it smelled, in his words, "mighty good."

I couldn't just leave him hanging; I send and receive a lot of packages and I don't want my stuff to end up in Alaska. So I opened up the box and there were these brownies, as fragrant as a cup of strong brewed coffee. A chocolate topping was in a little plastic container, so tightly wrapped I thought it was a precious stone.

So thoughtful, so sisterly, and just like Mrs. Mosley, who spent her last days in Tyler, Texas (see Sweetly Whipped: Egg-White Pies, page 121).

These brownies are heady and delicious.

BROWNIE LAYER:

¾ cup all-purpose flour

½ teaspoon baking powder

Pinch of salt

¾ cup walnuts or pecans

3 ounces unsweetened chocolate

2 tablespoons hot water

2 to 3 tablespoons instant coffee or espresso powder, such as Medaglia D'Oro

8 tablespoons (1 stick) unsalted butter

1⅓ cups granulated sugar

2 large eggs

1 teaspoon vanilla extract

TOPPING:

3 ounces semisweet or bittersweet chocolate

2 tablespoons unsalted butter

2 tablespoons light or dark corn syrup

1 tablespoon coffee liqueur, such as Kahlúa or Tia Maria or ¼ teaspoon vanilla extract

Preheat the oven to 350 degrees. Butter an 8- or 9-inch square baking or cake pan and dust lightly with flour, shaking out any excess flour.

Sift together the flour, baking powder, and salt. Coarsely chop the walnuts or pecans. Set aside.

Cut the chocolate into small pieces and set aside.

Combine the hot water and coffee or espresso powder in a small saucepan and stir until the powder is dissolved. Add the butter.

Place the pan over low heat and stir until the butter melts. Add the chocolate and beat briskly until the mixture is smooth. Remove from the heat and cool to lukewarm.

Combine the sugar and eggs in a medium mixing bowl. Using a handheld electric mixer set at medium-high or creaming speed, beat until light and lemony-colored, for 2 to 3 minutes, scraping down the bowl with a rubber spatula once or twice.

Add the chocolate-coffee mixture and the vanilla extract and beat 30 seconds more.

Using a wooden spoon, stir in the flour mixture and beat the batter briskly for a few seconds. Stir in the nuts and mix thoroughly.

Pour the batter into the prepared pan, and spread evenly with a spatula. Shake the pan gently to level the batter.

Set the pan on the middle oven shelf and bake for 20 to 25 minutes or until the brownies are puffy and crusty and a tester inserted in the center comes out moist but clean.

Place on a wire rack and let cool completely in the pan on the rack, at least 3 hours or longer.

Prepare the topping: chop the chocolate into small pieces. Place the butter in a small saucepan or skillet and melt over low heat. Stir in the chocolate and corn syrup and heat over low heat just until the chocolate melts, stirring constantly. Remove from the heat and stir in the liqueur or vanilla extract. Beat briskly until smooth and well combined.

To serve, run a metal spatula around the edge of the pan, and invert the brownie layer onto a wire rack, and then turn upright on the rack.

Place a sheet of wax paper on a cutting board and set the brownie layer on the paper, top side up. Spread with the topping and let set until it is hardened, for at least 2 hours, or put in a cool place and allow to remain overnight.

For serving using a serrated knife, cut into 2 × 2-inch square pieces.

Makes 24 brownies

Nuts About Nuts

The flavor of most nuts is enhanced by toasting. Before chopping, simply scatter the nuts on a jelly-roll or shallow roasting pan. Toast in a preheated 350-degree oven for 5 to 8 minutes.

Stir the nuts once or twice or shake the pan and watch carefully because they can burn quickly. Remove from the oven as soon as they are lightly browned and you detect the aroma of the roasting nuts. Transfer to a plate to cool and chop as directed in the recipe.

After toasting pistachio nuts, scatter the nuts on a tea towel and then rub briskly with the towel to remove the skins, or use a small sharp knife to cut off the skins. Don't blanch pistachio nuts to remove the skins; the hot water destroys flavor. ❧

TWO

Take the Cake

The moment word went out about an upcoming box supper, the collective pulse of our community in rural Alabama quickened. The traveling Watkins salesman stocked up on cinnamon, allspice, nutmeg, and cloves, as well as vanilla, lemon, orange, and almond extract, for he knew that most of the women would prepare a cake box. The women also bought fresh eggs, butter, and milk, and then went about cadging recipes from one an other.

Since the cakes were slated for public presentation, the baking was meticulous. Ovens were checked for accurate temperature, cake pans were inspected for correct size, and if they were not the right size, others were bought or borrowed. The butter and sugar were creamed vigorously by hand until fluffy and lemony-colored, and before long the batter was baking in the old cast-iron stoves, a sweet promise.

Early in the afternoon of the appointed day, each woman packed a main box supper with fried chicken, a biscuit or two, and perhaps potato salad. Then she lined a shoe box with crepe paper, nestled in four generous slices of cake, capped on the lid, and tied the box with ribbon. She wrote her name on the bottom of the cake box—out of plain sight.

Later that evening the box suppers were sold and enjoyed—right away. The cake boxes were lined up on a table at the church or school hosting the supper, their heady aroma accenting the din of the crowd. Prospective buyers would circle the table, trying to decide which cake box belonged to whom.

The fun came from the anonymity, for a buyer selected a cake box and then shared the dessert with the woman who had baked the cake. That in itself led to a lot of nudging and winking and joking about romances and marriages that had been sparked over cake at box suppers of the past, and ones that would likely ensue in the future.

Strictly speaking, this was not a sin-gles event, for both married and single women, young and old, came to these suppers, which generated almost as much excitement as a church revival or homecoming celebration. But if a single woman wanted a certain young man to buy her cake box, she could try to let him know which box belonged to her. Some of the women would whisper to an admirer that their cake box was tied with a certain color ribbon, or tell him to look for a little x mark or check at such and such place on the box.

At the end of the evening we walked home on those lonely country roads remembering divine coconut cakes, rich and sweet chocolate cakes, succulent caramel cakes, fragrant spice cakes, crumbly and tender pound cakes, all of which were baked and boxed with love.

Buttermilk Ginger Cake with Fresh Fruit Sauce

This light but aromatic cake is fragrant with nutmeg and fresh ginger, which years ago was thought to keep summer heat and thirst at bay. If you serve it with homemade vanilla ice cream and fresh fruit or berry sauce, you'll wish that summer never ends.

2 cups all-purpose flour
1/8 teaspoon salt
1 teaspoon baking powder
3/4 teaspoon baking soda
1 1/2 teaspoons grated nutmeg
1 3-inch piece fresh ginger
1 1/4 cups granulated sugar

12 tablespoons (1 1/2 sticks) unsalted butter, softened
3 large eggs, at room temperature
1 teaspoon vanilla extract
1 cup buttermilk (approximately), at room temperature
Fresh Fruit Sauce (page 55)

Preheat the oven to 350 degrees. Butter generously a 9 × 2-inch round cake pan or a 7-cup fluted pan or an 8 1/2 × 2 1/2-inch springform pan. Dust the pan with flour and shake out any excess flour.

Sift together the flour, salt, baking powder, baking soda, and nutmeg.

Peel the ginger, making sure to trim away and discard any woody part. Chop the ginger rather coarsely. You should have 1/4 cup chopped ginger. Add 2 tablespoons of the sugar, and chop very finely with a large knife or pulverize in a food processor.

Combine the ginger, remaining sugar, and butter in the bowl of a standing mixer fitted with the paddle attachment or use a large mixing bowl and a handheld electric mixer. Cream the mixture at medium-high or creaming speed until pale and fluffy, 3 to 5 minutes, scraping the bowl with a rubber spatula two or three times.

Add the eggs, one at a time, and beat 30 seconds after each addition. Add the vanilla extract and mix well.

Reduce the mixer to low speed. Add the flour and spices, alternately with the buttermilk, mixing only for a few seconds until blended.

After the last addition, beat the batter on low speed for 1 minute, scraping the bowl as needed. If the batter is very thick, add a little more buttermilk and stir to mix well.

Pour the batter into the prepared pan and spread the top evenly with a spatula. Shake the pan gently to settle the batter.

Place the cake on the lower oven rack and bake for 45 to 50 minutes, or until a cake tester or toothpick inserted in the center comes out clean and the cake is golden brown and puffy.

Remove the cake from the oven, place on a wire rack, and cool in the pan for 10 minutes. Run a metal spatula around the inside edge of the pan, invert the pan onto the rack, tap gently, and remove the pan. Place the cake top side up on the rack and cool completely.

If using a springform pan, unfasten the sides of the pan and remove. Carefully invert the cake onto the wire rack. Run the tip of a metal spatula between the bottom of the pan and the cake. When loosen, lift off the bottom of the pan. Place the cake top side up on the wire rack and cool completely.

Serve with Fresh Fruit Sauce.

Makes 8 to 10 servings

Variation: Substitute $1^{1}/_{2}$ to 2 teaspoons of finely crushed cardamom seeds for the nutmeg for an equally delicious flavor. In addition, $^{3}/_{4}$ cup plain low-fat yogurt diluted with $^{1}/_{4}$ cup water can replace the buttermilk.

Fresh Fruit Sauce

I made this sauce with a combination of peaches and blueberries, but diced mangoes or papayas or pitted cherries are fine, too. Allow about 3 cups of diced fruit for the sauce.

8 or 9 ripe fresh fruit, such as peaches, plums, or nectarines or 3 cups blueberries or blackberries, fresh or frozen

2 tablespoons lemon juice

$\frac{1}{2}$ cup (or to taste) granulated or golden baker's sugar (see Dark and Sweet, page 25)

$\frac{1}{2}$ cup water

1 teaspoon vanilla extract

2 tablespoons B&B or Benedictine liqueur

If using whole fruit, rinse, drain, peel, and cut into $\frac{1}{2}$-inch pieces. Discard pits. If using berries, rinse and remove stems.

Combine the lemon juice, sugar, and water in a medium saucepan. Bring to a boil and cook over high heat until the mixture thickens slightly, for about 3 minutes.

Add the fruit, reduce the heat to low, and cook, uncovered, 15 to 20 minutes, or until the sauce is thick and syrupy, stirring occasionally.

Stir in the vanilla extract and liqueur, remove from the heat, and cool the sauce completely before serving with the cake.

Makes about 3 cups

Patricia Stinson's Cardamom Swirl Coffee Cake (page 58) and my family's Buttermilk Ginger Cake (page 53) are usually spread with a cup or so of quick icings or glazes, or topped with fruit or whipped cream or custard, or crusted with nuts, sugar, and spice, or left plain and unadorned and delicious. These cakes are rich and spicy and don't need a heavy crown of frosting to boost flavor. And since the baking is done in one pan, you don't have to stack and frost cake layers—a time-saver.

But actually, though, making any cake today is far easier than it used to be, thanks to hefty standing mixers and gas- and electric-fueled ovens. We no longer have to beat a cake batter by hand for minutes on end, or spend hours stoking the old wood- or coal-burning stoves of yesteryear.

There's nothing plain about these cakes—they simply don't require much fuss. Set out any cake and you create a special atmosphere, for a cake makes festive occasions happier, and sad ones less so. We mark birthdays, weddings, anniversaries, graduations, new life, and death with a slice—or two—of cake, and we often bring out a cake just because it is a sweet pleasure.

"These are the kinds of cakes you can whip together, pack up, and take to a church or club meeting and enjoy with coffee or tea," says Patricia, depositing her gift on my kitchen table. "It's rich and moist but not too sweet. Children love it."

I had expected this type of cake from Patricia, primarily because she is involved in many community and church social events in Englewood, New Jersey, where she lives and sets a whirlwind pace.

She is an editor at a suburban New Jersey newspaper, helps coach her daughter's soccer teams, singlehandedly paints her rambling house, and is such a fearless swimmer that I am convinced that she can cross the English Channel in about the time it takes me to waddle across a municipal pool.

She has boundless energy, and I often wonder how her husband, Larry, and their two teenage children, Marcus and Juliana, keep up with her.

Patricia and I met more than two decades ago. At the time she was an editor at *Essence* magazine. I wrote a freelance article for the magazine and it was passed to her able hands.

Showing her usual adventurous streak, Patricia decided she wanted to meet the writer in person. Soon afterward she showed up at my place of work. She wasn't bearing a cake, but as I sat across from this outgoing women over lunch, I knew that a friendship was in the making.

"When I was growing up Aunt Theresa used to bake this cake at least once a week," says Patricia, who is a native of Edgewater, New Jersey, a little town near Burlington that is known for its bumper peach season. "It's the kind of cake you can serve when company is coming, take to a funeral, or enjoy yourself at home."

See Pots and Pans (page 1), for information on pan sizes.

Cardamom Swirl Coffee Cake

When Patricia gave me this recipe she said that she often changes the spice and comes up with a different flavor. I did just that. I substituted cinnamon for the cardamom and reached for a cup of hot apple cider—a great duo. On another occasion, raisins replaced the walnuts.

For a delightful citrus flavor, I used a tablespoon of grated lemon or orange peel or a combination of the peel in place of the cardamom. And for extra flavor and bite, I added a cup of coarsely chopped pistachios—skins removed.

And the cardamom version cried out for a good cup of coffee—the perfect partner.

But truthfully, all of these variations are delicious. That was the consensus last summer when I made two versions, packed them up, and took as a hostess gift to Vera Shorter, who had invited me to her lovely home in Vineyard Haven on Martha's Vineyard in Massachusetts.

Vera invited in friends and served one of the cakes, saving the other for our afternoon tea on her heavenly veranda. Her daughter, Beth Bagot, my friend and a former Alvin Ailey dancer, was home from Paris, where she now lives, and we would sit and talk, catch up on each other's life, drink tea, and nibble on cake, right up to cocktail time.

1½ to 2 teaspoons cardamom seeds (see Got a Crush, page 60) plus 1 tablespoon sugar if necessary
1 cup walnuts
2 tablespoons unsalted butter
1½ cups granulated sugar
2 cups all-purpose flour
1 teaspoon baking powder
1 teaspoon baking soda
⅛ teaspoon salt
8 tablespoons (1 stick) unsalted butter, softened
2 large eggs, at room temperature
1 teaspoon vanilla extract
1 cup sour cream, at room temperature
½ cup warm water

Preheat the oven to 350 degrees. Butter generously a 7-cup fluted mold pan or ring or a 9 × 2-inch round pan or an 8½ × 2½-inch springform pan. Dust the pan with flour and shake out any excess flour.

Lightly toast and then finely crush or grind the cardamom seeds until they are completely pulverized and powdery. If necessary, add a tablespoon of sugar to the nuts so that they will grind better. Coarsely chop the walnuts.

Melt the butter in a small skillet or saucepan. Remove immediately from the heat and stir in the cardamom, walnuts, and $1/2$ cup of the sugar; mix well. Set aside to use for the filling and topping.

Sift together the flour, baking powder, baking soda, and salt and set aside.

Combine the remaining sugar and butter in the bowl of a standing mixer fitted with the paddle attachment or use a large mixing bowl and a handheld mixer. Beat the mixture on medium-high or creaming speed for 3 to 5 minutes, scraping the bowl with a rubber spatula two or three times.

Add the eggs and beat 1 minute longer. Stir in the vanilla extract.

Set the mixer on low speed. Stir together the sour cream and water. Add the flour to the creamed mixture alternately with the sour cream mixture, mixing only for a few seconds until blended. After the last addition, beat the batter on low speed for 1 minute, scraping the bowl as needed.

Spoon or pour a little less than one-half of the cake batter into the prepared pan. Scatter half the cardamom mixture over the cake batter in the pan.

Fill the pan with the remaining batter. Using a butter knife, swirl the batter. Top with the remaining cardamom mixture and press the topping lightly into the batter with the back of a spoon.

Shake the pan gently to level the batter. Place the cake on the lower shelf of the preheated oven and bake for 45 to 50 minutes, until golden brown and puffy, or until a cake tester or toothpick inserted into the center comes out clean.

Remove the cake from the oven, place on a wire rack, and cool in the pan for 10 minutes. Run a metal spatula around the inside edge of the pan, invert the pan onto the rack, tap gently, and remove the pan. Place the cake top side up on the rack and cool completely.

If using a springform pan, unfasten the sides of the pan and remove. Carefully invert the cake onto the wire rack. Run the tip of a metal spatula between the bottom of the pan and the cake. When loose, lift off the bottom of the pan. Place the cake top side up on the wire rack and cool completely.

Makes 8 servings

Got a Crush
Cardamom and coriander seeds, juniper and allspice berries, and dried fruit, such as the star anise, release more essential oils and aroma when toasted and crushed.

Just scatter the seeds or spices over the bottom of a heavy skillet. Set over low heat and toast for 5 or so minutes, swirling pan a time or two.

Remove from the heat and crush the spices in a coffee grinder or with a mortar and pestle or enclose in a tea towel and crush with a rolling pin. ❁

Honey Carrot Cake

At least three friends and family members sent recipes for carrot cake, and I loved every recipe. Sharon Gethers's cake was spicy and moist, my brother John's recipe called for honey rather than sugar, and Rita Reid used pureed carrots to intensify the flavor.

A composite recipe follows, and this cake is healthful and scrumptious. I like to sprinkle the top of the cake with a couple tablespoons of brown crystallized sugar—my passion—which bakes into a glistening crust. Sharon Gethers's Cream Cheese Frosting (page 63) is also tangy and delicious with this cake, and so is a dollop of Honey Cream (page 242) or Perfectly Whipped Cream (page 74).

1 cup pecans, walnuts, or Brazil nuts
2¼ cups unbleached all-purpose flour
¼ teaspoon salt
½ teaspoon baking powder
1¼ teaspoons baking soda
½ teaspoon grated nutmeg or mace
1 to 1½ teaspoons ground ginger
2 cups shredded fresh carrots, well packed (from 2 or 3 large carrots)
¼ cup water

3 large eggs, at room temperature
1 cup honey, such as Golden Blossom
¼ cup granulated sugar
1 teaspoon vanilla extract
12 tablespoons (1½ sticks) unsalted butter, melted and cooled
2 tablespoons brown crystallized sugar, such as Sugar in the Raw (see Dark and Sweet, page 25), optional

Preheat the oven to 350 degrees. Butter generously an 8-cup ring or fluted pan or a 9 × 2-inch round cake pan or an 8½ × 2½-inch springform pan. Dust the pan with flour and shake out any excess flour.

Chop the nuts coarsely, toss with 2 tablespoons of the flour, and set aside. Sift together the remaining flour, salt, baking powder, baking soda, nutmeg or mace, and ginger. Set the flour mixture aside.

Place half of the carrots (1 cup) and the water in a blender or food processor and whirl until pureed and smooth. Set aside.

Combine the eggs, honey, sugar, and vanilla extract. Using a handheld electric mixer, beat on medium speed for about 1 minute. Add the melted butter, the pureed carrots and the shredded carrots, and beat on low speed 1 minute longer.

Stir in the flour and spices, adding about one-third at a time, and beat on low speed for just a few seconds after each addition. After the last addition, beat the batter on low speed for 1 minute, or until the batter is satiny and shiny, scraping the bowl at least once. Stir in the nuts and mix gently but until well combined.

Pour the batter into the prepared pan. Smooth the top with a spatula and shake the pan to settle the batter. If desired, sprinkle the top of the cake with the crystalized sugar.

Set the pan in the center of the lower oven rack and bake for 45 to 50 minutes, or until the cake is golden brown, springs back when touched in the center, or when a toothpick or knife comes out clean when inserted in the center.

Remove the cake from the oven, place on a wire rack, and cool in the pan for 10 minutes. Run a thin knife or spatula around the edges of the pan to loosen the cake, invert onto the rack, tap gently, and lift the pan off the cake. Set the cake top side up on the rack and cool completely.

If using a springform pan, unfasten the sides of the pan and remove. Carefully invert the cake onto the wire rack. Run the tip of a metal spatula between the bottom of the pan and the cake. When loose, lift off the bottom of the pan. Cool the cake on the rack, top side up.

Place the cake on a platter and spread with the desired glaze or topping.

Makes 8 to 10 servings

Cream Cheese Frosting

Sharon Gethers, a dear and supportive friend, who is a member of the theater support groups AULDELCO, sent this recipe for a quick-and-easy frosting that tops a carrot cake like love and marriage, as the song goes.

Sharon adds a dash of lemon juice for a tangy flavor, and replaces some of the cream cheese with butter. The frosting is smooth and creamy and delicious.

1 3-ounce package cream cheese, softened

3 tablespoons unsalted butter, softened

½ teaspoon vanilla extract

1 tablespoon lemon juice

2 cups confectioners' sugar, sifted

1 teaspoon water, or more if needed

In a medium bowl, combine the cream cheese, butter, vanilla extract, and lemon juice. Using a handheld electric mixer, beat on low speed until well blended. Gradually beat in the confectioners' sugar, and continue beating until of spreading consistency. If necessary, add a teaspoon or so of water for a creamier consistency.

Makes a generous 1¼ cups; enough frosting for one 9-inch cake

Chocolate Spice Cake with Creamy Chocolate Glaze

I met Amanda Thompson years ago and right away we decided that we were long-lost cousins. That was after we started exchanging childhood memories and learned that at the beginning of the last century both of our families had at one time lived in Clarke County in Alabama.

"And you know everybody in those little towns were kin to each other," says Amanda, who is church secretary at the Metropolitan A.M.E. Church in Harlem.

Her pastor, the Reverend James Lawrence, who was a guest at my marriage about one hundred years ago, nodded and said we sure look alike.

Amanda and I always talk about our common roots, and then we vow to go down South and search through court and church records and do our family tree, but we haven't had time yet. We will though.

But it doesn't matter anyway. She is a real sister, and a dear friend. And we both love this spicy, chocolate cake, which is a variation of a down-home devil's food cake. The batter also makes fingerlickin' cupcakes.

1 cup very hot strong brewed coffee
²/₃ cup unsweetened cocoa, such as Nestlé, Hershey's, or Ghirardelli (not Dutch-process)
1½ cups all-purpose flour
½ teaspoon baking powder
¾ teaspoon baking soda
¼ teaspoon salt
12 tablespoons (1½ sticks) unsalted butter, softened
1 cup light brown sugar, firmly packed
½ cup granulated sugar
2 to 3 teaspoons ground ginger
¼ to ½ teaspoon ground cloves
2 large eggs, at room temperature
1½ teaspoons vanilla extract
Creamy Chocolate Glaze (page 66)
1 cup coarsely chopped walnuts or pecans

Preheat the oven to 350 degrees. Butter generously an 8 × 3-inch round pan or an 8½ × 2½-inch springform pan. Dust the pan with flour and shake out any excess flour.

In a small bowl combine ½ cup of the hot brewed coffee and the cocoa and mix until smooth. Set aside. (Save the remaining coffee to stir into the batter.)

Sift together the flour, baking powder, baking soda, and salt and set aside.

Combine the butter, both sugars, ground ginger, and cloves in the bowl of a standing mixer fitted with the paddle attachment or use a large mixing bowl and a handheld electric mixer. Beat the mixture on medium-high or creaming speed for 4 to 6 minutes, scraping the bowl two or three times with a rubber spatula.

Beat in the eggs one at a time, scraping the bowl as needed.

Stir in the vanilla extract and cocoa and coffee mixture and beat 2 minutes, or until pale and fluffy. (Mixture may look curdled; which is all right.)

Set the mixer on low speed. Alternately add the flour and remaining brewed coffee to the creamed mixture, mixing only a few seconds after each addition, ending with the flour.

After the last addition, beat the batter on low speed for 1 minute, scraping the bowl as needed.

Pour the batter into the prepared pan. Smooth the top of the batter with a spatula and shake the pan gently to settle the batter.

Set the pan on the lower oven rack. Bake the cake for 45 to 50 minutes, or until a knife inserted in the center comes out clean, and the cake springs back when pressed lightly. The top of the cake may show thin crack lines, which is characteristic.

Remove the cake from the oven, place on a wire rack, and cool in the pan for 10 minutes.

Loosen the edges of the cake with a metal spatula, tap gently, and turn out of the pan onto the rack. Place the cake top side up on the rack and cool completely.

If using a springform pan, unfasten the sides of the pan and remove. Carefully invert the cake onto the wire rack. Run the tip of a metal spatula between the bottom of the pan and the cake. When loose, lift off the bottom of the pan. Cool the cake top side up on the wire rack.

Before serving, using a metal spatula, spread the top and sides of the cake with the Creamy Chocolate Glaze.

Let the icing set for about 20 minutes and then using your hand, cover the sides of the cakes with the chopped nuts (see Icing on the Cake, page 89).

Makes 8 to 10 servings

Creamy Chocolate Glaze

This is a rich and easy-to-make old-fashioned chocolate sauce. A tablespoon of brandy or cognac gives it a nice punch.

6 ounces good-quality bittersweet or semisweet chocolate
½ cup heavy cream or undiluted evaporated milk

2 tablespoons light corn syrup
1 tablespoon unsalted butter
1 tablespoon dark rum or brandy or ½ teaspoon vanilla extract

Cut or break the chocolate into ½-inch-size pieces and set aside. Combine in a heavy stainless steel saucepan the cream or milk, corn syrup, butter, and rum or brandy or vanilla extract. Place on medium heat and cook for about 5 minutes, or until the mixture is bubbling but not quite boiling.

Immediately move the pan from the heat and stir in the chocolate pieces. Whisk the glaze briskly until smooth. Cool completely and then spread generously over the cake or cupcakes.

Makes 1 generous cup; enough glaze for one 8-inch cake or 18 cupcakes

Chocolate Spice Cupcakes: Cupcakes pack up and go real quick, and you can use this same batter. Here's how:

Preheat the oven to 350 degrees. Butter generously and dust with flour eighteen muffin cups (½-cup size), shaking out any excess flour. Fill each cup about two-thirds full with batter, using a scant ⅓ cup of batter. If using two muffin pans, and there are unfilled cups, fill the empty cups with water.

If using two pans, set diagonally across from each other in the hot oven on the middle rack. Don't allow the pans to touch each other or the sides of the oven. Bake the cupcakes for about 20 minutes or until a tester comes out clean.

Cool the cupcakes in the pans on wire racks for 10 minutes. Run a thin metal spatula around each cupcake to loosen from the pans and then carefully lift out. Set the cupcakes on the racks, cool completely, and spread generously with Creamy Chocolate Glaze (recipe above). Top with chopped walnuts or pecans, if desired.

For a quicker topping, sprinkle the cupcakes liberally with brown crystallized sugar such as turbinado sugar (Sugar in the Raw) about halfway through the baking.

Makes 18 cupcakes

Banana Cake

When Irene Peoples was the director of a day care center in Queens, New York, the children under her care were fed a steady diet of books, but she occasionally rewarded everybody with a delectable cake from her kitchen, usually this absolutely divine Banana Cake. It is moist, spicy, and aromatic, and easy to carry.

"From the time I was ten years old I read at least four books a week," says Mrs. Peoples, who is now retired. "Education is all about books. When I worked with children I encouraged them to read all the time. That's what I did."

Mrs. Peoples is the mother of Camille Peoples, and mother and daughter are both members of the Literary Club at St. Albans Congregational Church. Both are passionate about food, and their annual Christmas dinner is a teamwork effort by two accomplished cooks. Camille makes twenty dozen cookies; Mrs. Peoples makes a fruit cake, a pound cake, sometimes a German chocolate cake, and several pies, plus the main entrée and the trimmings.

"I call my Banana Cake my rainy day cake," Mrs. Peoples says, laughing. "I bake it all the time. It is quick, easy to do, versatile, and smells good."

Maybe that's the reason why my neighbor Edith Collins rang my doorbell the moment I pulled this lovely cake out of the oven.

1 cup walnuts	2 tablespoons orange juice
1¾ cups all-purpose flour	2 large eggs, at room temperature
1 teaspoon baking soda	1 cup light brown sugar, firmly packed
1 teaspoon baking powder	¾ cup peanut or corn oil or a mixture
1 teaspoon ground cinnamon or allspice	of both oils
¼ teaspoon salt	½ cup sour cream
1½ cups coarsely mashed ripe bananas	2 teaspoons grated orange peel
(not pureed), 3 to 4 medium bananas	

Preheat the oven to 375 degrees. Butter generously a 9½ × 5 × 3-inch loaf pan or an 8 × 3-inch round pan. Dust the pan with flour and shake out any excess flour.

Coarsely chop the walnuts and toss with 2 tablespoons of the flour. Set aside.

Sift together the remaining flour, baking soda, baking powder, cinnamon or allspice, and salt, and set aside.

Combine the mashed bananas with the orange juice. Set aside.

Combine the eggs, sugar, oil, sour cream, and orange peel in the bowl of a standing mixer fitted with the paddle attachment or use a large mixing bowl and a handheld electric mixer.

Beat the mixture on medium-high or creaming speed for 2 to 3 minutes, scraping the sides of the bowl with a rubber spatula once or twice. Stir in the mashed banana-orange juice mixture and beat 1 minute longer.

Add the flour-spice mixture to the bowl, about one third at a time, and mix on low speed just until combined.

After the last addition, beat the batter on low speed for 1 minute. Using a wooden spoon, stir in the floured walnuts, and mix well but gently.

Pour the batter into the prepared pan. Shake the pan gently to settle the batter, and place on the lower rack of the hot oven.

Bake the cake for 50 to 55 minutes, or until a knife or toothpick inserted in the center comes out clean and the cake is puffy and golden brown.

Remove the cake from the oven, place on a wire rack, and cool in the pan for 10 minutes. Loosen the edges of the cake with a metal spatula, invert the pan onto the rack, tap gently, and remove the pan. Place the cake top side up on the rack and cool completely.

Spread the cake with Creamy Chocolate Glaze (page 66) or top with Nut Brown Glaze (page 70), or serve with a dusting of confectioners' sugar.

Makes 8 servings

Nut Brown Glaze

This silky glaze is an inspiration from sister Edna Lewis, who years ago, when she was a chef at a famous restaurant in New York City, topped plain yellow cake with a nutty burnt sugar glaze. Mrs. Lewis used heavy cream; I like the tangy flavor that old-fashioned buttermilk provides.

This glaze has a burnished flavor and a shiny deep amber color. It is great on both cookies and cakes, especially Banana Cake (page 68).

1 cup buttermilk
½ teaspoon baking soda
1½ cups dark brown sugar, firmly
   packed

2 tablespoons light corn syrup
4 tablespoons unsalted butter
½ teaspoon vanilla extract
2 tablespoons rum or brandy, if desired

Combine the buttermilk, baking soda, sugar, and corn syrup in a heavy 3-quart saucepan with a lid. Place the pan on medium heat, and cook, stirring, until the sugar dissolves, from 3 to 4 minutes.

Cover the pan, raise the heat, and boil the syrup for 3 minutes.

Uncover, reduce the heat to medium, and cook the syrup without stirring but swirling the pan, until it is as thick as honey, for 5 to 7 minutes.

Remove the pan from the heat and swirl in the butter, vanilla extract, and rum or brandy.

Set the pan on a wire rack, cool completely, and then spread on the cake. If the glaze becomes a little stiff, stir in a tablespoon of hot water or milk and beat until smooth.

Makes a scant 1½ cups; generous amount for an 8- or 9-inch cake

Orange Tea Cake

Whenever I visit my friend Shirley Brown, and her soul mate, husband Mel, I never get a moment's rest. Their friends come and go all the time, and the kitchen in their lovely home in Farmington Hills, Michigan, a Detroit suburb, is the favored gathering spot.

Shirley is a superb hostess, an art collector, generous to a fault, and thinks nothing of putting together a meal on a moment's notice, while never missing a beat of the topic at hand.

She is an excellent cook, and this delightful, moist cake is reason enough to gather in the kitchen, sip tea and coffee, and solve all of the world's problems.

Shirley is a beloved spiritual sister.

CAKE BATTER:

$1/2$ cup shelled pistachio nuts (see Nuts About Nuts, page 49)

$1^3/4$ cups all-purpose flour

$1/2$ teaspoon baking soda

1 teaspoon baking powder

$1/8$ teaspoon salt

12 tablespoons ($1^1/2$ sticks) unsalted butter, softened

$1^1/2$ to 2 tablespoons grated orange peel

1 cup granulated sugar

2 large eggs, at room temperature

1 teaspoon vanilla extract

$1/2$ cup sour cream

$1/2$ cup fresh orange juice

ORANGE SYRUP:

$1/3$ cup orange juice

$1/3$ cup granulated sugar or brown crystallized sugar (see Dark and Sweet, page 25)

2 or 3 tablespoons orange liqueur, such as Grand Marnier, or orange-flavored rum, such as Bacardi O

Preheat the oven to 350 degrees. Butter generously a 9 × 2-inch round pan or a 9 × 5 × 3-inch loaf pan or an $8^1/2$ × $2^1/2$-inch springform. Dust the pan with flour and shake out any excess flour.

Scatter the shelled pistachio nuts on a baking sheet. Set the pan in the oven on the middle shelf and toast the nuts for 5 to 7 minutes, stirring with a wooden spoon once or twice.

As soon as the nuts are lightly brown and fragrant, remove from the oven and transfer to a plate. Spread the nuts on a tea towel and rub briskly with the towel to remove the skins, or cut away the skins with a small knife.

Toss the nuts with 2 tablespoons of the flour and set aside.

Sift together the remaining flour, baking soda, baking powder, and salt and set aside.

Combine the butter, orange peel, and sugar in the bowl of a standing mixer fitted with the paddle attachment or use a large mixing bowl and a handheld electric mixer. Beat the mixture on medium-high or creaming speed for 3 to 4 minutes or until light and fluffy, scraping down the sides of the bowl with a rubber spatula once or twice.

Add the eggs one at a time, mixing about 30 seconds after each addition, scraping down the bowl as needed. Stir in the vanilla extract.

Mix together in a small bowl or cup, the sour cream and orange juice. Stir until well blended. Add the flour and sour cream-orange juice mixture alternately to the creamed mixture, mixing only until just blended.

Set the mixer on low speed and beat the batter for 1 minute, scraping down the sides of the bowl at least once.

Scatter the nuts over the batter, and mix just until blended. Pour the batter into the prepared pan. Shake the pan to settle the batter.

Place the pan in the center of the preheated oven on the middle shelf. Bake for 40 to 45 minutes or until golden brown, puffy, and a knife inserted in the center of the cake comes out clean. Set the pan on a wire rack but do not remove from the pan.

Prepare the orange syrup: Combine in a small saucepan the orange juice, sugar, and liqueur or rum. Set the pan over medium-high heat, stirring to dissolve the sugar. Bring the syrup to a boil and cook 1 minute.

Remove from the heat and pour the hot syrup over the cake in the pan. Cool the cake in the pan for 15 minutes. Run a metal spatula or knife around the edge of the pan to loosen the cake and then tap the pan gently.

Carefully turn out the cake onto a wire rack. Cool completely, right side up.

If using a springform pan, unfasten the sides of the pan and remove. Carefully invert the cake onto the wire rack. Run the tip of a metal spatula between the bottom of the pan and the cake. When loose, lift off the bottom of the pan. Cool the cake top side up on the wire rack.

Serve the cake with Perfectly Whipped Cream (page 74) or Vanilla Bean Ice Cream (page 216) or Burnt Sugar Ice Cream (page 211).

Makes 6 to 8 servings

Variation: This cake is also delicious made with either tangy lemon juice or sour or Seville oranges (see Sweet Citrus, page 245). Since lemon and Seville orange juice are tart, increase the sugar in the syrup to 1/2 cup, if desired, and proceed as directed in above recipe.

Perfectly Whipped Cream

When buying heavy cream be sure to check the date on the carton and buy the freshest possible. If the cream is not fresh, it will turn watery and thin when whipped.

1 cup heavy cream, chilled
1 to 2 tablespoons sugar, preferably
  superfine

1 to 2 tablespoons fruit liqueur or
  brandy or dark rum or $\frac{1}{4}$ teaspoon
  vanilla extract

Pour the cream into a medium-size mixing bowl. Set the bowl with the cream and the beaters from a handheld electric mixer in the freezer for 10 to 15 minutes.

When thoroughly chilled, stir in the sugar and liqueur or brandy or rum or vanilla extract.

Beat the cream until it mounds and forms soft peaks but no longer. If the cream is overbeaten, it becomes dry and grainy.

The whipped cream can be stored in the coldest part of the refrigerator in a container with a tight lid for 2 or 3 days.

Makes about 2 cups or 6 to 8 servings as a dessert topping

Black Walnut Pound Cake

Brenda Richardson was visiting the farmers' market at Union Square in New York City when she spotted a pile of aromatic black walnuts and decided to buy a big bag for yours truly.

A nice gesture, but so like Brenda, who has written and published more books than most people I know: seven at last count, and it is getting harder and harder to keep up with her creative work.

Brenda and I met years ago when we were journalism fellows at Stanford University. Both of us were newspaper reporters at the time; young mothers, we had our sons in tow, and we became friends, real fast. Brenda's son, Harlen, HP, as we call him, is only a couple months older than my son, Roy, who was two at the time. Brenda was living in Oakland, California, then and we never thought that someday we would be living within shouting distance of each other.

A few years ago, Brenda and her husband, Mark, and their two beautiful teenage children, Mark Junior and Carolyn, relocated to New York City, right near where I live. Hallelujah! Harlen, who is a young man now, still lives in California.

Brenda is a superb hostess, and at a recent gathering during the middle of the summer at her lovely home, long after she had bought me those black walnuts, I baked that cake for her, which she simply loved.

Black walnuts are native to the Americas and are highly appreciated by Native Americans. They have a rich and assertive flavor, and especially complement "plain" cakes left unfrosted, such as this delectable pound cake, which was inspired by a version in sister Edna Lewis's classic cookbook, *In Pursuit of Flavor*.

Maybe I dragged a little bit baking this cake because I knew I had my work cut out for me. Black walnuts are tough nuts to crack. They're covered with both a tough husk and shell, and it is far less time consuming and labor intensive to buy already cracked nutmeat, which is increasingly available at supermarkets during the holidays, sold in plastic bags.

But if you love hands-on tasks like I do—and Brenda knows I do—and can't resist the pleasure of cracking the nuts yourself, you'll need at least 7 or 8 pounds to guarantee 1 cup of nutmeat. And if you decide to gather the nuts during the fall of the year when they fall from trees, remember that they are covered with a yellow-green hull or husk that must be removed before you even get to the woody brown shell. A hammer or corn sheller works best for this. If you leave this outer husk on it eventually turns black and moldy, and can impart a sour flavor to the nutmeat.

After the husks are removed, the walnuts have to be washed and spread out on a screen and dried in a cool, dry place. But first check to make sure that there is nutmeat inside the nuts; sometimes it isn't because the trees are temperamental and some years don't bear fruit. Simply put the nuts in a tub or pan filled with water. Nuts that fall to the bottom have nutmeat inside. The floaters don't, so throw them away.

Some growers and sellers dry the nuts for 2 or 3 weeks, and others, like the Hammons Company of Stockton, Missouri, for at least three months. The nuts that Brenda bought me from the farmers' market had already been hulled and dried, so all I had to do was shell and crack.

I immediately ordered from Hammons a black walnut nutcracker that cost forty-five dollars; not cheap but it does split the nuts open. The day the intimidating gadget arrived, looking just like a rodent trap, I pulled out my bag of nuts from the freezer—where they should be kept to prevent the nutmeat from turning rancid—and soaked them in water for an hour to soften the shells.

I then drained and dried the nuts and got to work. I became concerned about the shells popping up and hitting me in the eye, but I don't own safety goggles, so I put on a pair of swim goggles. I then pulled on a pair of heavy duty work gloves to keep from staining my hands with the walnut shells. Three hours later—backed up by a hammer and a small metal skewer—I managed to extract the cup of nutmeat I needed for the recipe.

By that time I had mastered the art: split the nuts open with my overpriced nutcracker, wrap in a tea towel, and whack a couple times with the hammer. Use the point of the skewer to dig out pieces of nut left in the shell. Lord have mercy. As I nibbled on a few of the rich and pungent morsels that were almost winelike in flavor, I felt like doing a little dance. Tired, fingers aching, but exhilarated.

I even ignored my son, Roy, when he stopped by, took one look at me—I still had on my work getup—and the kitchen, which was splattered with black walnut shells, and said, "Mom, what fool's project are you involved with now?"

I just fixed myself a cocktail.

But I admit the next time I made the cake I grabbed the bag of nutmeat that I had ordered from Hammons and stored in the freezer. Not quite as rustic, but soon my kitchen was reeling with the same delightful aroma of the pungent, wild, delicious nuts.

1 cup black walnuts

2 cups cake flour

1/8 teaspoon salt

1/2 pound (2 sticks) unsalted butter, softened

1 1/2 cups light brown sugar, firmly packed

4 large eggs, at room temperature

2 teaspoons vanilla extract, or less

2 tablespoons brown crystallized sugar, such as turbinado or Demerara (see Dark and Sweet, page 25)

Preheat the oven to 325 degrees. Butter generously an 8-cup fluted pan or mold or a 9 × 2-inch round pan or an 8 1/2 × 2 1/2-inch springform pan. Dust the pan with flour and shake out any excess flour.

If in large pieces, coarsely chop the walnuts, toss with 2 tablespoons of the flour, and set aside.

Sift together the remaining flour and salt and set aside.

Combine the butter and sugar in the bowl of a standing mixer fitted with the paddle attachment or use a large mixing bowl and a handheld electric mixer. Beat the sugar and butter until light and fluffy, for about 6 minutes with the stand mixer and for 8 minutes with the handheld mixer, scraping the bowl two or three times with a rubber spatula.

Add the eggs one at a time, beating 30 seconds after each addition, scraping the bowl as needed. Stir in the vanilla extract.

Set aside 1 cup of the flour. Stir the remaining flour into the creamed mixture. Set the mixer on low speed and beat the batter for 2 minutes, scraping the bowl as needed.

If using the stand mixer, remove the bowl from the mixer. Stir in the walnuts and then carefully fold in the remaining cup of flour, mixing gently. Spoon the batter into the prepared cake pan. Shake the pan to settle the batter.

Sprinkle the top of the cake with the sugar. Place the pan in the center of the hot oven on the middle shelf.

Bake for 50 to 60 minutes or until the cake is golden brown, puffy, and a knife inserted in the center comes out clean but moist.

Remove the cake from the oven, place on a wire rack, and cool in the pan for 10 minutes. Run a metal spatula or knife around the edge of the pan to loosen the cake and then tap the pan gently. Carefully turn out the cake onto a plate and then set on wire rack, top side up. Cool completely.

If using a springform pan, unfasten the sides of the pan and remove. Carefully invert the cake onto a plate. Run the tip of a metal spatula between the bottom of the pan and the cake. When loose, lift off the bottom of the pan. Cool the cake top side up on the wire rack.

Makes 8 to 10 servings

Note: Black walnuts in the shell and nutmeat can be ordered from Hammons Pantry by calling: 1-800-872-6879. If not using immediately, store both the nutmeat and whole black walnuts in the freezer. The nutmeat will keep at least a year, and the whole nuts for two years or more. Expect to pay at least twice as much for black walnuts as for, say, shelled pecans or English walnuts.

Chocolate Pound Cake

When I sent out letters asking friends to contribute a favorite family recipe for this book, the first person to respond was K. Wise Whitehead. In a day or two she sent me a recipe for her mom's sweet potato pie, and followed up with five cake recipes, including this moist and velvety pound cake.

Not surprising. Little Sister, as I refer to her, tackles every task with zeal, and when I reflect on her accomplishments, I shake my head in wonder. A dozen years ago, while still in college, she lived in Africa for a year and worked for two months on a fishing boat cleaning fish, going up and down the river from Tanzania to Kenya. When she was in Kenya she lived in a hilltop hut with a blind woman, and one of her jobs was to fetch the water every day.

K. is now a senior producer at Metro TV in New York City, where she lives with her young son, Kofi Elijah, daughter, Mercedes, and her husband, Johnnie Whitehead.

She brought a world of experience to her job. She has worked for Golden Books and MTV Networks; in the mid-1990s, the Black Filmmaker Foundation (director Spike Lee was a judge), named her an emerging filmmaker. K. went on to make an award-winning film on domestic violence with the award.

She has made several documentary films and has also self-published two books of poetry that ring with images of food and comfort: *Red Zinger Love Starved Blues,* and *Soul Mates and Soul Food.*

Here's the real kicker: she is still just in her early thirties.

"My mother used to say that if you can't find a way to move the mountain, then go around or under it," says K., in a typical homily.

K.'s mom, Mrs. Bonnie Ruth Nix Wise, who lives in Washington, D.C., often bakes and serves this delicious cake, which was passed on to her by her mother.

1¾ cups cake flour	2 cups granulated sugar
⅔ cup unsweetened cocoa, preferably Dutch-process	4 large eggs, at room temperature
	1½ to 2 teaspoons vanilla extract
¼ teaspoon salt	1 cup sour cream, at room temperature
½ pound (2 sticks) unsalted butter, softened	Coffee Glaze (page 81) (see Note, page 80)

Preheat the oven to 325 degrees. Butter generously a 9 × 3-inch round or contour pan or a 9 × 3-inch springform pan. Dust the pan with flour and shake out any excess flour.

Set aside 1 cup of the flour. Sift together the remaining flour, cocoa, and salt and set aside.

Combine the butter and sugar in the bowl of a standing mixer fitted with the paddle attachment or use a large mixing bowl and a handheld electric mixer. Beat the mixture until light and fluffy, for 6 to 8 minutes, scraping the bowl two or three times with a rubber spatula.

Add the eggs one at a time, beating 30 seconds after each addition, scraping the bowl as needed. Stir in the vanilla extract. Add the sour cream and beat 1 minute longer.

Stir the flour-and-cocoa mixture into the creamed mixture. Set the beater on low speed and beat the batter for 2 minutes, scraping the bowl as needed.

Using a wooden spoon, carefully fold in the remaining cup of flour and mix gently. Pour the batter into the prepared cake pan. Shake the pan to settle the batter.

Place the pan in the center of the hot oven on the middle shelf. Bake for 60 to 70 minutes or until the cake is puffy and brown and a knife inserted in the center comes out clean but moist. The timing may vary; but watch carefully and don't overbake.

Remove the cake from the oven, place on a wire rack, and cool in the pan for 10 minutes. Run a metal spatula or knife around the edge of the pan to loosen the cake and then tap the pan gently. Carefully turn out the cake onto the wire rack and cool top side up.

If using a springform pan, unfasten the sides of the pan and remove. Carefully invert the cake onto the wire rack. Run the tip of a metal spatula between the bottom of the pan and the cake. When loose, lift off the bottom of the pan. Cool the cake top side up on the wire rack.

Spread the cooled cake with Coffee Glaze.

Makes 8 to 10 servings

Note: You can also use Honey Cream (page 242).

Coffee Glaze

Mrs. Wise usually serves her Chocolate Pound Cake (page 79) with a dusting of confectioners' sugar. This Coffee Glaze turns it into a mocha delight. If you like the glaze with an intense coffee flavor use 3 teaspoons of powder; if not, use 2 teaspoons or so.

1½ cups granlated sugar
2 to 3 teaspoons instant coffee or espresso powder (see headnote above)
2 tablespoons light corn syrup

1 cup water
2 tablespoons unsalted butter
1 tablespoon dark rum or brandy or coffee liqueur, such as Kahlúa, if desired

Combine the sugar, coffee, corn syrup, and 1 cup water in a 3-quart saucepan. Cook over medium heat, stirring, until the sugar dissolves. Cover the pan, place on medium-high heat, and boil for 3 minutes.

Reduce the heat to medium, uncover the pan, and cook the glaze 10 to 12 minutes or until thick and syrupy, swirling the pan, but not stirring. Remove the pan from the heat and stir in the butter and the rum, brandy, or liqueur, if desired.

Cool completely and spread over a 9-inch cake.

Makes about 1½ cups; for glazing 1 cake

Note: If there is leftover glaze, place in a small jar and refrigerate. It is delectable spooned over vanilla ice cream or plain yogurt and fruit.

Bitter but Sweet Remember when we had to reach for either Hershey's, Baker's, or Nestlé to satisfy our chocolate craving? No more.

Chocolates with brand names such as Valrhona, Lindt, Tobler, Callebaut, Scharffen Berger, and my favorite, Ghirardelli, now crowd supermarket shelves. And they range from semisweet to bittersweet to unsweetened, with the latter having no added sugar. Both semisweet and bittersweet chocolates have added sugar and the amount varies with the manufacturers. Generally bittersweet chocolate contains about 50 percent unsweetened chocolate and semisweet from 35 to 45 percent—not a big difference. And if you aren't a purist, you can use either bittersweet or semisweet in most recipes. I generally do.

These connoisseur chocolates are made like fine wine, from top-quality cacao or cocoa beans grown primarily in West Africa, Brazil, Venezuela, and Indonesia.

After the cocoa beans are roasted, chocolate liquor and cocoa butter are extracted from the beans' center cores, which are called nibs. The cocoa butter is set aside and the chocolate liquor is pulverized and refined during a process known as conching, which can last from several hours to several days, hence the higher price for the top-grade chocolates.

Bitter cocoa remains after the extraction, and this powdery residue is superb for baking cakes. It provides a more intense flavor to cake batters than bar chocolate, which is best for frostings, cookies, sauces, and candy making.

Most cocoa imported from Europe is treated to the "Dutch process," meaning that its acidity has been tempered with a substance similar to baking soda. This results in a smooth powder with a little higher content of cocoa butter, and a richer flavor than untreated cocoa, such as the old domestic standby, Hershey's.

When making a cake batter, don't substitute Dutch-process cocoa for unprocessed cocoa, or vice versa, because the cake won't rise properly. But if the recipes simply says "unsweetened cocoa," here's a guideline: Use baking soda as a leavening with untreated cocoa, and use baking powder with Dutch-process cocoa.

However, you can substitute one cocoa for the other in frostings, sauces, and candy, since no rising is required.

And ain't that sweet.❀

I had made the peach preserves, grated a fresh coconut, set out the butter, eggs, and milk, and sifted the flour. But when I measured out 5 cups of sugar I decided it was time to call my beautiful niece Toni, to see if we could put our heads together and "lighten up" her cake recipe.

My request was met with an expected chuckle, and then Toni sighed and said, "They'll just have to cut calories somewhere else, Aunt Joyce. This is not a cake you make all the time; just for holidays and special occasions."

She paused a moment and added, with just a hint of exasperation, as if I, of all people, should know this: "Those old Southern cakes are real rich and extravagant. That's what makes them so special."

They are showy and elaborate, often boasting three or four cake layers—and sometimes more—sandwiched with jam or jelly or preserves, or with a custard filling laced with bourbon, fruits, and nuts, especially raisins and pecans. Many are festooned with a boiled frosting that may never fluff up on a hot and humid day, but when that happens you simply spread on the soft icing the best you can, stick the cake in the refrigerator, and 2 hours later no one will notice that the cake is a little more homespun than usual. It's the cake that counts.

And for the Christmas holidays, fruitcakes are baked and soaked with bourbon, and treated to as much ritual and ceremony as in the Caribbean, where the cakes are spiked with rum and colored with burnt sugar.

In the Old South, two fruits, ironically imported from the tropics, pineapple and coconuts, reigned supreme in these cakes from the past, and Toni's version of the popular Southern coconut cake is sublime. The cake layers are spread with fresh peach preserves, scattered with coconut, stacked, covered with boiled frosting, and then blanketed with lightly toasted coconut. Toni says she created the cake to please those who wanted the aromatic peach filling cake, and the creamy coconut cake—both delectable Southern specialties—turned into one divine cake.

Toni is a part of my Gulf Coast family, and she was married to my brother John's oldest son, Lamar, who passed away suddenly after a tragic accident. At the time the couple was living in Los Angeles, having relocated there from the Gulf Coast, just like Aunt Mary had done three generations before.

Another of John's sons, Joe, and his lovely wife, Renee, moved to Los Angeles, and soon the brothers and their wives and children were hanging together like white on rice. Both Lamar and Joe were fine college football players—Joe made a splash as an NFL pro quarterback for several years—and they often indulged their passion for sports in each other's households, and food was always on the table.

Toni did most of the cooking, honing a talent that she began at age eight.

"There were three girls in my family," says Toni, who a few years ago moved back to the Mississippi Gulf Coast. "One of my sisters was a bookworm, the other was a tomboy, and I was the cook."

And she does cook with passion. When she was living in L.A., she often baked cakes and pies and carried them to her coworkers at the UCLA Medical Center, where she worked as a unit service coordinator. During the Thanksgiving-Christmas holiday season she would cook for days; split a baked 20-pound turkey down the middle, and share it and all the trimmings, plus three or four cakes and pies, with Joe and Renee, a time-pressed real estate broker.

They in turn would pick up the dinner and share the sumptuous meal with friends on Christmas Day, simply because both families wanted to branch out during the holiday season.

"When I think of those days in Los Angeles," says Toni, wistfully, "I remember the time when my family was happy and intact."

Coconut-Peach Cake

This elegant cake is perfect for a wedding reception. Very lightly toasted coconut adds a tawny color to the cake, but if you prefer a snowy pristine look, don't toast the coconut. Place the cake on a nice crystal platter and ring it with candied violets.

Toni likes the cake stacked with homemade peach preserves, but it is just as pretty, and delicious, with plum preserves made with black or Santa Rose plums, which turn into a delightful purplish-red color. So both recipes are included.

And on a hot, humid day, whipped cream is a fine covering for a coconut cake—a nice substitute for temperamental boiled icing. Recipes for both frostings are included.

CAKE LAYERS:

3 cups cake flour

1 tablespoon baking powder

1/4 teaspoon salt

1/2 pound (2 sticks butter), softened

1 1/2 cups granulated sugar

4 large eggs, at room temperature

2 teaspoons vanilla extract

1 cup whole milk, at room temperature

2 1/2 to 3 cups freshly shredded coconut, lightly toasted (see Cracking Coconuts, page 245)

PEACH OR PLUM FILLING:

1 1/2 cups Peach or Plum Preserves (page 272)

2 tablespoons peach brandy or peach schnapps

VANILLA ICING:

3 large egg whites, at room temperature (see Note below)

1 1/2 cups granulated sugar

1/3 cup water

2 tablespoons light corn syrup

1/4 teaspoon cider vinegar or cream of tartar

1 teaspoon fresh lemon juice

1 teaspoon vanilla extract

Preheat the oven to 350 degrees. Butter three 8 x 1 1/2-inch round cake pans. Dust with flour and shake out any excess flour.

Sift the flour with the baking powder and salt and set aside.

Combine the butter and sugar in the bowl of a standing mixer fitted with the paddle attachment or use a large mixing bowl and a handheld electric mixer. Beat the sugar and butter until light and fluffy, for 3 to 5 minutes, scraping the bowl once or twice with a rubber spatula.

Beat in the eggs one at a time, beating about 30 seconds after each addition, and scraping the bowl as needed. Stir in the vanilla extract. Set the mixer at low speed. Alternately add the flour and milk to the creamed mixture, mixing only until blended after each addition, ending with the flour.

After the last addition, beat the batter on low speed for 30 seconds, or until the batter is smooth and satiny.

Using a measuring cup, pour the batter into the prepared pans, dividing evenly. Shake the pans gently to settle the batter.

Place the cake pans in a triangular pattern in the hot oven on the middle shelf. Make sure that the cake pans don't touch. Bake the cake layers for 20 minutes, and then quickly change the position of the pans in the oven for even browning, shifting the pans from front to back and vice versa.

Bake for 5 to 7 minutes longer or until the cake layers are brown and puffy and a knife inserted in the center comes out clean, or until the layers pull away from the sides of the pan.

Remove the cake layers from the oven, place on wire racks, and allow to cool in the pans for 10 minutes. Don't turn off the oven.

Run a knife or metal spatula around the edges of the cake pans, tap gently, and carefully turn the cake layers out onto the wire racks and cool completely, top side up.

To toast the coconut: Scatter $1^1/_2$ to 2 cups of the coconut on a baking sheet or jelly-roll pan. Set the pan on the middle rack of the 350-degree oven. Toast the coconut for about 5 minutes, or until it is barely tinged golden brown, shaking the pan or stirring the coconut with a wooden spoon once or twice. Watch carefully and don't let the coconut burn or overbrown.

Use the remaining 1 cup of coconut for the filling, untoasted.

To make the Peach or Plum Filling: Combine the preserves and brandy or schnapps in a medium bowl. Beat briskly until well blended and smooth. Set aside.

To prepare the Vanilla Icing: Carefully crack the eggs one at a time and place the yolk and egg white into two separate small bowls, making sure that not one speck of yolk mixes in with the egg white. If the egg white is free of yolk, transfer it to a large spotless clean bowl for whipping. If the egg yolk drips into the egg white, discard that egg white and break another egg, using a clean bowl. Set aside the egg whites to warm to room temperature and return the yolks to the refrigerator (see Get the Whip, page 132). The egg yolks can be frozen and used in a custard, or scrambled for breakfast.

Have ready a long-handled wooden spoon, a pastry brush, a cup of hot water for brushing down sugar crystals from the sides of the pan, a candy thermometer, and a hand mixer with clean beaters.

When the egg whites reach room temperature, combine the sugar, $1/3$ cup water, and the corn syrup in a heavy 3-quart saucepan that has a tight-fitting lid.

Stir briskly with the wooden spoon to dissolve the sugar. Set the pan on medium heat and cook, stirring, until the sugar is completely dissolved. Cover the pan, raise the heat to medium-high, and cook for 3 minutes.

While the sugar is boiling, using the hand mixer set at medium-high speed, beat the egg whites until they are foamy. Sprinkle over the vinegar or cream of tartar and continue beating until the egg whites form soft peaks. Don't overbeat; this should take no more than 3 minutes. Set aside.

Uncover the pan, dip the pastry brush in the hot water, and wipe away any crystals on the inside of the pan. Attach the candy thermometer to the inside of the pan, raise the heat a bit, and cook the syrup, without stirring, until it reaches 238 to 240 degrees. (This should take about 4 minutes.)

Remove the syrup from the heat, let cool for 1 to 2 minutes, and then pour into the egg whites in a thin stream while beating on high speed. Continue beating until the icing is thick and glossy and holds a shape, for about 7 minutes.

Beat in the lemon juice and vanilla extract and spread the icing immediately over the cooled cake.

If the icing begins to harden, stir in a little of the hot water and beat briskly.

Makes 3 generous cups vanilla icing

To assemble the cake (Icing on the Cake, page 89): Place one cake layer top side down on a cake platter. Spread with half of the peach preserves or plum filling—$^3/_4$ cup—smoothing with a metal spatula. Sprinkle on $^1/_2$ cup of the untoasted coconut.

Place on the second layer, top side up, and spread with the remaining preserves and the remaining $^1/_2$ cup untoasted coconut. Top with the third layer, bottom side down. Secure the cake in place with metal skewers if it is leaning.

Spread the cake all over—sides and top—with the Vanilla Icing or with the Whipped Cream Frosting (page 93), swirling for a pretty effect.

Coat the cake all over with the toasted coconut, patting lightly with your hand.

Set the cake in a cool, dark place until ready to serve. Refrigerate any leftover cake.

Makes 10 to 12 servings

Note: If you aren't sure about the safety of the egg whites you plan to use in the icing, consider using pasteurized egg whites or reconstituted powdered egg whites instead. Powdered egg whites or meringue powder can be ordered from Wilton at 1-800-794-5866, or on line at www.wilton.com.

Icing on the Cake

Truth be told, few people like cakes festooned with garlands and rosettes of tinted confectioners' sugar frosting that have you digging forever for the heart of the cake. In fact, creativity puts the real icing on the cake, and you'll be surprised how a few embellishments, such as diced dried fruits, nuts, and candied peel, can turn a homemade cake into an artisan's delight.

Here are tricks of the trade that I learned years ago when I did food photography for *Ladies' Home Journal* magazine:

- Use a measuring cup to pour the batter into the prepared cake pans so that the same amount is placed in each pan. This way you end up with even layers, which look prettier when stacked and frosted.

- Make sure that the cake layers are real cool before frosting. Ideally, the layers should be baked one day, cooled thoroughly, wrapped in plastic or wax paper, and decorated the next.

- When you are ready to frost, if the layers are buckling or bulging on the top, use a long-bladed serrated knife (10- to 12-inch) and carefully cut off a thin slice, making each layer as level as possible.

- If you need to split cake layers so that you can end up with one of those dramatic Southern numbers, such as a pineapple or coconut cake that soars 5 to 6 stories, as my father used to say, here's how to do it: Using a ruler as a guide, insert long thin wooden skewers, or toothpicks, exactly halfway up the side of the cake layer in six to eight places. Then, resting the serrated knife against the sticks, cut the layer in half, using a long sawing motion. That's all.

  Inspect and brush off any crumbs. If there are a lot, melt a little jelly and brush the warm liquid over the crumbs, sealing them to the cake. Set the cake layers in the refrigerator for 10 to 15 minutes to allow the glaze to dry.

- A cold and thick frosting will cause the cake to pull off onto the spatula when you spread it. Stir the frosting and have it at room temperature. If it is real thick, add a little warm milk or cream to the frosting and beat briskly.

- Get out a nice cake platter, and even better, a footed or stand platter or a Lazy Susan type of turntable, so that you can move the cake around as you work and see what you are doing. Place a paper or cotton doily—if desired—on the platter and lay four strips of wax paper—3 or 4 inches wide—on the edge of the plate, overlapping, to catch drippings, covering the doily.

  Now stack: Place a cake layer upside down on the cake plate, bottom up. Using the metal spatula, spread the top of that layer with about $^3/_4$ cup filling or frosting, or the amount stated in the recipe. As you spread, try to keep the spatula on the icing and not on the cake, to prevent picking up crumbs.

  Place the next cake layer bottom side down, which should result in an even "fit" for a two-layer cake. For a three-layer cake, spread the top of the second layer with frosting, and place on the third layer, bottom side down.

- If the cake is lopsided and leaning precariously like the Tower of Pisa, gently straighten it up and insert a couple of thin metal skewers or wire cake testers from the top layer down to the cake plate. Thin knitting needles work just as well. Let the anchors remain in the cake until you are ready to serve, and then remove and cover the entry holes with a little frosting.

- To frost the sides, dip a metal spatula in warm water and dry it off. Spread a thin layer of frosting all over the cake, moving from the bottom to the top, bringing the frosting a little higher than the top, forming a rim. Try to keep the spatula on the frosting and not on the cake, and turn the cake around as you work. Chill the cake for about 30 minutes to allow the sealing to set.

- Frost the chilled cake generously with the remaining frosting, beginning from the bottom and moving to the top, again forming a little rim, but save about $^3/_4$ cup frosting for the top.

  Spread the remaining frosting across the top of the cake, connecting it to the rim, using a back-and-forth motion.

  Check to see that the frosting has been applied as evenly as possible.

- Several decorative options await. If you prefer a soft look, using the back of a tablespoon or a metal spatula, twirl the frosting in a circular motion, using a little more frosting as needed, for swirls and peaks. Do this on both the sides and the top.

For a smooth and sleek look, dip a metal spatula in warm water, shake off the excess, and smooth the top and sides of the cake.

Then, take a serrated knife and comb it across the top of the cake. Or, using a tablespoon with the bowl turned downward, make dimples across the top of the cake.

- To decorate the top with chopped nuts, first form a small circle of nuts in the center of the cake, followed by another larger circle, and then place a ring of nuts on the edge of the cake for three exquisite circles. Or, scatter the top with curled strips of Candied Citrus Peel (page 124), or form the peels into a circle on top of the cake.

  You can also make a little ring of chopped nuts in the center of the cake and place lines of nuts radiating from the center like spokes or flower petals.

- A cake decorated with a border or a pile of chocolate curls is also dramatic. To make the curls, wrap a 2- to 3-inch piece of good-quality semisweet or bittersweet chocolate in a small square of wax or parchment paper. Dip your hands in very warm water and dry off. Rub the chocolate briskly with your hands until you feel it warming and softening.

  Unwrap the chocolate but leave it on the paper and hold it in one hand. Holding a vegetable peeler in the other hand, cut into the chocolate, press down, and bring the blade toward you, creating long curls. The greater the pressure the fatter the curls.

  If the chocolate is not warm enough it will break off into splinters and will not curl. Cover it with the wax paper, warm your hands again, rub briskly, and try once more.

  If the chocolate is too soft the curls will collapse into strips, which you can allow to harden and scatter over the cake for a pretty effect.

- You can also coat the sides of the cakes with lightly toasted coconut or finely chopped nuts or toasted slivered almonds.

- When my son was growing up, I decorated his birthday cake with chocolate sprinkles and sparkling sugars and nonpareils that come in rainbow colors and numerous shapes.

  Fill the palm of your hand with the desired ingredient and press onto the side of the cake, moving your hand up and down and around the cake until it is covered.

- For an eye-stopping look, lay a paper doily on the top of a frosted cake. Sprinkle the paper all over with about 2 or 3 tablespoons confectioners' sugar, cocoa, or even brown crystallized sugar. Remove the doily and *voilà*, there is a pretty pattern!

Once a cake is decorated, place your lovely creation in a cool place and allow the frosting to set completely before serving. On a hot and humid day, chill the cake for about 30 minutes to set the frosting, and then place in a cool spot.

Before serving, remove the paper strips and wire anchors, if you used them. Leftover cake with a cream or whipped cream frosting should be refrigerated after serving. Keep other plain or frosted cake in a cool place, stored in a domed glass or tin cake keeper. ❀

Whipped Cream Frosting

When my son, Roy, was growing up, this was his favorite frosting for his birthday cake. It is quick and easy and delicious.

½ cup superfine sugar

2 tablespoons light corn syrup

2 tablespoons water or fruit juice, such as apple or pineapple

1 or 2 tablespoons dark rum, if desired

½ teaspoon vanilla extract

1½ cups heavy cream, chilled

Combine the sugar, corn syrup, and water or fruit juice in a small saucepan. Bring to a boil and cook 2 minutes, stirring.

Remove from the heat and stir in the rum and vanilla extract. Cool completely.

Pour the heavy cream into a large, chilled bowl. Stir in the sugar syrup. Chill the mixture, plus the beaters from a handheld electric mixer, for at least 30 minutes.

Then, beat the mixture until the cream mounds, just holding stiff but soft peaks. Don't overbeat. Spread the top and sides of the cake with frosting.

Makes about 3 cups; enough to generously frost a three-layer cake

Caramel Cake

Florida Ingram Brown must have sent me at least twenty recipes, and like the late Velma Mosley, forced me into the delicate task of selecting one or two for this book. Not easy, considering that Florida has been cooking virtually all of her life, and does so with unbounded enthusiasm and expertise.

She dines out all the time, has taken numerous cooking classes over the years, and can cite word for word dishes she made from this or that recipe thirty years ago.

Some of the recipes she sent me, like this Caramel Cake, date back to her childhood in Waverly Hall, Georgia, where she grew up on a farm. Florida recalls that years ago her mother and aunts would gather at her grandma's house during the Christmas holidays and "bake a whole bunch of cakes."

"Pineapple cake, coconut cake, caramel cake, chocolate cake, jelly cake, you name it," she says. "Then they would put all the cakes in one room. We didn't have to worry about putting the cakes in the refrigerator. They stayed cold; the house didn't have much heat."

Florida now lives in Altadena, California, just outside of Los Angeles, with her husband, Costello, who is a chemistry professor, and her two children, Eric, already a medical doctor, and Ninita, who is finishing up medical school. Florida is a lab technician, and a passionate cook.

This beautiful cake, with its shiny, glistening deep tan color and burnt flavor, was a favorite of my family, too.

Caramel frosting is not easy to do, and consider inviting a helper, for you have to move quickly and frost the cake before the icing hardens and loses its sheen. Actually, making caramel is a candy technique and before getting under way, please read Go Burn!, page 196, which outlines technique and safety tips.

And of course, every time you make this frosting it becomes easier and easier. So practice helps.

CAKE LAYERS:

2 cups all-purpose flour

2 teaspoons baking powder

1/8 teaspoon salt

12 tablespoons (1 1/2 sticks) butter, softened

1 1/4 cups granulated sugar

3 large eggs, at room temperature

1 teaspoon vanilla extract

3/4 cup whole milk, at room temperature

CARAMEL FROSTING:

3 cups granulated sugar

1½ cups whole milk or evaporated milk

1 tablespoon light corn syrup

¼ teaspoon cream of tartar or lemon juice

3 tablespoons water

2 large egg yolks

½ to 1 teaspoon vanilla extract

5 tablespoons cold unsalted butter, cut into pieces

½ cup pecan halves, if desired

Preheat the oven to 350 degrees. Butter two 8 x 1½-inch round cake pans, dust with flour, and shake out any excess.

Sift the flour with the baking powder and salt and set aside.

Combine the butter and sugar in the bowl of a standing mixer fitted with the paddle attachment or use a large mixing bowl and a handheld electric mixer. Beat the mixture on medium-high or creaming speed for 3 to 5 minutes or until light and fluffy, scraping the bowl once or twice with a rubber spatula.

Beat in the eggs one at a time, beating about 30 seconds after each addition and scraping the bowl as needed. Stir in the vanilla extract.

Alternately add the flour and milk to the creamed mixture, mixing on low speed only until blended after each addition, ending with the flour.

After the last addition, beat the batter on low speed for 30 seconds, scraping the bowl as needed. Using a measuring cup, pour the batter into the prepared pans, dividing evenly, about 2½ cups of batter per pan. Shake the pans gently to settle the batter.

Place the cake pans in the preheated oven on the middle shelf, diagonally across from each other. Make sure the pans don't touch.

Bake the cake layers for 20 minutes, and then quickly change the positions of the pans in the oven for even baking, shifting the pans from back to front and vice-versa.

Bake for 6 to 8 minutes longer or until the cake layers are brown and puffy and a knife inserted in the centers comes out clean, or until the cakes pull away from the sides of the pans.

Remove the cake layers from the oven, place on a wire rack, and cool in the pans for 10 minutes.

Run a knife or metal spatula around the edges of the cake pans, tap gently, and carefully turn out the cake layers on to the wire rack and cool completely, top side up on the rack. Frost and stack the cakes with the Caramel Frosting.

To make the Caramel Frosting: Have ready a pastry brush and cup of hot water for brushing down sugar crystals from sides of the pan, a candy thermometer, and a wooden spoon.

Clear the stovetop so that you have plenty of work space. Heat a saucepan of water on a back burner and keep it simmering. Set a metal spatula nearby. You'll need this when frosting the cake.

In a heavy 4-quart saucepan with a tight-fitting lid, combine $2^1/2$ cups of the sugar, the milk, and corn syrup. Cook over medium-high heat, stirring briskly and scraping the sides of the pan, until the sugar dissolves, for 3 or 4 minutes. Cover the pot and boil for 3 minutes.

Remove the pan from the heat. Add a few spoonfuls of the milk and sugar syrup to the egg yolks and beat briskly. Add a few more tablespoons of the syrup to the yolks, beat briskly, and then pour the egg mixture into the pot. Stir until the syrup is well blended. Set the pan back on the turned-off burner.

In a 1-quart heavy saucepan with a lid, combine the remaining $1/2$ cup of the sugar, the cream of tartar or lemon juice, and water. Place on medium-high heat and cook, stirring, scraping the sides of the pan, until the sugar dissolves, for 3 to 4 minutes.

Bring the mixture to a boil. Cover and boil for 3 minutes. Remove the lid, dip the pastry brush in water, and brush down the sides of the pan. Attach the candy thermometer.

Boil the syrup until it reaches 300 to 310 degrees, swirling the pan as it boils and turns deep golden brown with an amber glow. Immediately remove the pan from the heat, remove the thermometer, and pour the caramelized syrup into the pan holding the sugar and milk mixture. Stir vigorously with the wooden spoon until well blended.

Wash the thermometer under hot running water to clear off all syrup. Turn the heat back on under the pot. Bring the syrup to a boil. Cover the pan and boil for 3 minutes.

Dip the pastry brush in water and brush down the sides of the pan. Attach the candy thermometer inside the pan, and replace on the heat.

Raise the heat and boil the mixture, without stirring, but swirling the pan by the handle from time to time. Brush the sides of the pan with the damp brush a few times as the syrup cooks.

When the syrup reaches 220 to 222 (thread stage), immediately remove from the heat and swirl in the vanilla and the butter.

Cool pan on a wire rack 10 to 12 minutes, until the caramel is a little thicker than honey. Swirl pan from time to time; don't beat the frosting.

To assemble the cake: While the cake is cooling, spread strips of wax or parchment paper on a cake platter. Place one cake layer top side down on the cake platter, and set the other cake layer nearby. Also have handy the pan of hot water and the metal spatula.

As soon as the frosting is thickened, using a Pyrex cup, pour about $^3/_4$ cup over the cake layer on the platter and spread with the metal spatula.

Put on the second cake layer, top side up, and spread with the remaining frosting, smoothing with the metal spatula, starting at the bottom and smoothing upward. If the spatula begins to stick, dip in the pan of hot water and quickly wipe clean on the edge of the pan. If the frosting begins to harden, set it back on the hot burner and turn on the heat, very low, and stir gently.

If desired, scatter pecan halves in the leftover frosting and coat with caramel. Arrange them on the top of the cake while the frosting is still soft, making an attractive border. (Stir a few chopped nuts into any leftover frosting, pour into a buttered pan, cool, and enjoy as candy.)

Allow the icing to set and cool completely before serving the cake, but don't refrigerate. When ready to serve, carefully lift up the cake and remove the wax or parchment paper.

Store the cake in a cool place, preferably under a dome cake cover, or turn a big bowl upside down over the cake. The cake is best served the day it is made. After a day or so the moisture in the air will cause the sugar to harden and the frosting will begin to lose its shiny coating.

Makes 8 servings

Note: Nut Brown Glaze (page 70) is also delicious on this cake, and is not as challenging to do as caramel frosting.

Pineapple Iced Cake

There are many versions of pineapple cake but I must admit that I like Mama and Helen's recipe best. And since it is unique, it may have been a version passed on from Aunt Agnes or Grandma Addie. Helen no longer remembers.

Most recipes call for a filling made out of crushed pineapple, and either a boiled icing or butter cream for frosting. Helen and Mama made their cake a little differently.

They lightly glazed crushed pineapple and then mixed it with a thick syrup made out of sugar, milk, heavy cream, butter, and flavoring, and enriched with egg yolks. The creamy and luscious mixture was spread between the layers and then all over the cake as icing. The cake was sticky, tangy, and delicious. Raisins and pecans were often added to the filling, but over the years I have modified the recipe and now use other dried fruits.

I used to sit and watch them create this striking cake during the holidays, silently counting off the days to Christmas—when the cake was usually baked and served, and devoured.

CAKE LAYERS:

3 cups cake flour

2½ teaspoons baking powder

½ teaspoon baking soda

¼ teaspoon salt

½ pound (2 sticks) unsalted
   butter, softened

1½ cups granulated sugar

4 large eggs, at room temperature

1½ teaspoons vanilla extract

1 cup buttermilk, at room
   temperature

PINEAPPLE ICING:

1 can (20 ounces) unsweetened
   crushed pineapple, undrained

1¼ cups plus ½ cup granulated sugar

1½ cups milk

1½ cups half-and-half or heavy cream

½ teaspoon grated nutmeg or mace

1 teaspoon vanilla extract

3 large egg yolks

4 tablespoons unsalted butter, chilled
   and cut into pieces

FRUIT AND NUT FILLING:

1 cup dried cherries, cranberries,
   apricots, plums, peaches, or a
   combination of fruit

¼ cup bourbon or dark rum, or more if
   desired

⅔ cup pecans

Preheat the oven to 350 degrees. Butter three 8 x $\frac{1}{2}$-inch round cake pans, dust with flour, and shake out any excess.

Sift the flour with the baking powder, baking soda, and salt and set aside.

Combine the butter and sugar in the bowl of a standing mixer fitted with the paddle attachment or use a large mixing bowl and a handheld electric mixer. Beat the mixture on medium-high or creaming speed for 3 to 5 minutes or until light and fluffy, scraping the bowl once or twice with a rubber spatula.

Beat in the eggs one at a time, beating about 30 seconds after each addition and scraping the bowl as needed. Stir in the vanilla extract.

Alternately add the flour and milk to the creamed mixture, mixing on low speed only until blended after each addition, ending with the flour.

After the last addition, beat the batter on low speed for 30 seconds, scraping the bowl as needed.

Using a measuring cup, pour the batter into the prepared pans, dividing evenly. Shake the pans gently to settle the batter.

Place the cake pans in a triangular pattern in the preheated oven on the middle shelf. Make sure that the cake pans don't touch.

Bake the cake layers for 20 minutes, and then quickly change the positions of the pans in the oven for even baking, shifting the pans from back to front and vice versa.

Bake for 5 to 7 minutes longer or until the cake layers are brown and puffy and a knife inserted in the center comes out clean, or until the cakes pull away from the sides of the pans.

Remove the cake layers from the oven, place on a wire rack, and cool in the pans for 10 minutes. Run a knife or metal spatula around the edges of the cake pans, tap gently, and carefully turn the cake layers out onto the wire racks and cool completely, top side up.

Combine in a medium saucepan the crushed pineapple, juice from can, and the $\frac{1}{2}$ cup sugar. Bring to a boil, stirring. Reduce the heat to medium-low, and cook, uncovered, stirring occasionally, for 25 to 30 minutes or until the liquid evaporates and the pineapple is syrupy. Set aside.

Meanwhile, combine the milk, half-and-half or heavy cream, remaining 1 ¼ cups sugar, nutmeg or mace, and vanilla extract, in another large heavy saucepan. Place over medium-high heat and bring to a gentle boil, stirring. Reduce the heat to medium and cook the icing for about 15 to 20 minutes or until the mixture is thick and syrupy, stirring occasionally.

Place the egg yolks in a bowl and beat briskly with a whisk. Stir in a few tablespoons of the hot milk mixture and beat again. Add about 1 cup more of the hot milk to the egg yolks and whisk briskly.

Add the egg yolk mixture to the pan with the remaining milk and cook 5 minutes longer over medium heat, stirring constantly. Watch carefully and don't allow the icing to boil; the eggs will scramble.

When thickened, immediately remove the icing from the heat and pour through a strainer into a large bowl. Beat in the butter and then the reserved pineapple, mixing well.

Cool completely, stirring from time to time. If the icing is a little thin, chill for several hours or until it is of spreading consistency, or set in an ice water bath (see On Ice, page 237).

Prepare the filling: Finely chop the dried fruit and combine with the bourbon or rum in a small saucepan. Place the pan on medium heat and cook the mixture for 5 to 7 minutes, stirring, or until the dried fruit is just tender.

Remove the pan from the heat. Coarsely chop the pecans, mix with the dried fruit, and set aside.

To assemble the cake (see Icing on the Cake, page 89): Set aside about ¼ to ⅓ cup of the dried fruit filling to use as a decorative topping. Place one cake layer top side down on a cake platter. Spread with about ¾ cup of the pineapple icing. Scatter over half of the remaining pecan-and-dried-fruit mixture.

Place the second layer on, top side up, and spread with ¾ cup of the icing and the rest of the fruit-nut mixture. Top with the third layer, bottom side down, and spread the cake all over with the remaining icing.

Place the reserved nut-and-fruit filling on the top of the cake in a circle near the edge, forming a border.

Refrigerate the cake for about 30 minutes to set the icing.

Remove from the refrigerator before serving and allow to warm to room temperature.

Makes 12 to 14 servings

Cakes That Rise and Shine
A perfect cake is moist, even-textured, tender and velvety with soft crumbs and a smooth, slightly rounded top. Often the final product misses the mark, and usually because of inaccurate measurements, failure to follow the recipe directions, or incorrect techniques.

Follow these tips if you want your cakes to rise to the occasion:

- Read the complete recipe before beginning and follow the directions carefully.

- Assemble all the ingredients and have the eggs, milk, butter, flour, and sugar at room temperature. A cake made with cold ingredients rises poorly during baking.

- Set out the equipment needed, such as beaters, blenders, stirring spoons, sifter, and cake pans. Butter the cake pans or line with parchment paper as directed in the recipe.

- Preheat the oven.

- You can substitute low-fat plain yogurt for buttermilk, or almond extract for vanilla, but don't mess with the leavening agents, namely baking powder and baking soda, and don't substitute oil for butter or vice versa. Tampering with these ingredients can cause a cake to fall or bake into a foamy heap.

- Cakes made with ingredients high in acid, such as buttermilk, yogurt, sour cream, honey, molasses, unprocessed cocoa, or batters mixed with lots of spices or mashed fruits, require baking soda for leavening. The baking soda neutralizes the acid or spices so that the batter can rise.

- Cake batters leavened with only baking powder generally need 1 teaspoon of baking powder per cup of flour. I use Rumford baking powder, which is free of aluminum and doesn't have a strong metallic aftertaste.

- Well-creamed cake batter rises and shines. Cream the butter and sugar until the mixture is light, fluffy, and pale in color, for at least 3 minutes in a heavy-duty standing mixer, and for about 5 minutes with a handheld electric mixer.

- Cakes layered or frosted with meringue, vanilla icing, whipped cream, or custard must be kept refrigerated. Sit out the cake to warm to room temperature about two hours before serving. These cakes will stay fresh for three or four days.

  Store other cakes in tight-fitting domed containers in a cool, dark place. They will remain fresh for three or four days. If time is tight and you must bake a cake in advance, you can cool, wrap in plastic wrap and then in foil, and freeze, but the texture becomes tight and mealy, and the cake is never the same as before freezing.

  When ready to eat, unwrap the cake and thaw in the refrigerator overnight, and then let it sit at room temperature for two or three hours before serving. You can also thaw the cake in a microwave if you own such a gadget, but perish that thought.

- Fruitcakes baked and covered with a rum- or brandy-soaked cloth and then wrapped in foil will keep for months in a cool, dark place. ❀

West Indian Christmas Cake

Once on a cold winter morning, Chloe McKoy and I boarded a half-empty airplane at John F. Kennedy Airport, me en route to Guadeloupe in the French West Indies, and she on her way home, to the beautiful island of Nevis, both of us facing a change of planes in San Juan, Puerto Rico.

Of course the computer sat us right next to each other, and we took our seats, smiled, nodded, and said we would get seats to ourselves once airborne. Two middle-aged women of color: polite.

Then the talk began—about church, food, politics, family, children, cold winters, and how she was adjusting to her new life in New York, where her husband, the Reverend Leslie G. McKoy, had just been assigned as pastor of the Tremont Terrace Moravian Church in the Bronx.

Before we knew it we were leaving the plane in San Juan, scrambling to exchange phone numbers, having forgotten about changing seats, I caught a connecting flight to Guadeloupe and she went on to Nevis, and we have been friends ever since.

I now bake this heady fruitcake during the Christmas holiday and send it to dear friends, just like she does, following a tradition in the West Indian community.

The dried fruits for this cake are traditionally soaked in rum and port, and Chloe does this for several months in advance, topping off every month with the addition of 1 tablespoon of rum and 3 tablespoons of port. The flavors begin to meld after a couple of months, and after that ritual takes over.

When Chloe makes the cake she stirs a couple tablespoons of burnt sugar into the batter, which turns the baked cake a pretty tan color. Some bakers go heavy with the burnt sugar, and turn out what is traditionally known as the West Indian black cake, which is dark brown in color.

Once baked, a square of cheesecloth or muslin or linen is saturated with rum, squeezed out, and the cake is wrapped in the cloth and stored in a cool, dark place. Every so often the cake is unwrapped, the cloth is dipped in rum, and the ritual continues. By Christmas Day the cake is a delectable, moist delight.

Chloe prefers her cake without nuts, but I like a generous cup of coarsely chopped walnuts or pecans stirred into the batter; they add a crunchy dimension.

1 cup dark raisins

1 cup golden raisins

2 cups pitted prunes

2 cups currants

Grated peel from 2 medium limes or lemons

2 teaspoons allspice, preferably crushed berries

$\frac{1}{3}$ cup rum, white or dark, or fruit-flavored, such as orange or lemon

1 cup sweet ruby port wine

4 cups cake flour

1$\frac{1}{2}$ teaspoons ground cinnamon

1 teaspoon grated nutmeg or mace

$\frac{1}{4}$ teaspoon salt

1$\frac{1}{2}$ cups pecans or walnuts, if desired

1 pound (4 sticks) unsalted butter, softened

2 cups granulated sugar

8 to 10 large eggs, 1 pound by weight

3 to 5 tablespoons Browning or Burnt Sugar Syrup (page 106)

At least eight weeks before the holidays, or earlier, have available a large jar or glass or porcelain crock with a tight-fitting lid to use for soaking the fruit.

Chop or snip the raisins (if they are large) and the prunes. Place in the container. Add the currants, lime or lemon peel, and the allspice.

Pour in the rum and port, mix well with a large spoon, and then close the container with the lid. Place the jar or crock in a cool, dark place and allow the fruits to macerate and develop flavor for several weeks if desired, occasionally stirring and turning over the fruit in the liquid.

When ready to bake, preheat the oven to 275 degrees. Butter two 9 × 3-inch round pans, preferably with contour bottoms, or two 9 × 3-inch springform pans, dust with flour, and shake out any excess.

Sift together the flour, cinnamon, nutmeg or mace, and salt. Set aside. Coarsely chop the nuts and mix with the soaked fruit.

Combine the butter and sugar in the bowl of a standing mixer fitted with the paddle attachment or use a large mixing bowl and a handheld electric mixer. Beat the mixture on medium-high or creaming speed for 8 to 10 minutes, or until the mixture is light and fluffy and almost white in color, scraping the sides of the bowl with a rubber spatula several times.

Add the eggs, one at a time, and beat for about 30 seconds after each addition, scraping the bowl as needed. Stir in the Browning or Burnt Sugar Syrup and mix well.

Sprinkle 1 cup of the flour mixture over the fruit-and-nut mixture and stir until coated with the flour. Set aside 1 more cup of the flour.

Stir the remaining flour into the creamed mixture. Set the beater on low speed and beat the batter for 1 to 2 minutes, or until the batter is satiny and smooth, scraping the bowl as needed.

Using a wooden spoon, fold the fruit-and-nut mixture into the batter, mixing well but gently. Carefully fold in the remaining flour, mixing only until combined.

Using a measuring cup, pour the batter into the prepared cake pans, dividing evenly, using 6 to 7 cups of batter for each pan. Shake the pans to settle the batter.

Place the pans in the preheated hot oven on the middle shelf, diagonally across from each other, not touching.

Bake the cake for 1 hour, and then switch pan positions in the oven for even browning.

Bake 45 minutes to 1 hour longer, or until the cakes are golden brown, puffy, and a knife inserted in the centers comes out clean, but still moist. Don't overbake the cake.

Remove the cakes from the oven and place on wire racks.

Cool in the pan for 15 minutes. Run a metal spatula or knife around the edge of the pans to loosen the cakes and then tap the pans gently. Carefully turn the cakes out onto the racks. Cool completely, right side up.

If using springform pans, unfasten the sides of the pans and remove. Carefully invert the cakes onto the wire racks. Run the tip of a metal spatula between the bottom of the pan and the cake. When loose, lift off the bottom of the pan.

Cool the cakes top side up on the wire racks.

Dip a square of cloth into a little rum, squeeze out, wrap around the cakes, and then wrap the cake in foil. Store in a cool dark place. Unwrap the cakes every month or so and dip the cloth in rum again. Rewrap tightly.

Makes 2 cakes; 12 to 14 servings

Browning or Burnt Sugar Syrup

Browning is made from sugar that caramelizes until it liquefies and turns almost black, with a mahogany cast. This burnt sugar is not one bit sweet; as bitter as black coffee, and is used for coloring sauces and cakes. It also adds a nice edge to barbecue sauce.

This is a candy-making technique, and before attempting this recipe, read carefully Go Burn! (page 196) for safety tips and techniques.

The sugar is cooked until it reaches at least 340 degrees, but for deep coloring, it should reach 350 to 365 degrees. Since at this temperature the sugar will smoke, open a window for ventilation, and use a very heavy saucepan, preferably enameled cast iron. And bear in mind that the sugar is piping hot.

Have available a pastry brush, a cup of water, a candy thermometer, a wooden spoon, and heavy mitts or pot holders. And yes, undivided attention is required; and children should be kept out of the kitchen while you are doing this.

If burning sugar until it is almost coal black is intimidating, you can order Blue Mountain Country Burnt Sugar (Browning), from King Arthur Flour, a premier company. It's available in a 6-ounce jar for a few dollars (see Note).

1 cup granulated sugar	$\frac{1}{4}$ teaspoon cream of tartar or $\frac{1}{2}$
$\frac{3}{4}$ cup hot water	teaspoon lemon juice

Combine in a 1-quart heavy saucepan the sugar, $\frac{1}{4}$ cup of the water, and cream of tartar or lemon juice. Place the pan over medium-high heat and stir the mixture until the sugar dissolves. Cover the pan and boil for 3 minutes.

Remove the lid. Dip the brush in water and brush down the sugar crystals from the sides of the pan. Attach a candy thermometer inside the pan, making sure that it does not touch the bottom of the pan.

Cook the syrup, without stirring, but swirling the pan by the handle, until it reaches 350 to 365 degrees, frequently brushing the sides of the pan with the damp brush.

Remove the pan from the heat and carefully set on a wire rack. Cool the syrup for 2 or 3 minutes and then add the remaining $\frac{1}{2}$ cup of water a tablespoon at a time, carefully pouring it down the side of the pan. (If you add all the water at once the sauce may sputter and burn you.)

When all the water has been added, simmer the sauce for about 10 minutes, stirring occasionally. Cool and use as directed in your recipe. This syrup will keep for several months stored in a jar in the refrigerator.

Makes about ¾ cup

Note: King Arthur Flour can be reached by calling 1-800-827-6836 or on line at www.kingarthurflour.com.

THREE

Sweetie Pies

Once I shyly—well, almost—suggested to Frances Jackson that I could come out to Detroit and make the five pies for her annual Christmas dessert party while she made the rest of the sweets. Frances isn't exactly a pushover, and my offer was met with a hard stare, a cut of the eyes, but not a downright no. She mumbled something about schedule difficulties, tight kitchen space, and—jokingly I hope—about too many cooks handling the dough.

Truth is, I can't think of anything I would rather do in a kitchen than bake a pie. The signature of a good pie is a flaky and crisp piecrust and once you master the technique, the rest is easy as pie.

You can experiment with different flavorings and spices, throw in bits of grated orange or lemon peel, substitute various sugars, toss in nuts and raisins, add a dash of rum or brandy, and end up with a strikingly sweet temptation without a lot of fuss and bother. And there are so many variations: fruit pies and cobblers, creamy custard pies, rich but light and airy chess custard pies, earthy and full-flavored sweet potato, squash, and pumpkin pies. And if you bake the pie in a traditional straight-sided quiche pan, you end up with an elegant fruit tart that is especially delightful when shimmering with a sparkling glaze of jelly or preserves.

Actually, I should have known better than to try to crowd in on Frances's territory, but she does bake seventeen to eighteen desserts for her annual affair, and you would think that she would welcome a helping hand. In addition to the five pies, she makes three pound cakes, two or three cheesecakes, five chocolate cakes, one bourbon pecan cake, and an orange cake!

And I know from personal experience that hosting a dessert party for sixty-odd people during the busy holiday season is no piece of cake. Of course Sister Frances, as I call her, sets a mean table, but her schedule is kind of tight. She is a professor of nursing, her husband, Frank, is a lawyer, and both are involved in an array of activities at their church, John Wesley A.M.E. Zion.

But Frances and I share the same red dust of Alabama on our shoes (her parents migrated from Montgomery, Alabama, to Detroit after World War II) and we both are keenly aware of the immense pleasure of holiday baking.

Her holiday baking is a two-day marathon, and when she is done her lovely home is scented with all of those cakes, plus: a pecan pie, fresh strawberry pie, apple pie, sweet potato pie, peach cobbler, and an old-fashioned sweet but tart Lemon Meringue Pie (recipe follows).

"I also set out a platter of fresh fruits for the diehard dieters," she said smugly, "but almost everybody succumbs to my desserts during the party." No wonder.

Lemon Meringue Pie

1 baked single 9-inch Basic Piecrust
  (page 113)
4 large eggs
3 tablespoons cornstarch
3 tablespoons flour
1½ cups granulated sugar plus 5 to 8
  tablespoons, depending on
  sweetness desired
¼ teaspoon salt
1½ cups boiling water

Grated peel from 1 lemon
½ cup fresh lemon juice, from 2 or 3
  large lemons
1 tablespoon lemon liqueur, such as
  Limoncello or Liquori di Limoni
2 tablespoons unsalted butter
¼ teaspoon cider vinegar or cream of
  tartar
¼ teaspoon vanilla or lemon extract

Set aside the pie crust to cool.

Carefully crack the eggs one at a time and place the yolk and egg white in two separate small bowls, making sure that not one speck of yolk mixes in with the egg white. If the egg white is free of yolk, transfer to a large spotless clean bowl for whipping or to the bowl of a standing mixer. If the egg yolk drips into the egg white, discard that egg white and break another egg, using a clean bowl. Set aside the egg whites to warm to room temperature and return the yolks to the refrigerator (see Get the Whip, page 132).

Sift the cornstarch, flour, 1½ cups sugar, and salt into a heavy medium-size saucepan, preferably enameled cast iron.

Stir in the boiling water and grated lemon peel, whisking to combine well. Place the pan over medium heat, and cook, stirring constantly, until the filling is thick and smooth, about 3 minutes.

Remove the pan from the heat and stir in the lemon juice, 1 tablespoon lemon liqueur, and butter. Set aside.

In a medium bowl, beat the egg yolks briskly with a whisk until they are well blended. Add a few tablespoons of the hot filling to the egg yolks and mix well. Continue whisking in about half of the hot filling to the egg yolks, beating briskly after each addition.

Then pour the egg yolk mixture into the saucepan with the rest of the hot filling, and whisk until well blended. Place the saucepan back on the heat and cook over medium heat, stirring constantly, until the filling is quite thick, 3 to 5 minutes.

Remove the pan from the heat and press the filling through a fine sieve or strainer into a bowl. Set aside.

Preheat the oven to 350 degrees.

To make the meringue: Using a standing mixer fitted with the whisk attachment or a handheld electric mixer set at medium-high speed, beat the egg whites until they are frothy. Add the vinegar or cream of tartar. Increase the speed of the mixer to high. Add the remaining 5 to 8 tablespoons sugar in a steady stream and beat the egg whites until they are glossy and airy and just hold firm peaks. Stir in the extract and mix well.

Spoon the lemon filling into the baked pie shell and spread evenly with a spatula. Drop a heaping cup of the meringue over the pie filling, and spread with a metal spatula, making sure that the meringue seals the edge of the piecrust. This prevents weeping and shrinkage during baking.

Spread the remaining meringue all over the pie filling and to the edges, and then swirl with the back of a spoon to make peaks.

Place the pie on the middle shelf of the preheated oven and bake 12 to 15 minutes, or until the meringue is lightly brown. Don't overbake.

Cool the pie on a wire rack, and then chill before serving.

Makes 6 to 8 servings

Variation: For an equally bracing flavor, substitute $1/2$ cup lime juice or sour orange juice, from Seville oranges (see Pickin' Fruit, page 243) for the lemon juice.

Basic Piecrust

When making a piecrust, the butter or shortening or lard has to be "cut" into the flour with either two knives, a gadget called a pastry blender, or with your hands, and this has to be done with minimal handling and as quickly as possible. You can also place the flour and butter or shortening or lard in a food processor and pulse until the mixture resembles coarse cornmeal, but I prefer to do this by hand.

If the fat in the dough melts from the heat of your fingers or from the action of the utensils, the pastry ends up tough and flat and not flaky. So don't hesitate to stick the dough back in the refrigerator to chill at any point.

If your kitchen is small and your workstation is jammed up next to the stove, don't turn the oven on until you are ready to bake the piecrust. A hot stove will warm up a small kitchen in no time, and melt the piecrust butter.

The key to a flaky and crusty piecrust is to use ice water and have all the ingredients and the mixing bowl as cold as possible. Add a teaspoon of cider vinegar to the water and the protein in the flour, gluten, will relax and roll out better.

Then, dip your fingers in ice water, dry off, rev up your heart, and mix the dough rapidly but with a "light" hand.

After mixing the dough, place it in the refrigerator to chill for at least 30 minutes or as long as an hour.

You can also chill the dough overnight or freeze. But the fat will congeal and you have to let the dough warm up at room temperature for about 20 or so minutes before rolling it out.

This can get tricky. If you let the dough sit out too long it will soften and begin to ooze butter. So watch carefully.

The following recipe makes pastry for a two-crust 9- or 10-inch pie, or for two single 9- or 10-inch pies or tarts.

For a one-crust or single pie or tart crust, use half the recipe, or make two single crusts and freeze one for later use. Generally, once a pie is baked, the crust tastes best at room temperature and shouldn't be refrigerated, especially fruit and berry pies.

However, egg and milk–based custard and cream pie fillings require refrigeration and taste best chilled. After chilling, you can let these pies sit at room temperature for 20 or so minutes before serving to warm up the pastry for better flavor.

Custard and cream pies will keep three or four days in the refrigerator. Cover tightly with foil or plastic wrap. But don't freeze these pies; the fillings break down and become watery.

Fruit and berry pies are fine for two or three days at room temperature, but if you plan to keep them around longer, cover with plastic wrap or foil and refrigerate. And these pies freeze well and will remain fresh for two or three months. Let warm to room temperature before serving.

8 tablespoons unsalted butter, chilled	5 to 8 tablespoons ice water, or as
6 tablespoons vegetable shortening,	needed
chilled	1 teaspoon cider vinegar
2¼ cups all-purpose flour	1 lightly beaten egg white
¼ teaspoon salt	

Cut the butter into ½-inch pieces and place in a large, shallow mixing bowl. Add the vegetable shortening. Sift the flour and salt into the bowl and mix well.

Chill the flour mixture for 30 to 40 minutes.

Gather the chilled flour mixture in the palms of both hands and rub handfuls together briskly, letting the mixture drop back into the bowl through your fingers, alternating rubbing the dough with your fingertips. Continue doing this until the mixture resembles coarse cornmeal. This should take no longer than 5 minutes.

Place 5 tablespoons of the ice water in a small cup. Stir in the vinegar. Sprinkle the ice water over the dough 1 tablespoon at a time, lifting with a fork to dampen all over. After adding 5 tablespoons of the water, squeeze a little of the damp dough with your fingertips; if it doesn't hold together add more water, a tablespoon at a time, until the dough just clings together but is not mushy and wet.

Quickly stir together the damp dough with a fork and gather into a disk or ball. Turn the dough out onto a lightly floured work surface. Using the heel of your hand, smear the dough two or three times in a forward motion to evenly distribute the butter and shortening. (Don't overwork the dough; it will become tough.)

Form the dough into a ball, dusting lightly with flour if it sticks. Wrap the dough in plastic wrap or wax paper and chill for 30 minutes to 1 hour.

To form the piecrust, place the dough on a lightly floured work surface and divide into two parts, one slightly larger than the other. Use the larger piece for the bottom crust and the smaller part for the top. Return the smaller portion to the refrigerator.

Lightly dust the rolling pin with flour. For best results, always roll outward; not back and forth, using a light touch. Lift the dough slightly and turn it to make sure that it is not sticking to the work surface or canvas. Roll again, pick up the dough, rotate, and continue doing this until the dough is a wide circle of even thickness. For a 9-inch or 10-inch pie or tart crust, roll out the larger piece of dough into an 11- to 12-inch circle and as thin as possible, no more than $1/8$ inch thick.

If the dough sticks, dust it with a little more flour, or cover the rolling pin with a stockinette or lay a sheet of wax paper over the dough and then roll it out. If the dough begins to ooze butter at this point, place the dough back in the refrigerator and chill for 5 to 10 minutes.

Lightly flour the rolling pin again, and carefully roll the circle of dough around the pin, lift up, and unroll the dough onto the pie pan. Do not stretch the dough. Use your fingers to fit the dough snugly into the pie pan.

Prick the bottom and sides of the piecrust with a fork so that the dough can expand as it bakes. Brush lightly all over with the beaten egg white, which keeps the pie shell from becoming soggy during baking. Freeze or chill the pie shell while rolling out the top crust.

Roll out the remaining half of dough the same way into an 11-inch circle. Fill the chilled piecrust generously with filling. Using the rolling pin, carefully lift up the top crust and place it over the filling.

Firmly press the bottom and top edges together. Using kitchen scissors, trim the dough $1/2$ to $3/4$ inch below the edge of the pie pan. For a pretty border design, roll up the dough on the rim of the pie pan and pinch all around with your fingers, making a flute design.

Or, press the trimmed pastry flat against edge of pie pan. Press the fork tines into the crust without going completely through, scoring the edge. A scallop design is also pretty: Stand or roll up the edge of pastry on the rim and press all around with the back of a spoon, making indentations.

Prick the top crust all over with a fork or cut several slits or a fancy design to let out steam during the baking. Bake the pie according to specific recipe directions and cool on a wire rack.

See directions below for a partially baked or fully baked pie crust or shell.

Flour Power: In a Pinch

Wheat flours are classified according to their content of a protein called gluten. Flours high in gluten are called "hard," while those with low gluten are classified as "soft" flours. Unbleached an "bread" flours are high in protein; flours marked as "cake" or "pastry" are low in gluten and are soft flours.

Right in the middle of the field is good old reliable all-purpose flour, a mixture of both soft and hard flour, which in my book works best for pie crusts. It rolls out into a soft and pliable dough that is easy to handle.

But if a recipe calls for all-purpose flour and all you have is unbleached all-purpose, don't put off making that pie. A tip: substitute two or three tablespoons of cornstarch for an equal amount of flour called for in the recipe, and the crust will end up soft and flaky. All butter rather than a mixture of butter and vegetable shortening works best with piecrusts made with unbleached flour.

And in a pinch, if all you hve on hand is cake flour, and you just got to get that peach pie going, right now, go for it! In the South, piecrusts are often made from soft wheat flours—White Lily and Martha White are popular brands—and this flour is very similiar in protein content to cake flour.

Soft wheat flour, and especially pastry flour, bakes into delicate, tender crusts, and the dough should be well chilled before rolling. An equal amount of vegetable shortening or lard and butter is best for piecrusts made from soft wheat flour, rather than all-butter.

Another hint: the next time you make a double piecrust from all-purpose flour, substitute $1/4$ to $1/3$ cup of fine-grained stone-ground cornmeal for an equal amount of flour. Real fine for blueberry or cranberry pies and cobblers. ❈

Partially or Fully Baked Single Pie or Tart Crust

Crusts that are partially or fully baked are best for pies and tarts made with custard or fruit and berry fillings, since they don't become soggy and soft during baking.

However, a single pie or tart crust will buckle and shrink and bake unevenly if it is baked unfilled. To prevent this, you have to bake the crust "blind," using what is known as a pastry weight. Here's how:

Basic Piecrust (page 113) for one crust   1 egg white

Fit the pie dough into the pie pan, prick the bottom and sides of the crust with a fork, and crimp the edge. Chill the crust at least 30 minutes or longer, or freeze for 15 minutes or longer.

Preheat the oven to 400 degrees.

Cover the crust with a sheet of foil—heavy duty works best—or parchment paper, and then fill the pan with about 3 cups of dried beans, peas, rice, or macaroni forming the pastry weight. The dried beans, peas, rice, or macaroni can be stored in a container and used over and over again.

Set the piecrust on the lower oven shelf, the hottest part of the oven.

For a partially baked piecrust, bake 15 to 16 minutes or until the crust is set and dry. Carefully remove the weight, including the foil or paper. If there are air bubbles, gently prick with a fork to deflate.

Bake the crust 3 to 4 minutes longer or until just lightly brown.

Remove the crust from the oven, cool the crust for a few minutes, and then brush liberally with egg white.

For a fully baked shell, cover the crust with the pastry weight and bake for 20 minutes. Carefully remove the pastry weight, including the foil or paper. If there are air bubbles, gently prick with a fork to deflate.

Bake the crust 5 to 8 minutes longer, or until the pastry is golden brown and crisp. After 5 minutes watch the crust carefully! It can overbrown quickly and turn acrid in flavor.

Remove the crust from the oven, and set on a wire rack.

Let the crust cool for a few minutes, and then brush with the beaten egg white.

Chewing the Fat

A piecrust can be made with butter or vegetable shortening or a combination of the two fats. During my childhood in the South, the most delectable and flaky piecrusts ever were made with home-rendered lard and an equal amount of freshly churned butter.

Piecrusts made with both butter and vegetable shortening or lard are flakier than all-butter piecrusts, which are crumbly, but especially winsome with fruit pies and cobblers.

When making an all-butter piecrust, simply substitute additional butter for the shortening called for in the recipe, using 6 tablespoons chilled butter for the vegetable shortening, for a total of 14 tablespoons, and proceed as directed for Basic Piecrust (page 113). All-butter crusts are especially delicious with fruit pies or tarts.

However, all-butter crusts do require a little more skill to handle, since the butter oozes quicker than the shortening or lard.

Crusts made with sour cream and a couple tablespoons of confectioners' sugar are delectable with fruit pies and also make a fine "bottom" for cheesecakes.

The choice is yours. A little something to chew on. ✿

Sour Cream Pie or Tart Crust

This soft and pliable dough is great with fruit pies and tarts. Confectioners' sugar gives it a little sweet edge, which balances the sour cream note.

I prefer the smooth texture of this piecrust to those made with cream cheese, which, despite my best efforts, always end up just a little bit pebbly because the cheese never quite blends in with the flour.

1¼ cups all-purpose flour	chilled
2 tablespoons confectioners' sugar	1 teaspoon cider vinegar
⅛ teaspoon salt	¼ cup sour cream
8 tablespoons (1 stick) unsalted butter,	2 tablespoons ice water, or as needed

Sift the flour, sugar, and salt into a large, shallow bowl. Cut the butter into ½-inch-size pieces, place in the bowl, and mix well.

Chill the flour mixture for 30 to 40 minutes.

Gather the chilled flour mixture in the palms of both hands and rub handfuls together briskly, letting the mixture drop back into the bowl through your fingers, alternating rubbing the dough with your fingertips. Continue doing this until the mixture resembles coarse cornmeal. This should take no longer than 5 minutes.

Stir the cider vinegar into the sour cream and mix well.

Sprinkle the sour cream mixture over the dough, 1 tablespoon at a time, lifting with a fork to dampen all over. Squeeze a little of the damp dough with your fingertips; if it doesn't hold together add the water, a tablespoon at a time, until the dough just clings together but is not mushy and wet.

Quickly stir together the damp dough with a fork and gather into a disk or ball.

Turn the dough out onto a lightly floured work surface. Using the heel of your hand, smear the dough two or three times in a forward motion to evenly distribute the butter and shortening. (Don't overwork the dough; it will become tough.)

Form the dough into a ball, dusting lightly with flour if it sticks. Wrap the dough in plastic wrap or wax paper and chill for 20 minutes to 1 hour.

Roll the dough into a 12-inch circle for a 9-inch pie pan, or into a 13-inch circle for a 10-inch tart pan. Carefully transfer the dough to the pan (see Basic Piecrust, page 113).

Trim the dough to $^1/_2$ to $^3/_4$ inch beyond the edge of the pie or tart pan. For a tart pan, fold the overhang inward and press against the side of the pan to form a ridge to reinforce the edge. For a pie pan, stand the overhang on the rim of the pan, and flute with fingertips or crimp with a fork.

Bake the pie according to the specific recipe directions. (See Partially or Fully Baked Single Pie or Tart Crust, page 117)

I was thumbing through the box of papers the late Velma Mosley had sent me before she died when I noticed for the first time a recipe for a custard pie that was made with buttermilk, egg yolks, grated orange peel, and orange juice, and then blended with softly whipped egg whites.

I was intrigued, although I knew that whipped egg whites star in many of the favorite dishes of the Old South, from lemon meringue pies to boiled icing to the famous Lady Baltimore Cake, which often calls for seven or eight egg whites.

But this recipe was different; it was virtually a soufflé in a pie shell. And since I had all the ingredients on hand, in less than an hour the pie was glowing in my oven, puffy, aromatic, seductive. The pie baked into a soft creamy custard that was topped with a light, soufflé-like layer. I took one delicious bite and immediately called my friend.

At the sound of my voice I felt her enthusiasm picking up. Mrs. Mosley was a nurse and community activist, lived her last days in Tyler, Texas, and brought boundless energy to every challenge. She fought for equal housing, schools, and streetlights in her community, and did so while carrying covered dishes to her local church, or hosting a flea market at her home to raise money for the needy.

Right off she said that her pie was an old family recipe, and that it was simply a variation of the chess pie, which is popular today in the South. The story goes that during slavery a brother created the chess pie, and when queried about his culinary triumph, replied, "Jes pie," hence its name, chess pie.

"Honey," Mrs. Mosley said, "this is just another example of our history that has gone with the wind."

Shortly afterward, another cookbook arrived in the mail, and this time from the untiring scholar and culinary historian Karen Hess. The book, less than one hundred pages, is titled *What Mrs. Fisher Knows About Old Southern Cooking* (Applewood Books) and is billed as "The first African-American cookbook from 1881."

Karen edited and wrote the historical notes for the book, which was written by a sister named Abby Fisher, who was born in Alabama probably in the 1830s.

Excited, I hurried through the book, and on page 25 was a coconut pie, made just like Mrs. Mosley's pie: Separate the eggs; make a custard with the yolks, add milk or cream, flavoring, and then fold in softly beaten egg whites.

I called Mrs. Mosley again.

"These are the type of pies we made when we didn't have much in the house and wanted something sweet," she said, laughing. "Necessity has always been the mother of our invention."

Mrs. Mosley was a beacon of light. I miss her wit, charm, generosity, and most of all, her zest for life, which she lived to the fullest.

Sweetie Pies

Orange Buttermilk Pie

Last summer Norma Boucher had a series of late Sunday afternoon dinner parties at her brand-new beautiful apartment in Rochdale Village in Queens, New York.

Norma is a tennis player and coach, and her game seems to be connecting friends. She asked me to bring a dessert. I made this pie and topped it with candied orange peel. It was a winner.

1 fully baked single 9-inch Basic
    Piecrust (page 113)
3 large eggs
1¼ cups granulated sugar
1 tablespoon all-purpose flour
1 tablespoon grated orange peel
1 teaspoon vanilla extract
½ to 1 teaspoon ground cinnamon
⅛ teaspoon salt

½ cup freshly squeezed orange juice
4 tablespoons unsalted butter, melted
    and cooled
1 cup buttermilk
¼ teaspoon cider vinegar or cream of
    tartar
2 to 3 tablespoons candied orange peel
    slivers (see Candied Citrus Peel,
    page 124)

Set aside the piecrust to cool.

Carefully crack the eggs one at a time and place the yolk and egg white into two separate small bowls, making sure that not one speck of yolk mixes in with the egg white. If the egg white is free of yolk, transfer to a large spotless clean bowl for whipping or to the bowl of a standing mixer. If the egg yolk drips into the egg white, discard that egg white and break another egg, using a clean bowl. Set aside the egg whites to warm to room temperature. (see Get the Whip, page 132).

Preheat the oven to 350 degrees.

Transfer the egg yolks to a large bowl and beat briskly for a few seconds with a wire whisk. Add the sugar, flour, orange peel, vanilla, cinnamon, and salt and whisk again. Whisk in the orange juice and butter and beat again until blended. Stir in the buttermilk and mix well. Set aside.

Sprinkle the vinegar or cream of tartar over the egg whites. Using a standing mixer fitted with the whisk attachment or a handheld electric mixer, beat the whites at medium-high just until they hold slight peaks.

Stir in a large spoonful of the egg whites into the filling and mix well. Fold in the remaining egg whites, and mix gently but thoroughly until blended. Pour the filling into the prepared pie shell.

Cover the edges of the crust with strips of foil to prevent overbrowning. Place the pie on the lower shelf of the hot oven and bake for 35 to 40 minutes or until puffed and brown, firm, and a knife comes out almost clean when inserted in the center.

Remove the pie from the oven, top with the candied orange peel. Cool on a wire rack and serve at room temperature.

Makes 6 servings

Candied Citrus Peel

My favorite recipe for these crunchy, sweet, but slightly tart strips comes from my Aunt Mary, who was an expert candy maker.

I love to scatter the peel on the top of custard and sweet potato pies while they are still warm. The aromatic sugar melts a little and seeps into the pie, imparting a sweet but tart flavor. A jar of candied peel makes a nice hostess gift, especially during the Christmas holidays.

3 large oranges or 4 large lemons
1 cup granulated sugar plus $1/4$ cup, for coating

1 cup water
1 tablespoon light corn syrup
$1/2$ teaspoon vanilla extract

Rinse the fruit well. Using a small sharp knife or vegetable peeler, cut off the peel into $1/2$-inch-wide strips, avoiding the white pith, which has a bitter taste. Cut the strips into thin strawlike or matchstick slivers.

Place the peel in a medium saucepan, cover with cold water, bring to a boil, and blanch for 5 minutes.

Drain the peel, discard the cooking water, and rinse with cold water. Return the peel to the pan, cover with cold water, and simmer for 20 to 25 minutes, or until just tender. Drain, rinse with cold water, and return to the pan.

Add the 1 cup sugar, water, corn syrup, and vanilla extract. Bring to a boil, stirring until the sugar dissolves.

Cook the peel, uncovered, on low heat for 30 to 35 minutes, or until tender, and the syrup is thick and the peel is translucent and candied.

Pour the syrup and peel through a sieve and drain well. (Save the syrup. Boil it down and use as a topping for ice cream or cake. It is especially delicious when flavored with melted chocolate or orange liqueur, or both.)

Spread the well-drained peel on a sheet of wax or parchment paper and allow to dry in a sunny or warm spot for at least an hour. Sprinkle the peel with the remaining $1/4$ cup sugar, and toss to cover all.

Transfer the peel to a doubled sheet of paper towel, spread out and continue drying at room temperature for several hours.

Store the candied peel in an airtight jar or container. The peel will keep at room temperature for about a week; if keeping longer, refrigerate.

Makes 1 cup

Right On!

PASTRY FOR MAKING PIES OF ALL KINDS

One pound of flour nicely sifted to quarter pound of butter and one quarter pound of lard, one teaspoonful of salt, fine, mixed in flour while dry; then with your hands rub the butter and lard into the flour until thoroughly mixed, then add enough cold water and mix with your hands so as to make pastry hold together, be sure not to have it too wet; sprinkle flour very lightly on pastry board, and roll pastry out to the thickness of an egg-shell for the top of fruit, and that for the bottom of fruit must be thin as paper. In rolling pastry roll to and from you; you don't want more than ten minutes to make pastry.

Excerpted from the first African-American cookbook from 1881:
***What Mrs. Fisher Knows About Old Southern Cooking,* Applewood Books**

Brown Sugar Pie

My sister, Helen, sent me this recipe, which she said Aunt Agnes passed on to her years ago. And since I like to "top off" pies, I scattered the almost-baked pie with a coating of lightly toasted almonds tossed with butter and sugar. I baked the pie for a few more minutes, just until the sugar melted and glazed the almonds.

1 fully baked single 9-inch Basic
    Piecrust (page 113)

3 large eggs

4 tablespoons unsalted butter,
    softened, plus 1 tablespoon unsalted
    butter, melted

1 cup heavy cream or half-and-half

$\frac{1}{8}$ teaspoon salt

1 teaspoon vanilla extract

$\frac{1}{2}$ teaspoon grated nutmeg, or to taste

$\frac{1}{2}$ cup granulated sugar

$\frac{3}{4}$ cup dark brown sugar, firmly packed

1 tablespoon flour

1 tablespoon fine-grained cornmeal,
    preferably stone-ground

$\frac{1}{4}$ teaspoon vinegar or cream of tartar

$\frac{1}{2}$ cup slivered almonds, lightly toasted

2 tablespoons brown sugar, preferably
    brown crystallized sugar (see Dark
    and Sweet, page 25)

Set aside the piecrust to cool.

Carefully crack the eggs one at a time and place the yolk and the egg white into two separate small bowls, making sure that not one speck of egg yolk is mixed in with the egg white. If the egg white is free of yolk, transfer to a large spotless clean bowl for whipping or to the bowl of a standing mixer. If the egg yolk drips into the egg white, discard that egg white, and break another egg, using a clean bowl. Set aside the egg whites to warm to room temperature and return the yolks to the refrigerator (see Get the Whip, page 132).

Preheat the oven to 350 degrees.

Combine the softened butter and heavy cream or half-and-half in a small saucepan. Heat, stirring, for a few minutes over low heat, just until the butter melts and the cream is warm. Remove the pan from the heat and stir in the salt, vanilla extract, and nutmeg and mix until just blended. Set aside.

Transfer the egg yolks to a large mixing bowl and beat briskly for a few seconds with a wire whisk. Add both sugars, the flour, and the cornmeal and whisk again. Pour the warm cream mixture over the egg yolk and sugar mixture, and beat briskly until smooth. Set aside.

Sprinkle the vinegar or cream of tartar over the egg whites. Using a standing mixer fitted with the whisk attachment or a handheld electric mixer, beat the whites on medium-high speed just until they hold slight peaks. Stir a large spoonful of the egg whites into the filling and mix well. Fold in the remaining egg whites, and mix gently but thoroughly until blended. Pour the filling into the prepared pie shell.

Cover the edges of the crust with strips of foil to prevent overbrowning. Set the pie on the lower shelf of the preheated oven and bake for 25 minutes or until puffy and golden.

Stir together the almonds, melted butter, and sugar. Spread the mixture over the top of the pie.

Bake the pie 5 to 10 minutes longer, or until a knife inserted in the center comes out almost clean.

Remove the pie from the oven, set on a wire rack, and cool completely before serving.

Makes 6 servings

Chess Tart

When I was collecting recipes for my book *Soul Food: Recipes and Reflections from African-American Churches,* John Wesley sent me a recipe for chess pie that has been in his family for almost sixty-five years.

John is the music coordinator at the Macedonia Baptist Church in Arlington, Virginia, and he recounted in his letter a funny anecdote about trying to mix the pie filling in a heavy–duty mixer. Every time the filling would separate during the baking, forcing John back to the kitchen again.

Finally John got out an old wire whisk, mixed the filling by hand, and the pie blended and stayed that way.

"So much for technology," John wrote, with just a hint of sarcasm.

John's pie has become my favorite "fancy" summer dessert, which I have modified with whipped egg whites and bake in a fancy tart pan. I love the tart sweetness of this pie, and yes, mix the filling briskly with a wire whisk or fork for best results.

1 fully baked single 10-inch Tart Crust
   (page 117)
4 eggs
1 to 1¼ cups granulated sugar
Pinch of salt
½ cup heavy cream or half-and-half

1 tablespoon finely grated lemon peel
½ cup freshly squeezed lemon juice
   (from 2 or 3 large lemons)
¼ teaspoon cider vinegar or cream of
   tartar

Set aside the tart crust to cool. (You can also use a 9-inch baked piecrust.)

Carefully crack the eggs one at a time and place the yolk and the egg white into two separate small bowls. If the egg white is free of yolk, transfer to a large spotless clean bowl for whipping or to the bowl of a standing mixer. If the egg yolk drips into the egg white, discard that egg white, and break another egg, using a clean bowl. Set aside the egg whites to warm to room temperature. (see Get the Whip, page 132).

Preheat the oven to 350 degrees.

Transfer the egg yolks to a large mixing bowl and beat briskly with a wire whisk for a few seconds. Add the sugar and salt and whisk again.

Add the heavy cream or half-and-half and beat briskly until smooth. Stir in the lemon peel and lemon juice and mix until blended. Set aside.

Sprinkle the vinegar or cream of tartar over the egg whites. Using a standing mixer fitted with the whisk attachment or a handheld electric mixer, beat the egg whites at medium-high speed just until they hold slight peaks. Stir a large spoonful of the egg whites into the filling and mix well. Fold in the remaining egg whites, and mix gently but thoroughly until blended.

Pour the filling into the prepared pie shell. Cover the edges of the tart pan with strips of foil to prevent overbrowning. Set the pan on the middle shelf of the preheated oven and bake for 25 to 30 minutes, or until the custard is firm and puffy and set in the center. Don't overbake the pie; it will continue to cook as it cools.

Remove the pie from the oven and cool on a wire rack.

Serve at room temperature, or chill for 15 or 20 minutes, if desired.

Makes 5 or 6 servings

Angel Pie

A while back I took a copy of my book *Soul Food* to Eve Bryan, an antiques dealer, who holds forth every Saturday and Sunday at the world-famous Sixth Avenue Flea Market in Chelsea.

As she was thumbing through the cookbook, carrying on in her lyrical Jamaican voice, up walked John James, a client and friend.

Eve pushed the book at him and said in her commanding way, "This book is fabulous. Why don't you invite Joyce to speak at the club?"

And he did. John's twin brother, Aldon, is the president of the prestigious National Arts Club of New York City, and so began our friendship.

The last time the James brothers came to dinner I set up a table on my terrace and lit candles. Aldon James had requested pan-fried chicken but I mustered up molasses-baked chicken instead and not a morsel was left. Dessert was Buttermilk Ginger Cake (page 53), homemade ice cream, and this Angel Pie, which I made from a recipe that John sent me.

An old Southern favorite—the James brothers hail from Maryland—Angel Pie is basically a meringue pie shell filled with lemon curd, and topped with either fresh fruit or whipped cream, or both—sweetly whipped egg whites at their best.

4 large egg whites, at room temperature
1/2 teaspoon cider vinegar or cream of tartar

1/8 teaspoon salt
1 cup superfine sugar
1 teaspoon vanilla extract

PIE FILLING:

4 egg yolks
1 cup granulated sugar
1/3 cup lemon juice or sour orange juice from Seville oranges (see Pickin'

Fruit, page 243)
1 tablespoon grated lemon or orange peel

TOPPING:

2 cups fresh strawberries or raspberries
1/3 cup granulated sugar, or more if desired

1 to 2 tablespoons fruit liqueur, of choice
1 cup heavy cream, well chilled

Carefully crack the eggs one at a time and place the egg white into a small bowl and the egg yolk in the top of a double boiler. If the egg white is free of yolk, transfer to a large spotless clean mixing bowl for whipping or to the bowl of a standing mixer. If the egg yolk drips into the egg white, discard the egg white and break another egg, using a clean bowl. Set aside the egg whites to warm to room temperature and return the yolks to the refrigerator while preparing the meringue crust (see Get the Whip, page 132).

Preheat the oven to 250 degrees. Line a baking sheet with parchment paper. Turn a 9-inch pie plate upside down on the paper, and use as a guide to draw a perfect circle in the center of the paper. The circle will be used as an outline to form the meringue shell. Set the paper-lined baking sheet aside.

Sprinkle the vinegar or cream of tartar and salt over the egg whites. Using a standing mixer fitted with the whisk attachment or a handheld electric mixer, beat the egg whites on medium-high speed until foamy and soft.

Gradually add the sugar in a steady stream, and continue beating the egg whites at high speed until the meringue is glossy and holds rather stiff, shiny peaks. If using a stand mixer, turn off the mixer and scrape the bowl with a rubber spatula from time to time so that the egg whites are evenly beaten.

Add the vanilla extract to the stiffly beaten egg whites and mix well. Spread about three fourths of the meringue evenly over the circle on the parchment paper, mounding the egg whites about 2 inches high. Then, using a tablespoon, drop the remaining meringue near the edge of the circle, and swirl upward with the back of the spoon, forming a rim of peaks for the crust.

Set the crust on the middle shelf of the oven and bake for 1 hour and 30 minutes or until the crust is crisp and firm, pale cream in color but not browned. (If the meringue crust is not crisp after this time, turn off the oven and let remain in oven from 40 to 60 minutes longer. Don't open the oven during this time.)

Set the baked meringue crust on a wire rack and cool completely before filling with the custard. (The crust can be made the day before and kept in a cool place.)

To make the filling: Remove the egg yolks from the refrigerator and using a handheld electric mixer on medium-high speed, beat until thick and lemon-colored. Gradually beat in the sugar.

Stir in the lemon or sour orange juice and the grated lemon or orange peel. Cook over hot water—not in—stirring constantly, until the custard is thick and bubbles begin appearing, about 8 to 10 minutes. The mixture should be thick enough to mound slightly when dropped from a spoon, and to show resistance when stirred.

Remove the custard from the heat and cool completely, stirring occasionally to release steam. Chill the filling at least 2 hours or longer.

If using strawberries, discard leaves and cut the fruit into quarters; leave the raspberries whole. Combine the berries with 3 tablespoons of the sugar and chill until ready to use.

Combine the liqueur, heavy cream, and the remaining 2 tablespoons of sugar in a well-chilled bowl (see Perfectly Whipped Cream, page 74). Beat the heavy cream until it forms soft peaks, but don't overbeat.

At serving, spoon the filling into the meringue crust, spreading evenly. Spoon over the fruit, and top with the whipped cream. Cut into wedges for serving.

6 servings.

Get the Whip

Egg whites yield greater volume when beaten at room temperature, not icy cold. But there's a catch: separate the eggs while they are still cold because they get real runny at room temperature. And even a speck of egg yolk, butter, or grease can prevent egg whites from whipping into shape. Return the egg yolks to the fridge, and set the egg whites on the kitchen counter to warm up.

When you are ready to whip: Set out a large spotlessly clean stainless steel bowl or the bowl of a standing mixer to use to beat the egg whites, a small bowl to use to transfer the egg whites to the whipping bowl, and another small bowl for the egg yolks. This way, if you accidentally drop a little of the egg yolk into the egg white when cracking the egg, you can simply discard that egg white, and not the whole batch of egg whites.

To separate the eggs, tap the center of an egg on the rim of one of the small bowls and make an even crack. Hold the egg over the bowl. Using your thumb, gently part the crack, crosswise, and let the egg white fall to the small bowl underneath, while keeping the egg yolk in one of the halves.

Carefully transfer the yolk from one half shell to the other, letting any additional egg white fall into the bowl. Place the egg yolk into the other small bowl.

Now, transfer the egg white in the small bowl to the large bowl, which will be used for the whipping. Crack the remaining eggs in the same way: drop the egg white into one small bowl, the yolk into another small bowl, and then transfer the egg white to the larger bowl.

Let the bowl of egg whites warm to room temperature, away from draft, for about an hour. If you are pressed for time and want to warm up the egg whites quickly, set the bowl in a pan of warm water and swirl the bowl gently until the eggs are no longer frigid. But watch this carefully; egg whites scramble quickly, so remove the bowl from the water in a hurry.

To whip, sprinkle the egg whites with a few drops of cider vinegar, or a pinch of cream of tartar, a white powder that comes from fermented grape juice. Vinegar and cream of tartar are high in acid, and stabilize the egg whites so that they can rise and shine. But don't use strongly flavored red wine or balsamic vinegar.

Using an electric mixer, preferably a handheld model set at medium-high speed, move the beaters in a circular pattern in the bowl, and beat the egg whites without stopping just until they hold slight but glossy peaks. If you use a standing mixer, you have to turn off the mixer a couple times, and using a rubber spatula, scrap the bowl so that the egg whites are evenly beaten. Use softly whipped egg whites to fold into cake batters, pies, and puddings.

Here's how to fold: Using a rubber spatula or a wooden spoon, place the beaten egg whites on top of the batter or filling. Cut down to the bottom of the bowl with the edge of the spatula or spoon and bring up some of the filling or batter and place on top of the egg whites. Gently continue this cutting and lifting motion until the egg whites are evenly combined with the filling or cake batter, turning the bowl as you work.

If you are making meringue topping or a meringue piecrust, once the eggs are frothy and foamy, gradually add the sugar and beat on high speed until the peaks are glossy, quite firm, almost stiff, but airy and elastic. The sugar acts as a stabilizer and prevents the egg whites from deflating quickly and you can beat the whites until quite stiff.

But don't get carried away. After the peaks turn glossy and firm, beat much longer and you end up with dry, grainy, deflated egg whites. ❀

Put out a cinnamon-infused apple pie and before you can get all bluesy and patriotic and start humming a few stanzas of Ray Charles's version of "America," the pie will be long gone. I know few people who can resist a creamy sweet potato pie, especially when it is topped with a ring of caramelized pecans, evoking sweet but bitter memories that our ancestors brought this root over on those slave ships. And no dessert is more soul-satisfying than a rich and spicy peach pie or cobbler, whether with a cup of tea or coffee in mid-afternoon, or as the memorable sweet offering at a joyful family reunion.

If you combine molasses with a few eggs, a cup of cream, and a handful of pecans, you have the makings of an aromatic molasses pecan pie straight from my birthplace, Choctaw County in Alabama. Since a box of cocoa, a few bars of cooking chocolate, and a package of coconut are staple ingredients, they provide the perfect reason to stir together an old-fashioned chocolate cream pie, or a tangy coconut pie, and both are so fine.

And isn't it difficult to reach for a basket of peaches on a summer day at the market, when you know you can turn a quart of berries into a glorious pie or cobbler in no time, too? Don't sweat; buy both. That's what Jasper McGruder did when he was growing up in Waverly,

New York—a little town of five thousand people near the Pennsylvania border—when the pie man came around hawking lemon meringue, chocolate, apple, coconut custard, and cherry pies.

"I remember never wanting to share mine," said Jasper, and that must have been tough too, considering that he was one of fourteen children!

Jasper's great-grandfather sought refuge and was welcomed in Waverly in the 1840s, fleeing the state of Virginia and slavery. In fact, getting this information out of him was like pulling taffy candy; Jasper, I think, is the only African-American I ever met whose family was "free" before the Civil War.

But he is so modest and cool, that just by listening and talking to him, you'd never guess that he is a consummate actor, a fine director, has a deep knowledge of all kinds of music, hosts a rhythm and blues show on WBAI radio, and besides that, is a cook extraordinaire.

"His talent boggles the mind," says his wife, Sharon, also an actress, who doesn't seem to mind that Jasper has literally pushed her out of the kitchen.

Jasper has a wide repertoire of recipes—couldn't help but use that word—and it was a little hard choosing only a couple to feature in this book. He makes sophisticated cheesecakes, soaks strawberries in port wine for a fabulous upside-down cake, and turns out a creamy and luscious sweet potato pie that has me wondering if the guy didn't really grow up down home.

In the end though, I had to go with his delectable peach pie or cobbler, primarily because it is elegant, aromatic, and delicious—an evocative but provocative mélange of flavors.

"Somebody passed the recipe on to me and I have added my personal touches over the years," said Jasper in his modest way. "So many influences shape my cooking: friends from college, people I have met in the theater, my travel. But if you add a little brandy or cognac and some brown sugar to this pie, you get real deep flavor."

But none of our old-time desserts are slackers.

Summer Peach Pie

I prefer pies to cobblers because I like to have my pie filling squeezed in between two layers of buttery but flaky pastry. Jasper prefers cobblers, which he says, highlight the fruit more. Actually, there is not much difference between the two. A fruit or berry pie has both a bottom and top crust, while the filling for a cobbler is placed in a deep dish or pie pan, and covered only with a top crust.

So in the name of diplomacy, recipes for both desserts follow, using the same peachy filling.

Dough for 1 double 9-inch Basic
　Piecrust (page 113)
9 or 10 ripe medium-size fresh
　peaches (about 2½ pounds)
2 tablespoons lemon juice
2 tablespoons brandy
1 teaspoon vanilla extract

¾ cup granulated sugar, or to taste
¼ cup light brown sugar, firmly packed
1 teaspoon grated nutmeg, or to taste
1½ teaspoons ground cinnamon
2 tablespoons flour
1 large egg
4 tablespoons unsalted butter

Cut off slightly more than half of the dough for the bottom crust. Return the remaining half to the refrigerator.

Dust the work surface lightly with flour and roll out the larger piece of dough into an 11- to 12-inch circle. Lift the crust carefully with the rolling pin and place the pastry into a 9-inch glass pie pan. Trim the dough about ¾ inch below the edge of the pie pan. Prick the crust all over with a fork. Brush the crust with a little of the egg white and chill.

Preheat the oven to 400 degrees.

Rinse the peaches, remove the stems, peel and cut into eighths, discarding the pits. (You should have at least 4½ cups of the sliced fruit.) Place the peaches in a large glass bowl and toss with the lemon juice, brandy, and vanilla extract.

Combine both sugars, the nutmeg and cinnamon. Set aside 2 or 3 tablespoons of the sugar-spice mixture to use for a topping.

In a small bowl, combine the bulk of the sugar-spice mixture and the flour. Add the egg and beat until well blended. Pour the sugar-egg mixture over the peaches, and mix well.

Pour the peaches into the chilled crust. Use a large spoon and tuck the slices snugly and tightly together. Cut the butter into bits and scatter over the peaches.

To make a quick lattice crust: Roll out the remaining dough roughly into a 12-inch square on a lightly floured work surface. Cut the dough into twelve strips, each 1 inch wide.

Twist six of the strips and lay across the pie in a row, spacing evenly. Twist the remaining strips and lay across the pie in the opposite direction, to make a diamond pattern.

Cut off the ends of the pastry strip evenly with the bottom crust. Press the ends of the strips to the edge of the crust to seal. Roll up the edge of the crust on the pie pan rim and pinch or crimp together.

Brush the pastry top with the remaining egg white.

Place the pie on the lower shelf of the hot oven and bake for 40 minutes. (Place a sheet of foil on the oven floor to catch drippings, and if the edges of crust begin to brown too quickly, cover with strips of foil.)

Sprinkle on the sugar-spice topping and continue baking for 15 to 20 minutes or until the crust is golden brown and the pie is bubbly and thickened.

Remove from the oven and cool to lukewarm on a wire rack.

Makes 6 to 8 servings

Peach Cobbler

Using the dough for a single 9-inch Basic Piecrust, roll out into a 12-inch square or circle, depending on the shape of baking dish.

Place the dough on a baking sheet and chill while making the pie filling, using the same ingredients and following the recipe directions for Summer Peach Pie (page 136).

Generously butter a 9-inch round or square shallow baking dish (1½-quart size). Pour the peach filling into the baking dish, arranging as neatly as possible.

Remove the dough from the refrigerator and place over the peaches. Using scissors or a knife, trim the edges of the dough, leaving about $^1/_2$ inch of the pastry hanging over the rim of the pan all around.

Neatly tuck under the edge of the dough and press against the inside rim of the pan. Flute the edge of the dough with your fingertips, or crimp with a fork, pressing against the baking dish.

Prick the top of the pastry all over with a fork or cut tiny slivers in several places, to allow steam to escape during baking. Brush the pastry with a little beaten egg white.

Set the cobbler on the lower shelf of the hot oven and bake for 25 minutes. Sprinkle the top with the reserved spice-sugar. (Place a sheet of foil on the oven floor to catch drippings, and if the edge of the crust browns too quickly, cover with strips of foil and continue baking.)

Bake for 20 to 25 minutes longer or until the pastry is golden brown, the cobbler is hot and bubbly, and the filling has thickened. Cool to lukewarm on a wire rack before serving.

Makes 6 to 8 servings

Variations: Substitute $4^1/_2$ cups blueberries, blackberries, pitted cherries, or sliced nectarines for the peaches.

Apple-Cranberry Pie

Janice Mosley remembers that a friend told her about the St. Albans Congregational Church in Queens, New York, so she went one Sunday, and the next, and finally, every Sunday. She soon joined the church.

Right away she became a member of the church's Literary Club, got involved with the women's day activities, and started volunteering at the nursery on Sundays.

"But what I like most about this church is the bonding," says Janice, a schoolteacher. "At St. Albans our history is every day, not just in February during Black History month. It is a real progressive church."

Janice also carries covered dishes to various church events, especially apple pie, which is made with brown sugar and spices. For Thanksgiving dinner last year I boosted the flavor with tangy cranberries and shouted, "Hallelujah!"

Dough for 1 double 9-inch Basic
  Piecrust (page 113)
3 pounds tart cooking apples, about 6
  or 7 (see A Is for Apples, page 243)
1 cup fresh or frozen cranberries
2 tablespoons orange juice
3/4 cup light brown sugar, firmly
  packed, or to taste, depending on
  sweetness of apples

1/2 cup granulated sugar
1 to 2 teaspoons ground cinnamon
1/2 to 1 teaspoon grated nutmeg
2 tablespoons flour or cornstarch, or
  1 tablespoon each
1 teaspoon vanilla extract or 2 or 3
  tablespoons liqueur, such as Grand
  Marnier, Cointreau, or B&B
2 tablespoons butter

Lightly flour a work surface. Cut off slightly more than half of the dough for the bottom crust. Roll out the larger half of the dough into an 11- to 12-inch circle. Lift carefully and place the pastry into the pie pan. Trim the pastry, leaving from 1/2- to 3/4-inch overhang all around. Prick the crust with a fork, brush with the egg white, and chill.

Preheat the oven to 400 degrees.

Peel and core the apples and cut into 1/8-inch-thick slices. Place the apples in a large bowl. Rinse and drain the cranberries and remove the stems. Combine the cranberries, apples, and orange juice.

Add both sugars, the cinnamon, nutmeg, flour or cornstarch, and vanilla extract or liqueur. Mix gently but combine well. Spoon the fruit mixture into the pastry shell.

Cut the butter into little pieces and dot over the pie filling. Roll out the remaining pastry into an 11-inch circle. Place the top crust over the apples. Using a sharp knife or kitchen scissors, trim the edges of the top pastry, leaving from $1/2$- to $3/4$-inch overhang.

Press the edges of the bottom and top shell firmly together. Stand the pastry edge on the rim of the pie pan. Crumple with your fingers to make a pretty border, or crimp edge with a fork.

Brush the top lightly with the remaining egg white. Set the pie on the lower shelf of the hot oven. Place a sheet of foil on the oven floor to catch dripping.

Bake the pie for 50 minutes or until golden brown and crusty.

Remove from the oven and let rest at least 20 minutes before serving. Best served warm or at room temperature.

Makes 6 to 8 servings

Honey Apple Tart

I was just about to close the book on fruit pies when Ann Birchett called and told me not to forget her open-face apple pie. How could I?

I met Ann when I first arrived in New York City years ago, and she promptly invited me to her elegant home on Convent Avenue in Harlem, where we have shared many feasts.

Now that she's an octogenarian, her pace has slowed, but not her thoughts and goodwill. She is a dear friend, just like family, and I was pleased to bake this tart recently when she and her husband, Charles (Butch), celebrated their sixtieth wedding anniversary.

This lovely apple pie is baked in a straight-sided tart pan, lightly perfumed with ginger, and glazed with honey. It is delightful and delicious. If you don't have a tart pan, use a 9- or 10-inch pie pan.

I used Ida Red apples in this recipe, but there are many other suitable varieties of apples, and I used sour cream pastry for the crust (page 119), which provided it with a delightful tangy accent (see A Is for Apples, page 243).

1 fully baked single 10-inch Sour
    Cream Tart Crust (see page 119)
2 pounds small tart apples, about
    5 to 6
1 tablespoon lemon juice
1 teaspoon ground ginger
4 to 6 tablespoons unsalted butter

⅓ cup light brown sugar, firmly packed,
    preferably crystallized brown sugar
    (see Dark and Sweet, page 25)
⅓ cup honey, such as clover or
    wildflower
1 to 2 tablespoons apple brandy, such
    as Calvados

Set aside the tart crust to cool.

Meanwhile, rinse the apples, peel, core, and cut lengthwise into thin slices. Put the apple in a large glass bowl and sprinkle with the lemon juice and ginger, tossing gently to cover all over.

Melt the butter in a large stainless steel skillet. Add the apple slices and mix well, coating all over with the butter.

Cook the apples gently over medium heat, turning, until they begin to lose their juice and are slightly translucent, 5 to 6 minutes. (If you don't have a skillet large enough to hold the apples, do this in two steps, using half the butter each time.)

Remove the apples from the heat. Using a slotted spoon, and pressing out as much juice as possible, place the apples back in the bowl, leaving the juice in the pan. (If the apples are real juicy, press at least twice so as to collect the juice.)

Add the sugar, honey, and brandy to the juice in the pan. Place on medium-high heat and bring to a quick boil. Cook for 3 or 4 minutes, stirring, or until the syrup is bubbly and thick. Remove from the heat and set aside.

Preheat the oven to 400 degrees.

Arrange the apples in the pastry shell in a tight concentric circle, overlapping the slices, creating a daisy wheel pattern.

Pour half the honey syrup over the apples, spreading evenly with a spatula. Cover the edges of the tart pan with strips of foil to prevent overbrowning.

Set the pie on the lower shelf of the hot oven and bake for 35 to 40 minutes, or until the apples are tender and lightly browned. Place a sheet of foil on the oven floor to catch drippings.

Spoon the remaining syrup over the apples, spreading evenly. Return the tart to the oven and bake for 5 minutes longer or until the honey is glazed.

Remove the tart from the oven and cool on a wire rack until the juices set and stop bubbling.

Serve the pie warm with Perfectly Whipped Cream (page 74), or with Honey Cream (page 242), if desired.

Makes 4 to 5 servings

Sweet Potato Praline Pie

Several years ago for Thanksgiving dinner, Aldon and John James asked me to bake a few sweet potato pies for their annual private party at the National Arts Club in New York City, where Aldon is the residing president. The next year the request rose to a half-dozen pies, and after that a dozen.

And by that time I was totally consumed with a project involving a culinary creation that I simply adore. Then I was faced with the challenge of making several exciting variations of this humble pie.

"But don't get too carried away," said Aldon, "we just plain love sweet potato pie."

And so do I. At its best, a sweet potato pie is creamy with a subtle caramel flavor, and warmed with spices and a hint of spirits, either dark rum or brandy.

This past year I presented Aldon and John with three variations: one with a praline topping, another scattered with candied orange peel, and a third festooned with lemon caramel.

"They were all so delicious we couldn't decide what variation we liked best," said John.

Several recipes came in for sweet potato pie; this pie is real popular in our community. This version was inspired by my friend K. Wise Whitehead's "Mom's Sweet Potato Pie" recipe.

Thank you, Mrs. Bonnie Ruth Nix Wise.

1 partially baked single 9 inch Basic
    Piecrust (page 113)
2 pounds sweet potatoes (about 4 or 5
    small)
4 tablespoons unsalted butter, melted
1 cup granulated sugar, or to taste
2 medium eggs

$\frac{1}{2}$ teaspoon vanilla extract
1 teaspoon ground ginger
1 teaspoon ground allspice
2 tablespoons dark rum or brandy
$\frac{1}{2}$ cup evaporated milk, undiluted, or
    half-and-half

PRALINE TOPPING:

2 tablespoons unsalted butter
2 tablespoons brown sugar, preferably
    brown crystallized sugar (see Dark
    and Sweet, page 25)

$\frac{1}{2}$ to $\frac{2}{3}$ cup coarsely chopped
    pecans
$\frac{1}{4}$ teaspoon vanilla extract

Set aside the crust to cool.

Meanwhile, scrub and rinse the sweet potatoes. Cut away the eyes or sprouts and discard. Place the unpeeled sweet potatoes in the top of a steamer and cook over boiling water for about 30 minutes or until tender.

Preheat the oven to 350 degrees.

Remove the cooked potatoes from the pan and drain. Peel while still warm. Using a fine strainer that is at least 6 inches in diameter, force the potatoes through the sieve into a large mixing bowl or the bowl of a standing mixer fitted with the paddle attachment, pressing hard with a rubber spatula.

Using 2 cups of the mashed potatoes, beat on low speed until they are light and fluffy. (Use the leftover mashed potatoes in pancake or biscuit batter.) Add the butter, sugar, eggs, vanilla extract, ginger, allspice, and rum or brandy.

Beat on medium-high speed for 2 or 3 minutes until the filling is smooth and creamy and well blended. Add the milk or half-and-half and beat on low speed until well blended.

Pour the filling into the pie shell and spread evenly with a knife or spatula.

Set the pie on the lower shelf of the preheated oven and bake for 25 minutes.

Meanwhile prepare the praline topping: Combine in a small saucepan the butter and sugar. Place on medium-low heat and heat stirring until the butter melts and the mixture is well combined. Stir in the pecans and vanilla extract, mix well, and remove from heat.

Carefully remove the pie from the oven and set on a wire rack. Using a tablespoon, place a small circle of the nut mixture in the center of the pie. Spoon another larger circle of nuts near the edge of the pie, creating two rows of nuts. Spoon the syrup in the pan over the nuts and over the top of the pie.

Return the pie to the oven and bake for 20 to 25 minutes longer or until the pie is lightly browned around the edges and a knife inserted into the center comes out clean. Don't overbake.

Cool the pie completely on a wire rack before serving. For best flavor and to set the filling, chill the pie 30 to 40 minutes. However, many sweet potato pie lovers prefer the pie served at room temperature.

Makes 6 servings

Variation 1: Add $\frac{1}{3}$ cup fresh orange juice to the mashed sweet potatoes. Omit the praline topping and scatter the top of the pie while it is still warm with 3 or 4 tablespoons of Candied Citrus Peel, made with orange peel (page 124).

Variation 2: Add 2 teaspoons grated lemon peel to the mashed sweet potatoes. Omit the praline topping. Cool the pie completely at room temperature. Before serving, scatter the top with Caramel Threads (page 170).

Butternut Squash Pie

Bernice Lewis went home to Suffolk, Virginia, sat down with her mother, Thelma Faulk, and came back to New York City with this delightful recipe for squash pie. Bernice and I then got together and recounted the Sunday dinners of our youth, both of us remembering homemade ice cream, home-brewed peach and blackberry brandy, coconut and fruit cakes, sweet potato pies, and in Bernice's family, an exquisite Butternut Squash Pie.

I grew up on the red clay of southern Alabama, where sweet potatoes grew supreme, sporting an orange pulp just like butternut squash. But the two vegetables really don't taste alike. Sweet potatoes are more fibrous and homey, while butternut squash has a subtle, ethereal flavor—perfect foil for spices.

Bernice is the first cousin of my dear friend Brenda Richardson, and is a real sister, just like Brenda. Bernice lives in Forest Hills, Queens, and is an active member of Amity Baptist Church in Jamaica, where I was treated to a royal welcome during a book signing for *Soul Food: Recipes and Reflections from African-American Churches*.

1 partially baked single 9-inch Basic Piecrust (page 113)

1½ to 2 pounds butternut squash (to make 2 cups mashed cooked squash)

2 medium eggs

1 cup granulated sugar

1 tablespoon flour

2 tablespoons light molasses (not dark molasses)

½ teaspoon ground cinnamon

½ teaspoon ground ginger

½ teaspoon grated nutmeg

½ teaspoon vanilla extract

1 cup undiluted evaporated milk or 1 cup heavy cream or half-and-half

Perfectly Whipped Cream flavored with dark rum (page 74)

Set aside the piecrust to cool.

Preheat the oven to 375 degrees.

Rinse the squash well, wipe dry, and cut away any blemishes. Cut the squash in half crosswise and then cut in half lengthwise, yielding 4 pieces. Using a spoon, scoop and remove the seeds and fiber from the cavity and discard.

Lightly butter a roasting pan and pour in $^1/_4$ to $^1/_2$ inch of water. Place the squash cut side up in the pan. Set the pan on the lower shelf of the preheated hot oven and bake the squash for 35 to 40 minutes or until tender, turning over the squash halfway through the cooking.

Remove the squash from the heat and cool for a few minutes. Scoop out the pulp and place 2 cups of the squash in the bowl of a standing mixer fitted with the paddle attachment or in a large mixing bowl. (Refrigerate the remaining squash and use in another dish; it is delicious in a soup or salad.)

Add the eggs and sugar to the squash. Using the standing mixer or a handheld electric mixer, beat the squash on medium speed until smooth and fluffy. Add the flour, molasses, cinnamon, ginger, nutmeg, and vanilla extract and beat again until well blended.

Add the milk or cream and beat the filling on low speed until well combined.

Pour the filling into the partially baked pie shell.

Set the pie on the middle oven shelf and bake for 40 minutes or until the custard is firm and just set in the center. (Don't overbake; the pie will continue to cook as it cools.)

Remove the pie from the oven and cool on a wire rack. Chill if desired, and serve with the rum-flavored whipped cream.

Makes 6 to 8 servings

Spicy Molasses Pecan Pie

My sister-in-law, Laura, sent me this recipe from Choctaw County, in Alabama, triggering memories of the molasses breads, cakes, and puddings that Mama made during my childhood. Daddy used to help our neighbor, Mr. Ras, make syrup during the late fall, and his reward was a few gallons of molasses that carried us through the winter.

Laura's inventive recipe is similar to the popular Southern pecan pie, but hers is spicy, creamy, and a little heady from the molasses.

Recently I baked this pie for Brenda Richardson and her family, and the next day, Brenda called and said, "I am so accustomed to the traditional pecan pie that I didn't think I was going to like this pie. But I sure do."

It is delicious.

1 partially baked single 9-inch Basic Piecrust (page 113)
4 tablespoons unsalted butter
1 cup granulated sugar
3 large eggs
1/4 to 1/3 cup light molasses (not dark molasses)
2 tablespoons lemon juice

1 teaspoon grated nutmeg or mace
1/2 teaspoon ground cloves
1 teaspoon vanilla extract
1/2 cup heavy cream or undiluted evaporated milk
1 generous cup pecan halves
Vanilla Bean Ice Cream (page 216) or Perfectly Whipped Cream (page 74)

Set aside the piecrust to cool.

Preheat the oven to 350 degrees.

Place the butter in a small skillet or saucepan and heat over medium-low heat until it melts, turns light brown, and gives off a nutty aroma, about 5 minutes. Remove the pan immediately from the heat and pour the butter into a large mixing bowl.

Add the sugar to the butter and mix well with a wooden spoon. Beat in the eggs one at a time, mixing well after each addition. Stir in the molasses, lemon juice, nutmeg, cloves, and vanilla extract and mix until the filling is well blended. Add the heavy cream or milk and beat until smooth.

Pour the filling into the prepared pie shell. Spread the pecan halves on top of the pie.

Place the pie on the middle shelf of the preheated oven and bake for 35 to 40 minutes or until the pie is golden brown and puffed, and a knife comes out clean when inserted into the center. (Watch the pie carefully. If it overcooks it can become gummy.)

Cool on a wire rack until the pie is set. Serve at room temperature topped with the vanilla ice cream or whipped cream.

Makes 6 servings

Cocoa Cream Pie with Candied Almonds

I am absolutely sure that I arrived in New York City on the Greyhound bus more than three decades ago with my sister's recipe for chocolate cream pie packed in my Samsonite luggage, a gift from my brother C. L., who lived in Detroit.

When I was growing up in southern Alabama, Helen was a cook at a local café, and she made magical desserts from chocolate, and most times with a box of Nestlé or Hershey's cocoa and a few bars of Baker's chocolate.

A chocolate cream pie is quick and easy to do, and can take many variations. Most times Helen stirred a cup of freshly grated coconut into the cooked filling, spooned on meringue, and browned the topping quickly in a hot oven.

If you make the pie in a metal tart pan, you can top the filling with a layer of sliced bananas: brush the bananas with a little melted butter, sprinkle on sugar or apricot preserves, and caramelize for a few minutes under a hot broiler.

I like this pie without meringue, with a crisp golden crust holding a soft and mushy filling, and ringed with candied almonds and dabs of whipped cream.

You can substitute 2 to 3 tablespoons of cornstarch for the flour in the filling for a satiny finish, but flour is the traditional thickener for this pie.

1 fully baked single 9-inch Sour Cream Piecrust or 10-inch Sour Cream Tart Crust (page 119)
½ cup unsweetened cocoa, preferably Dutch-process (see Bitter but Sweet, page 82)
4 tablespoons all-purpose flour
1 cup granulated sugar
Pinch of salt
½ teaspoon ground cinnamon

2 cups milk
4 tablespoons unsalted butter
1½ teaspoons vanilla extract
3 large egg yolks
Perfectly Whipped Cream (page 74)
Candied Almonds (see recipe for Candied Pecans, page 205, and use lightly toasted blanched almonds instead of pecans)

Set aside the crust to cool.

Combine the cocoa, flour, sugar, salt, and cinnamon in a heavy medium-size saucepan. Stir in the milk, whisking to combine well.

Place the pan over medium heat and bring to a gentle boil. Cook, stirring constantly, for about 5 minutes or until the mixture is thick and smooth.

Remove the pan from the heat and whisk in the butter and vanilla extract. Beat the mixture thoroughly.

Place the egg yolks in a small bowl and beat briskly for a few seconds. Stir a few tablespoons of the hot milk mixture into the egg yolks and mix well. Continue whisking about half of the hot filling into the egg yolks, beating briskly after each addition. Then, pour the egg yolk mixture into the saucepan with the rest of the hot milk mixture and beat until well blended.

Place the saucepan back on the burner and cook over medium-high heat, stirring constantly, until the filling comes to a boil again, for about 5 minutes.

Remove the pan from the heat and immediately pour the filling through a fine strainer into a large bowl. Set the bowl in an ice water bath (see On Ice, page 237) and chill thoroughly, stirring occasionally.

Spoon the chilled custard into the baked pie or tart shell. Drop mounds of whipped cream on top of the pie, garnish with the Candied Almonds, and serve right away.

If you make this pie in advance, you must refrigerate, but let the pie sit at room temperature and allow the pastry to warm up for 20 or so minutes before serving.

Makes 6 servings

Devil's Food Cake Pie

Every year in late November or early December, my brother John sends me a 15- to 20-pound box of pecans fresh off the trees in Biloxi and Gulfport. The deliveryman always greets me rattling the box, letting me know that he knows about my little annual cache. So I pass over a doggie bag full, happy to do so, despite the shakedown. Those guys really are great.

This past year John sent along this wonderful pie recipe, which is almost like a brownie in a pie shell. It is delicious served with whipped cream, or with Caramel or Burnt Sugar Sauce, and a scattering of pecans or toasted pecans.

Chocolate lovers will go mad for this cake pie.

1 fully baked single 9-inch Basic
    Piecrust (page 113)
6 ounces good-quality bittersweet or
    semisweet chocolate
2 tablespoons unsalted butter
3 large eggs
3 tablespoons all-purpose flour
1/8 teaspoon salt
1/2 cup light brown sugar, firmly packed

1/2 cup dark flavored honey, such as
    buckwheat
2 teaspoons vanilla extract
1/4 cup bourbon or dark rum or brandy
Caramel or Burnt Sugar Sauce (page
    234) or Perfectly Whipped Cream
    (page 74)
1 cup pecan halves or toasted peanuts

Set aside the crust to cool.

Preheat the oven to 350 degrees.

Chop the chocolate into small pieces. Melt the butter in a medium saucepan. Remove the pan from the burner and stir in the chocolate. Set the pan in a large skillet of hot water and stir over low heat until the chocolate melts and is smooth.

Remove the saucepan from the skillet, and set aside to cool.

In a large mixing bowl, whisk together the eggs, flour, salt, sugar, honey, and vanilla extract. Stir in the melted chocolate mixture and beat to combine well. Add the bourbon or rum or brandy and mix well. Pour the filling into the baked pie shell and smooth with a spatula.

Set the pie on the lower rack in the middle of the preheated oven. Bake for 25 to 30 minutes or until the pie is barely set in the middle and a tester comes out almost clean but moist when inserted in the center. (Don't overbake; it will become gummy. The pie will continue to cook as it cools.)

Place the pie on a wire rack and cool completely.

Top each serving with the burnt sugar sauce or the whipped cream and sprinkle over the pecans or peanuts.

Makes 6 servings

Variation: Substitute $1/4$ cup coffee liqueur, such as Tia Maria or Kahlúa, for the rum, brandy, or bourbon, for a divine mocha pie.

Three Sisters Coconut Pie

While working on this book I received an e-mail from a stranger, who told me to be sure to include a coconut custard pie in my upcoming dessert cookbook. She then continued with a few paragraphs of applause. Don't we love fan mail, and don't we love and appreciate girlfriends!

At that very moment I was wrestling over three recipes for coconut pie: from Brenda Richardson, from her cousin, Bernice Lewis, and from pal Norma Boucher, the tennis player and coach.

All three of the women are dear friends, and I love all three recipes. So the following recipe is a composite, using Brenda's nutmeg and Bernice's buttermilk; the cream of coconut is from Norma, who hails from beautiful Jamaica in the Caribbean.

There may have been a few sighs when I explained the compromise, but not one sister put her hands on her hips. Smile.

1 partially baked 9-inch Basic Piecrust
   (page 113)
3 large eggs
$^2/_3$ cup granulated sugar
3 tablespoons flour or cornstarch
$^1/_4$ cup coconut cream, such as Coco
   Lopez or Coco Goya

2 cups buttermilk or undiluted
   evaporated milk
Pinch of salt
1 teaspoon vanilla extract
$1^1/_2$ cups sweetened flaked coconut
$^1/_2$ teaspoon grated nutmeg, or to taste

Set aside the piecrust to cool.

Preheat the oven to 350 degrees.

Combine the eggs, sugar, and flour or cornstarch in a large bowl. Beat briskly with a whisk until well blended. Stir in the coconut cream, milk, salt, and vanilla extract, mixing until blended. Add the coconut and stir again.

Pour the filling into the partially baked piecrust. Sprinkle the top of the pie with the nutmeg.

Set the pie on the middle oven shelf and bake in the preheated oven for 30 to 35 minutes, or until the pie is puffy and light golden, and a knife inserted in the center comes out almost clean. Don't overbake.

Remove the pie from the oven and cool completely on a wire rack.

If you must chill, bring to room temperature for 20 or so minutes before serving.

Makes 6 servings

Variation: Toss $1^1/_2$ cups freshly shredded coconut with 2 tablespoons sugar and substitute for the sweetened flaked coconut (see Cracking Coconuts, page 245).

FOUR

Puddings and Custards: So Smooth

Years ago as a child I would sit eyes wide open when my sister, Helen, pulled a banana pudding out of the oven: a glass baking dish holding a layer of vanilla wafers on the bottom, topped by a creamy custard and banana slices, which supported a towering mound of golden brown meringue. The bananas were ripe but not overly, the wafers retained a little of their crispness, the custard was creamy but not too thick, and the meringue never wept. The creation was sublime, and I could hardly wait.

Eventually I began to appreciate other custards and puddings, and although most didn't match the banana pudding for sheer drama, they did in flavor. The principal ingredient is the humble egg, which is paired with milk or cream, and after that, you are limited only by your imagination.

You can add fruit, spices, nuts, chocolate, liqueurs, molasses, coconut, coffee, or tea; top with sauces made from jellies, jams, rum, brandy, or bourbon; or enjoy with a generous dab of flavored whipped cream.

And if you add a grain—either bread, rice, or noodles—then you have what is collectively referred to as old-fashioned puddings, for these types of desserts have been around since time immemorial. In biblical days, grains and oats were sweetened with honey and spices and turned into gruels, perhaps our first puddings. And in Africa, way before the arrival of the Europeans, our ancestors made mush and porridge and fufu, forerunners of puddings, from yams, cassava, millet, and barley.

While some puddings and custards are warming and comforting, others are exquisite and sophisticated: Just think of a winter night and a soulful bread pudding laced with fruit and served with a bracing bourbon sauce. But what could be more cooling on a hot summer day than a rice pudding topped with an exquisite, lacy "burnt" sugar coating, or an elegant fruit-topped cheesecake? And yes, cheesecake is a custard not a cake batter.

But a banana pudding is a showstopper, understandably the favorite dessert of Grace Ingleton, whose dining table displays her broad cultural horizon.

Grace was born in Panama to West Indian parents who ventured there in the early 1900s to work on the infamous canal. She emigrated to New York City in 1953, became a nursing educator and art consultant by profession, and is so passionate about food that until this day she has saved copies of *Gourmet* magazine dating back to the 1960s.

Along the way she met and married a brother from the South, discovered soul food, and need we say more.

"I love banana pudding," Grace says, laughing, "but when you think about it, it really isn't much different from the pineapple flans, coconut custards, and plantain puddings that we make in the Caribbean. People of the African diaspora cook the same way, basically because we had the same ingredients and same circumstances."

This recipe is creamy with a spicy edge from homemade Gingersnaps. Lemon Vanilla Wafers (page 13) are also delicious in this pudding, and so is almost any other plain cookie.

New Banana Pudding

4 eggs
1 cup granulated sugar plus $^1/_2$ cup
3 tablespoons flour
$^1/_8$ teaspoon salt
$2^1/_2$ cups milk
1 teaspoon vanilla extract

2 tablespoons dark rum
12 to 15 Gingersnaps (page 36)
2 or 3 very ripe medium bananas
$^1/_4$ teaspoon cider vinegar or cream of tartar

Generously butter a $1^1/_2$-quart baking dish and set aside.

Carefully crack the eggs one at a time and place the yolk and the egg white in two separate small bowls. If the egg white is free of yolk, transfer to a large spotless clean bowl for whipping or to the bowl of a standing mixer. If any egg yolk drips into the egg white, discard that egg white and break another egg, using a clean small bowl. Set aside the egg whites to warm to room temperature and return the yolks to the refrigerator until ready to use (see Get the Whip, page 132).

Combine the 1 cup sugar, flour, and salt in the top of a double boiler over hot water. Whisk in the milk, mixing well. Bring the milk almost to a boil, cooking until it is hot and bubbly and begins to thicken, stirring occasionally. This should take 5 to 7 minutes. Remove the pan from the heat.

Whisk the egg yolks until just blended. Add the vanilla extract.

Add 2 or 3 tablespoons of the hot milk to the egg yolks and beat again. Stir another cup of the milk into the egg yolks and mix again. Now add the egg mixture to the milk in the double boiler and mix well.

Set the pan back on the heat and cook the custard over boiling water 10 to 12 minutes, or until it is very thick and creamy, stirring constantly. Watch this carefully, for you don't want the eggs to scramble.

When it is very thick, immediately remove the custard from the heat and stir in the rum.

Pour the custard through a strainer into a large bowl. Set the bowl in an ice water bath (see On Ice, page 237), and stir occasionally until chilled.

Meanwhile, preheat the oven to 350 degrees.

Spread $1/2$ cup of the custard on the bottom of the buttered dish. Top with the Gingersnaps and spoon over another $1/2$ cup of custard.

Peel the bananas and cut crosswise into $1/4$-inch-thick slices. Top the custard and Gingersnaps with the sliced bananas, overlapping if necessary. Spread the remaining custard evenly over the bananas.

Prepare the meringue: Sprinkle the egg whites with the vinegar or cream of tartar. Using an electric mixer on medium-high speed, beat the egg whites until foamy. Gradually add the remaining $1/2$ cup sugar, about 2 tablespoons at a time, and beat on high speed until the peaks are stiff and shiny, but not dry. This should take about 5 minutes; don't overbeat.

Spread a generous cup of the meringue over the filling, and smooth it to the edge of the baking dish. Spread on the rest of the meringue and using the back of a tablespoon, swirl for a decorative effect.

Place the pudding on the middle shelf in the preheated oven. Bake 12 to 15 minutes or until the meringue is tinged golden brown. Cool the pie completely on a wire rack, and then chill for several hours, or overnight, if desired. Serve cold.

Makes 6 to 8 servings

I still can't remember exactly when Mama gave me her old bread board, but it is sitting now on a table in my cramped apartment kitchen, filled with fruit and produce, actually more of a graceful, sloping trough than a board, about a foot wide and twice as long, slick from use, gnarled and pitted from age, evocative with memories.

It is possible that the board was passed on to Mama by Aunt Agnes or Grandma Addie, but sometime in the late 1970s or early 1980s, she gave it to me during a visit home. I remember boarding the airplane with the board tucked under my arm, for there was a remark or two from the flight attendants, like, "Where did you find that old relic? Sure make up some good biscuits, though."

And as I think of those comments, in my mind's eye I can see Mama now: It is Saturday morning and the busy pace of our household has slowed a bit. Her hands are dusted with flour, she is silent with thoughts, leaning over the old bread board. She sticks one pan of biscuits in the oven for breakfast, and another pan for the bread pudding that she will make the next day before church service.

Early on Sunday morning a cast-iron skillet is generously buttered, a simple custard is made with eggs, sugar, canned milk, and vanilla or lemon extract; the day-old baked biscuits are placed in the bottom of the skillet, sometimes topped with slivers of fruit, usually dried peaches or apples; the custard is poured over, and soon our kitchen is filled with fragrant aromas.

I was thinking of this recently when Pat Mack sent me a recipe for Biscuit Bread Pudding (page 163), which was passed to her by her father, the late Benjamin Holmes. At one time her dad was the head chef at the Walter Reed Hospital in Washington, D.C., ran a catering concern on the side, and worked hard to survive.

"There was a bunch of us—six children," says Pat, who has a large extended family in metropolitan Washington, D.C. "We had the necessities, and there was always food in the house."

Mr. Holmes would take leftover bread, whisk together eggs and reconstituted dried milk or canned milk, add sugar and flavoring, and make something sweet, delicious, and soul-satisfying from everyday staples, just like Mama did.

As the years passed and after Pat got married, she began to fiddle with her father's basic bread pudding recipe. She and her brother Wendell opened a catering firm—now defunct—and her cooking became more and more inventive.

Buttermilk, which she likes for cooking, was used in the custard. Regular walnuts were sprinkled on top of the pudding for extra crunch, and then she got bold and jazzy and switched to aromatic black walnuts. Brown sugar eventually squeezed out some of the white sugar. And when

Puddings and Custards: So Smooth

time permitted, leftover rolls were replaced by baked-from-scratch buttermilk biscuits. The results: The comforting dessert from her childhood was now sophisticated and delicious.

"I make this bread pudding at least five or six times a year for family gatherings," says Pat, a legal secretary and events planner who now lives in Upper Marlboro, Maryland, with her husband, Clinton, a retired policeman. "And if I don't bake it, the family wants to know why. It is the memories and tradition that matter."

Biscuit Bread Pudding

The first time I baked this pudding I called over my glamorous friend and neighbor, Edith Collins, who has a critical eye for food and fashions. She slid into my kitchen with customary élan, I set out dessert plates, and we dug in.

"What did you put in this pudding?" she exclaimed, "It is absolutely delicious."

I demurred and said, "It wasn't me; it was my dear friend Pat Mack."

This crusty bread pudding calls out for a fruit topping. I like Raspberry Sauce (page 165), or, as suggested by Pat Mack, gently poached pears. A good recipe is Pears Noires (Chocolate Pears) (page 256). The pears are poached in a delightful orange-flavored sauce, and the chocolate is stirred in at the last moment. If desired, omit the chocolate; if not, add it and enjoy the succulent combination, which turns the dessert into a chocolate bread pudding!

6 to 10 baked Buttermilk Biscuits
   (page 166), preferably day-old
3 large eggs
¾ cup granulated sugar
½ cup light brown sugar, firmly
   packed, plus ¼ cup
2 tablespoons all-purpose flour
2 tablespoons unsalted butter, melted

1 teaspoon ground cinnamon
½ teaspoon grated nutmeg
1 teaspoon vanilla extract
⅛ teaspoon salt
2 cups buttermilk
1 cup coarsely chopped walnuts, or
   less if desired

Generously butter a 2-quart glass or porcelain baking dish (an 8 × 12-inch pan works nicely).

Slice the biscuits in half crosswise with a serrated knife and place the bread in the bottom of the baking dish, cut side down. Set aside. If you like your bread pudding with a lot of custard, use six biscuits; if you prefer more bread, add a few more biscuits.

Place the eggs in a large mixing bowl and beat until just blended. Stir in the granulated sugar, ½ cup of the light brown sugar, the flour, butter, cinnamon, nutmeg, vanilla extract, and salt and whisk again. Add the buttermilk and mix well.

Pour the custard over the biscuits. Press the bread down with the back of a spoon, making sure that the bread absorbs the custard and is soaked through. Let the custard stand at room temperature for 30 minutes, occasionally ladling the custard over the biscuits.

Preheat the oven to 350 degrees.

Toss together the walnuts and the remaining $1/4$ cup brown sugar and scatter over the top of the bread pudding.

Set the baking dish inside a large roasting pan or cast-iron skillet. Bring a kettle of water to a boil. Carefully pour the water into the roasting pan, about halfway up the sides of the baking dish, creating a water bath (see In Hot Water, page 180).

Set the pan on the middle shelf of the preheated oven. Bake for 40 minutes or until the pudding is puffy and browned around the edges, firm in the center, and no longer runny. A knife inserted in the center should come out almost clean.

Remove the pudding from the oven and the water bath and set on a wire rack. Cool the pudding to room temperature and serve, or chill, if desired.

Makes 8 servings

Note: Black walnuts are especially delicious in this pudding, but they have a robust flavor and if you use them you may want to reduce the amount to $1/2$ cup.

Raspberry Sauce

I especially like bread puddings topped with fruit sauces infused with a little liqueur, and I love raspberries. This sauce is also delicious with the Biscuit Bread Pudding (page 163).

2 or 3 tablespoons granulated sugar, or
   to taste
¼ cup water
1 tablespoon lemon juice

2 cups fresh or frozen raspberries
1 or 2 tablespoons raspberry or cherry
   fruit brandy, such as framboise or
   kirsch

Combine the sugar, water, and lemon juice in a small saucepan. Place on medium-high heat and bring to a boil, stirring until the sugar dissolves. Boil 2 or 3 minutes longer, or until the syrup thickens slightly. Remove from the heat and cool.

Combine the syrup, raspberries, and fruit brandy in a blender or food processor. Puree or pulse the mixture until smooth.

Pour the sauce through a fine strainer before serving.

Makes about 2 cups

Buttermilk Biscuits

I used cream of tartar in the recipe instead of baking powder, a technique learned from the great cook and cookbook author Sister Edna Lewis. The biscuits are tangy, crunchy, and delicious.

2 cups all-purpose unbleached flour

1/4 teaspoon salt

1/2 teaspoon baking soda

2 teaspoons cream of tartar

6 tablespoons unsalted butter, chilled

2/3 cup buttermilk

Preheat the oven to 425 degrees. Lightly butter a baking sheet and set aside.

Sift the flour, salt, baking soda, and cream of tartar into a large bowl. Add the butter. Using a pastry cutter or two knives, cut in the butter until the mixture resembles coarse cornmeal.

Add the milk and stir the batter lightly with a fork. Turn the dough onto a floured board or pastry cloth and knead lightly four or five times.

Roll out or pat the dough into an 8-inch circle, about 1/2 inch thick. Using a 2-inch biscuit or cookie cutter or a glass rim dipped in flour, cut the dough into rounds. Gently reroll the scraps and cut again into rounds until all the dough has been used.

Place the biscuits on the baking sheet, allowing a little space between each. Set the pan on the lower shelf of the hot oven and bake for 12 to 15 minutes or until golden brown.

Remove from the oven and set on a wire rack. Cool for a few minutes in the pan, and then take them from the pan and put on the rack to cool completely.

Makes 16 to 18 biscuits

Bread Pudding with Whiskey Sauce

This wonderful recipe for old-fashioned New Orleans–style bread pudding was sent by Earlene Spiller. Her beautiful daughter, Anya, is married to my brother John's handsome son, my nephew, Cleve, who is named for our father, Daddy Cleve, as we called him.

A few years ago Earlene returned home to Biloxi on the Gulf Coast after spending thirty-two years teaching school in Prince William County in Alexandria, Virginia. She spends her days now caring for her aging parents, singing in the chorus with the Gulf Coast Opera, going to crab boils at Cleve and Anya's lovely home, attending concerts, and enjoying the beautiful scenery.

"I grew as an adult in Prince William County and metro Washington, D.C., and I have a lot of friends there," says Earlene. "But this is home, and I always missed it. It is peaceful being around water. And I love the food down here."

This is a straightforward Southern-style bread pudding, and since I love apples baked in custard, this was the fruit of my choice. But a generous cup of freshly shredded coconut, diced plums or peaches, or a cup of well-drained crushed pineapple or fruit cocktail can replace the sliced apples.

6 slices white, firm-textured day-old
   bread or 2 large rolls
3 large eggs
1¼ cups granulated sugar
2 cups milk
1 tablespoon (3 teaspoons) vanilla
   extract
½ teaspoon ground cinnamon or

grated nutmeg, or to taste
Pinch of salt
1 large baking apple (see A Is for
   Apples, page 243)
½ cup dark or golden raisins
5 tablespoons unsalted butter
Whiskey Sauce (recipe follows)

Preheat the oven to 400 degrees.

Cut the crusts from the bread, and using a serrated knife, cut into ½-inch cubes. You should have 2 cups of bread cubes. Spread the bread on a baking pan or cookie sheet. Set the pan in the preheated oven on the middle shelf and toast lightly, turning over as needed, for about 5 minutes. Don't overbrown the bread.

Remove the bread from the oven and set aside.

Reduce the oven temperature to 350 degrees. Generously butter a 1½-quart shallow baking dish and set aside.

Combine the eggs and sugar in a large bowl and beat with a whisk until well blended. Whisk in the milk, vanilla extract, cinnamon or nutmeg, and salt, mixing well. Stir in the toasted bread cubes, and mix well.

Let the bread-milk mixture stand at room temperature for 30 minutes, stirring occasionally to saturate the bread with the custard. Peel the apple, core, and thinly slice.

To assemble the pudding: Place the apple slices in the buttered dish. Top with the raisins. Carefully pour over the bread-milk mixture.

Cut the butter into small pieces and scatter over the top of the custard. Set the baking dish inside a large roasting pan or cast-iron skillet. Pour hot water into the pan to reach about halfway up the sides of the baking dish, creating a water bath (see In Hot Water, page 180).

Set the pan on the middle shelf of the preheated oven. Bake 45 to 50 minutes or until the pudding is puffy, lightly browned, and firm in the center. A knife inserted in the center should come out almost clean.

Remove the pudding from the water bath and cool on a wire rack to room temperature. Serve with Whiskey Sauce or Caramel or Burnt Sugar Sauce (page 234), ladling the sauce over each serving of the bread pudding.

Makes 6 to 8 servings

Whiskey Sauce

This bracing and creamy sauce is also delicious with Biscuit Bread Pudding (page 163). Teetotalers can leave out the booze but the sauce won't taste quite as good.

1 large egg yolk
4 tablespoons unsalted butter
½ cup granulated sugar

1 cup heavy cream or undiluted
  evaporated milk
¼ to ⅓ cup bourbon

Combine the egg yolk, butter, and sugar in the top of a double boiler over hot water. Beat in the heavy cream or milk or cream until smooth.

Bring the sauce to a quick gentle boil, stirring frequently, until the sauce thickens, begins bubbling, and coats a spoon, 3 or 4 minutes. Watch carefully and don't let the sauce curdle.

Immediately remove the sauce from the heat and whisk in the bourbon.

Makes about 1 ¼ cups

Raisin-Rice Pudding with Caramel Threads

W hat I love about cooking," says Irene Peoples, of Hollis, Queens, in New York, "is that you can start with practically nothing and at the end something comes out that is pretty and delicious. You are an artist. Cooking turns everybody into an artist."

This is especially true when applied to her magical rice pudding, which is no more than last night's leftover rice turned into a creamy and soft-baked custard perfumed with raisins.

Irene and her loving daughter, Camille, are artisans and scholars. Both are excellent cooks and they bake scrumptious cakes and cookies for days for their family's annual Christmas party.

Both mother and daughter are voracious readers and members of the Literary Club at St. Albans Congregational Church in Queens.

For extra crunch, I topped Irene's rice pudding with lemony Caramel Threads, a perfect match.

4 large eggs

³/₄ cup granulated sugar

2 tablespoons unsalted butter, melted and cooled

3 cups milk

1¹/₃ cups cooked rice

1¹/₂ teaspoons vanilla extract

2 teaspoons grated lemon peel

1 teaspoon grated nutmeg

²/₃ cup dark raisins

CARAMEL THREADS:

¹/₂ cup granulated sugar

1 tablespoon lemon juice

1 tablespoon light corn syrup

2 tablespoons water

Preheat the oven to 350 degrees. Generously butter a 1¹/₂-quart baking dish and set aside.

In a large bowl, combine the eggs and sugar and beat with a whisk until well blended. Stir in the butter and mix well. Whisk in the milk, mixing until blended, but don't incorporate the bubbles by beating the mixture too much.

Add the rice, vanilla extract, lemon peel, nutmeg, and raisins and stir to combine.

Pour the custard into the buttered dish. Set the dish inside a large roasting pan. Pour enough hot water into the roasting pan to reach about halfway up the side of the dish, creating a water bath (see In Hot Water, page 180).

Set the pan on the middle shelf of the preheated oven. Bake the pudding for 20 minutes or until it is just slightly thickened.

Using a large spoon, stir the pudding gently but thoroughly to redistribute the rice. Bake for another 25 to 30 minutes, or until the pudding is puffy and firm in the center. A knife inserted in the center should come out almost clean.

Remove the pudding from the oven and the water bath and cool on a wire rack.

Prepare the Caramel Threads: Have available a long-handled wooden spoon, a pastry brush, and a cup of water. In a heavy, small saucepan or skillet, combine the sugar, lemon juice, corn syrup and 2 tablespoons water. Place the pan on medium-high and bring to a boil, stirring with the wooden spoon until the sugar dissolves (see Go Burn!, page 196).

Cover the pan and cook 3 minutes. Remove the lid. Dip the brush in the water and wash down the side of the pan.

Cook the syrup, swirling the pan, for 3 to 4 minutes, or until the syrup is amber or the color of deeply brewed tea. Don't allow the syrup to burn.

Immediately remove the pan from the heat, pour the syrup into another pan, and set aside to cool for 2 to 3 minutes, or until the syrup begins to thicken.

Using a fork, drizzle the caramel over the rice pudding. If the caramel in the pan hardens, stir in a teaspoon of water and heat over low heat.

Serve the pudding lukewarm, or chill and serve.

Makes 6 servings

AS RICH AND SMOOTH AS SILK:
CHEESECAKES AND SOUFFLÉS

Often I tease Pat Mack and Alfreda Holmes—two sisters—that their family is perfect for a Norman Rockwell calendar, tinted African-American and all-American.

Pat and Alfreda have four brothers, and they are the middle sisters in a rousing family of six siblings, all of whom live in Capital Beltway communities. And they hang together so tight, that I am sure that their parents, the late Alice and Benjamin Holmes, must be smiling from the heavens.

At least a half-dozen times a year the siblings and their spouses and children, and now the third generation's children, gather for spirited picnics, cookouts, ball games, concerts, and family dinners. And if you count that cousins often join the Holmes clan, as they call themselves, the crowd grows to fifty family members real quick.

Food galore is on hand, and each household chips in and brings something. Their father worked as a chef for years and everybody cooks in this family. One of the brothers, Wendell, a minister, once ran a catering business with Pat, and he stands guard over the slabs of ribs, making sure that they are barbecued to perfection. Butane-fed fish and turkey fryers are heated up, and at least a dozen homemade pies and cobblers are set out, sweet and inviting.

Pat bakes a delicious Biscuit Bread Pudding (page 163). Alfreda bakes hot rolls and a delectable cheesecake, which is creamy, slightly tart with a lemony edge, rich but not heavy and dense, the perfect dessert for a festive gathering.

"Our parents imparted to us a sense of values," says Alfreda, "and they told us to always stay connected."

They do.

Cheesecake Divine with Strawberry-Apricot Topping or Strawberry-Lemon Caramel Topping

Alfreda had a home repair emergency during the recent Christmas holidays and didn't have time to bake her divine cheesecake, which she usually gives as a gift to a circle of dear friends. So she gave the friends a gift certificate for her cake. The idea is that whenever they want the cake, say for the starred item at a family dinner, they can give her a few days' notice and she will bake and deliver her gift. So novel, and so loving.

And I love this creamy, delicious cheesecake, and so does my tester and neighbor, Edith Collins. I made several variations: On one occasion I swirled 3 or 4 ounces of semisweet chocolate into the batter, and on another, swirled in a generous half-cup of raspberry preserves, and the next time I used apricot preserves. All were delicious.

Since cheesecake is a custard, it will split and crack if it gets too hot during the baking, or if it remains in the oven until it is firm in the center. So follow the recipe directions closely and remove the cheesecake from the oven while it is still wiggly in the center.

However, Alfreda covers her cake with a delightful strawberry topping that covers all fault lines anyway. So no sweat.

1¼ cups, or more, cookie, cake, or graham cracker crumbs

2 tablespoons sugar, granulated or light brown

2 to 3 tablespoons unsalted butter, melted

1 pound whole-milk ricotta cheese, at room temperature

1 pound cream cheese, at room temperature

1½ cups granulated sugar

Grated peel of 1 large lemon

4 large eggs, at room temperature

1 cup sour cream

2 to 3 teaspoons vanilla extract

1 cup heavy cream

3 tablespoons all-purpose flour

Strawberry-Apricot Topping (recipe follows)

Strawberry-Lemon Caramel Topping (recipe follows)

Preheat the oven to 350 degrees. Butter the bottom of a 9 × 3-inch springform pan. Mix together in a small bowl the crumbs, sugar, and butter.

Press the crumbs on the bottom of the pan, and a little ways up the sides of the pan (see Note below). Set the piecrust in the oven and bake 5 to 6 minutes or until lightly tinged with brown. Set the crust aside to cool on a wire rack.

Increase the oven temperature to 450 degrees.

Combine the ricotta, cream cheese, sugar, and lemon peel in the bowl of a standing mixer fitted with the paddle attachment or use a large mixing bowl and a handheld electric mixer. Beat the mixture on medium speed until it is smooth and creamy, about 2 minutes.

Add the eggs, sour cream, and vanilla extract, and beat again until well mixed.

Stir in the heavy cream and beat the mixture on low speed until just blended. Sprinkle over the flour and mix well.

Pour the filling into the prepared pan. Place the pan on the middle shelf of the hot oven and bake for 15 minutes, only.

Immediately reduce the oven temperature to 275 degrees. Bake the cheesecake for 45 to 50 minutes longer, or until it is set around the edges but still soft and spongy in the middle. Watch the cake carefully at this point. If it remains in the oven until the center is set, the cake will expand and split or crack.

Remove the cake from the oven and set on a wire rack. Cool the cheesecake in the pan for 15 to 20 minutes. Gently run a thin metal spatula around the sides to loosen the cake from the pan.

Finishing cooling the cake in the pan 1 hour longer. Remove the sides of the cake pan. Cover the cheesecake with plastic or foil and chill thoroughly, from 6 to 8 hours or overnight.

If desired, at serving, loosen the cake from the bottom of the cake pan with a thin metal spatula. Slide the cake on to a serving platter.

Spoon over the Strawberry-Apricot Topping. (You can also use Strawberry-Lemon Caramel Topping, page 175.)

Makes 10 to 12 servings

Note: If you prefer the crust to go higher up the sides of the pan, add another ¹/₂ cup crumbs to the mixture.

Strawberry-Apricot Topping

Fresh blueberries, raspberries, or sliced peaches or plums are just as delicious, and pretty, as strawberries as a topping. It's your choice.

2 cups fresh strawberries

¹/₄ cup apricot preserves or orange marmalade

2 tablespoons orange-flavored liqueur, such as Grand Marnier or Cointreau

Wash, drain, and dry the strawberries. Discard the leaves. Cut the fruit into halves or quarters. Arrange the fruit in tight circles on top of the cheesecake.

Combine the apricot preserves or orange marmalade and 2 tablespoons orange-flavored liqueur in a medium saucepan.

Set the pan over medium-high heat and cook for few minutes to warm the preserves or marmalade, stirring briskly. Pour the syrup over the strawberries, spreading all over.

Makes 2¼ cups

Strawberry-Lemon Caramel Topping

I love caramel topping; it adds a nice crunch. And the lemon in this topping complements the lemony edge of the cheesecake.

2 cups fresh strawberries

1 cup granulated sugar

¹/₄ cup lemon juice

2 tablespoons light corn syrup

¹/₃ cup water

Wash, drain, and dry the strawberries. Discard the leaves. Cut the berries into halves or quarters. Arrange the fruit in tight circles on top of the cheesecake.

Have available a long-handled wooden spoon, pastry brush, and a cup of water. In a heavy, 1^1/$_2$-quart saucepan, combine the sugar, lemon juice, corn syrup, and ^{1}/$_3$ cup water. Place on medium-high heat and bring to a boil, stirring until the sugar dissolves. (See Go Burn!, page 196).

Cover the pan and cook 3 minutes. Remove the lid. Dip the pastry brush in water and wash down the side of the pan.

Cook the syrup, swirling the pan, 3 to 4 minutes, or until the syrup is amber or the color of deeply brewed tea. Don't allow the syrup to burn.

Immediately remove the pan from the heat, pour into another pan, and set aside to cool for 2 to 3 minutes, or until the syrup begins to thicken.

Using a fork, drizzle the caramel over the strawberries. If the caramel in the pan hardens, stir in a teaspoon of water and heat over low heat.

Makes 2½ cups

Sweet Potato Cheesecake

Years ago when Florida Ingram Brown's children were growing up, every time I visited her home in Altadena, California, she was on a treadmill, shuttling them about to their various lessons and classes: swim team, tennis, piano, soccer, tutors. And then at the end of the day she would put this wonderful meal on the table, often featuring some dish she had learned to make at her own numerous cooking classes. To say that this was a busy household is an understatement.

But enough of the soapbox. This delectable Sweet Potato Cheesecake is just one of the more than two dozen recipes that Florida dug out; some dog-eared, others splattered, but all sent with love. Florida and I have known each other forever.

This inventive cheesecake has a creamy, spicy, sweet potato filling supporting a lush cream cheese topping. When my neighbor and tester, Edith Collins, took a bite of this cheesecake she said something corny like "heavenly." A little hyperbolic perhaps, but this cheesecake is sublime.

Dough for 1 single Sour Cream
   Piecrust (page 119)
1 teaspoon peanut or corn oil
3 or 4 medium sweet potatoes, about
   1½ pounds
¾ cup light brown sugar, firmly packed
4 tablespoons melted unsalted butter

½ teaspoon ground cinnamon
¼ teaspoon grated nutmeg or mace
2 large eggs, at room temperature
½ cup heavy cream
2 tablespoons cognac, brandy, or dark
   rum

CHEESECAKE BATTER:
2 (8-ounce) packages cream cheese,
   softened
½ cup granulated sugar
2 large eggs, more, at room temperature
2 tablespoons all-purpose flour

Pinch of salt
Grated peel of 1 small orange or large
   lemon
1 teaspoon vanilla extract
Cinnamon sugar, optional

Preheat the oven to 400 degrees. Remove the sides from an 8½ × 2½-inch or 9 × 3-inch springform pan and set aside.

Lightly flour the work surface. Using a lightly floured rolling pin, roll out the dough into a 12-inch circle. Fit the pastry circle over the bottom lid of the pan.

Using scissors, trim the pastry about 1 inch beyond the rim of the lid. Fold the overhanging pastry toward the center of the pan. Carefully fit the side of the pan over the pastry-lined bottom lid and fasten. Using your fingertips, press the overhanging dough snugly against the sides of the pan, moving all around.

Chill the pastry at least 20 minutes or longer. Line the pan with a sheet of foil or parchment paper and fill with a pastry weight. (See Partially or Fully Baked Single Pie or Tart Crust, page 117).

Bake the crust in the hot oven for 15 minutes or until it is lightly tinged with brown. Remove from the oven and carefully lift out the weight. Set the pan on a wire rack. Brush the crust generously with egg white.

When cooled, lightly oil the sides of the pan with the oil. Set aside.

Meanwhile, scrub and rinse the sweet potatoes. Cut away eyes or sprouts and discard. Place the unpeeled sweet potatoes in the top of a steamer and cook over boiling water for about 30 minutes or until tender.

Reduce the oven temperature to 350 degrees.

Remove the cooked potatoes from the steamer and drain. Peel while still warm. Using a fine strainer that is at least 6 inches in diameter, force the potatoes through the sieve into the bowl of a standing mixer fitted with the paddle attachment or into a large mixing bowl, pressing hard with a rubber spatula.

Using the standing mixer or a handheld electric mixer, beat the potatoes until they are light and fluffy. Add the sugar, butter, cinnamon, and nutmeg or mace. Add the eggs and beat until well blended. Add the heavy cream and beat on medium-low speed for 2 to 3 minutes, or until the filling is smooth and creamy and free of lumps. Stir in the cognac or brandy or rum and mix well.

Pour the sweet potato mixture into the prepared cake pan. Set the pan on the lower shelf of the preheated oven and bake for 20 minutes.

Remove the pan from the oven and set it on a wire rack. Reduce the oven temperature to 325 degrees.

Prepare the cheesecake batter: In a large mixing bowl, combine the cream cheese, sugar, and eggs. Using an electric mixer set on medium speed, beat the batter for about 2 minutes, or until light and fluffy.

Stir in the flour, salt, lemon or orange peel, and vanilla extract. Beat 30 seconds longer, or until well blended.

Carefully pour the cream cheese batter over the sweet potato filling. Sprinkle the top with a dusting of cinnamon sugar, if desired (see Note below).

Set the cake in the center of the oven on the middle shelf. Bake for 45 to 50 minutes or until the cake is puffed, firm around the edges, lightly browned but still a little soft in the center. Remove the cheesecake from the oven and cool on a wire rack for 15 to 20 minutes. Then, carefully run a thin metal spatula around the edge of the cake to unloosen it from the pan.

Cool the cake in the pan 40 to 50 minutes longer. Remove the sides of the pan and chill the cheesecake several hours or overnight.

If desired, at serving, loosen the cake from the bottom of the cake pan with a thin metal spatula. Slide the cake onto a serving platter.

Makes 8 to 10 servings

Note: Combine 2 to 3 tablespoons brown crystallized sugar, such as Sugar in the Raw (turbinado sugar) with $1/2$ teaspoon ground cinnamon. Sprinkle the cheesecake top with the scented sugar, if desired.

In Hot Water Custards or puddings that cook too fast or at too high temperature end up curdled, watery, and thin. To temper the heat, set the baking dish in a larger pan, and then pour in very hot water halfway up the baking dish—but no higher—creating a water bath. Set the pan on the middle oven rack.

A 12-inch cast-iron skillet, about 3 inches deep, is a perfect container for a water bath. (The water bath water level should not extend much above $1^1/_2$ inches—if too much water is used, it will lower the temperature of the custard and slow down the baking.)

To test a custard or pudding for doneness, insert a knife in the center and if it comes out just about clean with a little moisture or beads clinging to the blade, the custard is done. If the knife comes out too clean, the custard is likely overcooked.

Remember, the custard will continue to cook as it cools, so remove it immediately from the water bath and cool on a wire rack. Some cooks remove the custard from the oven when it is just about done—still wiggly in the center—and let it finish cooking in the water bath, but you have to watch this carefully, or the custard will overcook.

After a while though, you will develop a feel for when the custard is perfectly baked, and the dazzling dessert will come out of the oven satiny, silky, and smooth.

Cool note: Bread puddings, rice puddings, cheesecakes, and soufflés are all custard-based, made with eggs and milk or cream, and should be kept in the refrigerator. Cover the dish first with plastic wrap or foil. If desired, bring to warm temperature before serving, or warm up in the microwave or set in a preheated 350-degree oven for 10 to 15 minutes.

Don't freeze these desserts; the custard breaks down and turns watery. I know; you can buy frozen cheesecakes. But those are loaded with fillers and thickeners, the reason why they withstand freezing. Thank goodness ours aren't. ❦

Chocolate Soufflé

A while back, my friend Todd Beamon, then a magazine editor, was supervising a photo shoot in southwest France, and I was there to chronicle the event. It was a cocktail party at the château owned by Benedictine S. A., the liqueur producer, and Todd decided he would pour the champagne in the glasses as the photographer snapped away, assuming a real hands-on role.

Next to me on the sidelines was Monsieur Pierre, who, as Todd gingerly removed the foil wrapper and wire caging from the champagne, whispered over and over that the cork was going to turn into a missile and break the beautiful antique chandelier that hung above our heads, from a ceiling that must have soared forty feet.

But suddenly, there was a little pop, and a stream of smoke wiggled snakelike from the mouth of the champagne bottle as Todd danced the cork between his fingers, having performed the feat with aplomb.

Pierre took a deep breath and slumped in his seat, relieved. Todd caught my gaze and I think he winked. I smiled at monsieur and wanted to say, but didn't: "Not only does this brother know how to open a bottle of champagne, he can burn. Him bad. He's a foodie."

I was thinking of that moment in France when Todd's recipe for this elegant soufflé arrived in the mail. It is a chocolate lover's delight: a luscious custard scented with chocolate and a hint of coffee, lightened with beaten egg whites, and baked until it rises looking like a majestic top hat. This soufflé is elegant and homespun at the same time, just like Todd. And as smooth as silk.

"You know," says Todd over the phone from his home in Silver Spring, Maryland, "over the years I have played with different types of chocolates; sometimes I serve the soufflé with a hot fudge sauce, at other times with a coconut custard sauce and sometimes with a whiskey sauce."

Todd, who is a copy editor at *The Journal Newspapers Inc.,* a suburban newspaper serving counties in northern Virginia and Maryland, stops for a few seconds and I reflect, remembering that he loves a challenge. Todd is the divorced father of two beautiful young daughters, Kamaria and Gabrielle, and a couple years ago he took a six-week course in hair braiding so that he could tend their locks when they stay with him on weekends and holidays!

"And you know," he says again, "this is a real special dessert, for special occasions. I only make it two or three times per year."

I love chocolate and this puffy, dramatic dessert graces my table quite often. Soufflés really aren't difficult to do. The key is properly beaten egg whites, which should be folded gently but thoroughly into the custard.

But soufflés do fall fast. Time the dessert so that it finishes baking after the table has been cleared and your guests are seated waiting for "the star."

The chocolate custard for the soufflé can be made the day before, refrigerated, returned to room temperature when ready to bake, and then folded with the whipped egg whites.

I like this soufflé with a big spoonful of Whiskey Sauce (page 169) but a Caramel or Burnt Sugar Sauce (page 234) or Chocolate Fudge Sauce (page 236) is also delicious. And your guests may just want a big scoop of Perfectly Whipped Cream (page 74).

3 tablespoons granulated sugar or brown crystallized sugar plus $\frac{1}{2}$ cup granulated sugar, or more

3 large egg yolks

5 egg whites, at room temperature

4 ounces semisweet chocolate (not unsweetened)

3 tablespoons unsweetened cocoa

$\frac{1}{4}$ cup brewed coffee

1 tablespoon unsalted butter

2 tablespoons liqueur, such as B&B, or dark rum or brandy

1 teaspoon vanilla extract

$\frac{1}{2}$ teaspoon cider vinegar or cream of tartar

Generously butter a $1\frac{1}{2}$-quart baking or soufflé dish. Sprinkle the dish with 1 tablespoon of the 3 tablespoons sugar, coating the bottom and sides all the way to the rim of the dish.

You'll need three of the egg yolks for the custard and 5 egg whites for the meringue. (Discard the leftover egg yolks or refrigerate and scramble for breakfast.)

Carefully crack the eggs one at a time and place the yolk and the egg white into two separate small bowls. If the egg white is free of yolk, transfer to a large spotless clean bowl for whipping or to the bowl of a standing mixer. If the egg yolk drips into the egg white, discard that egg white and break another egg, using a clean bowl. Set aside the egg whites to warm to room temperature and return the yolks to the refrigerator until ready to use (see Get the Whip, page 132).

Preheat the oven to 425 degrees.

Chop the chocolate coarsely and place in a large metal or ovenproof bowl. Set the bowl in a skillet of hot water and place on medium heat.

Add 2 tablespoons granulated sugar, the cocoa, coffee, butter, liqueur or rum or brandy, and the vanilla extract. Heat the mixture until the butter and chocolate melt, stirring briskly. This should take only 3 or 4 minutes.

Remove the pan from the heat. Beat the three egg yolks for a few seconds, and pour into the chocolate mixture.

Beat the chocolate mixture until well blended and smooth. Remove the bowl from the pan of water and set aside.

Sprinkle the egg whites with the vinegar or cream of tartar. Using the standing mixer fitted with the whisk attachment or a handheld electric mixer, beat the egg whites on medium-high speed until foamy. Gradually add the remaining sugar, about 2 tablespoons at a time, and beat on high speed until the peaks are stiff and shiny, but not dry. This should take about 5 minutes; don't overbeat. (If using the standing mixer, turn off the mixer a couple times, and scrape the bowl so that the egg whites are evenly beaten.)

Stir a generous cup of the beaten egg whites into the chocolate custard and mix well. Spoon the remaining egg whites over the custard and quickly fold the two mixtures together, mixing gently but until well blended.

Spoon or pour the mixture into the prepared baking dish. Run your thumb around the inside edge of the soufflé, making a little dent. This will help the soufflé rise and form a top-hat effect.

Set the dish on the lower oven shelf. Immediately lower the oven temperature to 375 degrees.

Bake the soufflé for 23 to 25 minutes, until it is puffed and has risen about 2 inches above the rim of the dish. To test for doneness, quickly insert a metal skewer or thin knife into the puff down the side of the dish; if wet particles cling to it; the soufflé is not quite done.

Bake the soufflé a few minutes longer or until a skewer or knife comes out almost clean. But don't overbake the soufflé. When you take it out of the oven, a few moist beads should be visible on the top.

Remove the soufflé from the oven and serve immediately.

Makes 4 to 5 servings

FIVE

Homemade Candies: Real Sweet

Aunt Mary had six pecan trees in her backyard and whenever she declared a truce with one of her neighbors—who often said she put on airs—she would treat the redeemed to a box of her homemade candy.

She would beribbon the candy box, and then scoot over to whatever neighbor she was no longer angry with, and render her peace offering. Sometimes she would make succulent little morsels of pecan praline, at other times it was thin-as-a-dime peanut or pecan brittle, and on other occasions, velvety fudge, toothy caramels, or little creamy squares that she simply called brown sugar nut candy.

Smiles were exchanged, the candy was sampled and generously praised, but invariably in a matter of minutes Aunt Mary was discussing the fine points of confection making, the kind of talk that got her into trouble in the first place.

She was in her sixties then, and if I close my eyes I can see her now, standing, her arms akimbo, a Lucky Strike cigarette stuck in her mouth. I remember a clear late fall day during the Thanksgiving holiday, and out in the distance I could see the silvery waters of the Mississippi Gulf Coast.

She begins talking: "Nothing ruins a batch of praline or brittle candy like humidity, so don't try to make it unless the weather is cool and dry; to make fine brittle you really have to let it cool until it is just warm to the touch and then pull; add a pinch of baking soda to your praline syrup to soften it up because it shouldn't be as hard as brittle; if you don't get rid of the sugar crystals on the sides of the pan you'll end up with a grainy mess," and on and on.

I watch my dearly beloved aunt, my heart skipping beats, as the smile freezes on Mrs. Ward's face. In a few minutes we head on back home, but as soon as we are out of earshot, she whispers to me: "Next time I'll take over arsenic," and then breaks out laughing.

And so began my love affair with candy making and giving, two uncomplicated pleasures.

Basically, all candies are made alike: a sugar syrup is boiled to a certain temperature or until it reaches a specific consistency, depending on whether you are making, say, creamy fudge, or tooth cracking brittle or lollipops (see Hot and Syrupy Stages, page 207).

Other than sugar, you only need a few ingredients—perhaps a little butter, chocolate, nuts, bits of dried fruit, egg whites for divinity and marshmallows, and a flavoring or two. And once the technique is practiced a few times, even the most fancy or elaborate-sounding candy is within the scope of the home candy maker.

But the real pleasure of homemade candy is the gift giving, for even the most jaded soul rarely resists hand-crafted sweets, especially Aunt Mary's confections. Here are favorite recipes:

Southern Pralines

There is much debate about the origin of this renowned candy, but none is more provocative than a passage from the book *African Heritage Cooking* (Macmillan Publishing Co.), written in 1971 by Helen Mendes.

I quote: "The marketplaces of West Africa were enlivened by the voices of women calling out the praise of the cakes they baked for sale. They also sold candies made out of sugar cane, which they pulled and boiled to extract the syrupy liquid. Later, many of these women, both slave and free, earned a tidy sum of money selling pralines, as these candies were called, in the streets of Brazil and the United States."

I first saw the above quotation in Jonell Nash's wonderful cookbook, *Essence Brings You Great Cooking* (Amistad, 1999).

This delicious confection requires quick work; invite a helper.

1½ to 2 cups pecans	2 tablespoons light corn syrup
2 cups granulated sugar	½ teaspoon vanilla extract
½ teaspoon baking soda	2 tablespoons unsalted butter
1 cup buttermilk, at room temperature	2 to 3 tablespoons milk or cream

Clear the range top of all pots and pans so that you can have plenty of work space.

Have ready a long-handled wooden spoon, a pastry brush, a cup of hot water to brush down sugar crystals from the sides of the pan and a candy thermometer (see Go Burn!, page 196). Also have handy two tablespoons to use for dipping and dropping the candy.

Line 3 baking sheets with parchment paper or foil, butter generously, and set near the stove on a counter or table. (Don't use wax paper; the candy will stick to it.)

Chop the pecans coarsely and set on the stove.

Combine in a heavy 4-quart saucepan, the sugar, baking soda, buttermilk, and corn syrup. Place the pan on medium-high heat and bring the syrup to a boil, stirring with the wooden spoon until the sugar is completely dissolved, 3 or 4 minutes.

Cover the pan and boil the syrup without stirring for 3 minutes. Remove the cover. Dip the pastry brush into the water and brush down the sides of the pan. Attach the candy thermometer to the inside of the pot.

Cook the syrup without stirring until it reaches 225 degrees, frequently brushing down the pan with the damp brush, and swirling the pan.

Quickly scatter the pecans over the syrup and continue cooking until the syrup reaches 236 degrees or the soft ball stage and is deep amber in color, swirling the pan as the syrup cooks.

Watch carefully, because the candy cooks quickly at this point and can burn.

Slide the candy from the hot burner to an off-burner. Remove the thermometer. Add the vanilla extract and butter, and swirl the pan until combined. Let the candy cool for 1 minute, then move one of the pans to the stove.

Using the two tablespoons, and working quickly, dip and fill one tablespoon with the candy and use the second spoon to push the candy onto the baking sheet, dropping the nuggets about 2 inches apart. You will probably need all three baking sheets.

If the candy in the pan begins to harden, stir in a couple tablespoons of milk or cream, turn the heat to medium, stir briskly, and when the candy is smooth, drop by tablespoonfuls onto the baking sheet.

Place the baking sheets with the candy on wire racks, set in a cool place, and let stand until firm, crunchy, and the consistency of hard fudge, for at least an hour or longer.

The pralines can be stored in airtight containers for a week or so.

Makes about 2 ½ dozen pralines

TOOTHSOME PLEASURES: PRALINE, BRITTLE, AND OTHER BURNT CANDIES

Even today my oldest brother, John, lives only a few hundred feet from where Aunt Mary's old house once stood, and of all my siblings, he and I hold the strongest memories of this indomitable woman.

John left our home in Choctaw County in Alabama and went to live with Aunt Mary shortly after high school, and when I was teenager I visited her often. But as I reflect, it was actually Mama who encouraged my visits, for although her personal relationship with Aunt Mary was on and off, there was begrudging admiration. For despite her antics, Aunt Mary was generous and gregarious.

Late in life she married a jazz trumpet player, John Collins, who was from a rather prominent New Orleans family. I had never before heard light-skinned Negroes refer to themselves as "Creole," and the first I heard him use the word I wondered what exotic foreign country he came from.

Aunt Mary came from a little hamlet on the Tombigbee River in Clarke County, Alabama, where she and all of her six siblings, including Daddy, fled between 1915 and 1920, fearing raging floods and starvation. Daddy went to Mobile and became a dock worker. Aunt Mary migrated to the Mississippi Gulf Coast, then to Los Angeles, and eventually returned to the Biloxi-Gulfport area, where she met and married Uncle John.

By my late teen years she had the enviable freedom to pursue her interests: cooking, fishing, crossword puzzle contests, homemade candy. But she enjoyed most her "buddies," a tight circle of a half-dozen late-middle-aged women who seemed to know everything about everybody and each other.

They loved Aunt Mary's candy and she gifted them often, passing it out in little boxes—pralines, peanut brittle, caramels, coconut fudge, candied pecans or almonds, each candy more delicious than the next, all bearing her signature goodness. And occasionally she would give a little demo, usually under the pretense that she needed a helping hand.

More than once I watched her pour hot boiling brittle syrup on a well-oiled piece of plywood—her candy board as she called it—and then quickly slip on a pair of white gloves, the kind Mama wore to church. In a matter of minutes she was pulling the brittle, and soon it was glistening like a new dime, and just as thin. After the candy was cooled, she broke it into delectable shards.

I fell helplessly under her spell.

My nephew, John Junior, who is my brother John's son, grew up within hollering distance of Aunt Mary and still lives in Biloxi. John Junior and his wife, Brenda, sent this recipe for Pistachio Brittle in her memory:

Pistachio Brittle

Brittle is cooked longer than pralines, and since it is made without the addition of milk or heavy cream, the final candy is as slick and clear as glass, whereas pralines are fudgelike and creamy.

Peanut brittle is a Southern favorite, but this version with pistachio nuts is just as delicious.

2 cups pistachio nuts in shells
1½ cups granulated sugar
½ cup water

½ cup light corn syrup
2 tablespoons unsalted butter
1 teaspoon vanilla extract

Preheat the oven to 350 degrees.

Shell the pistachio nuts. (Pistachios sold in their shell have better flavor than most shelled nuts and are worth the extra effort.) Spread them in a single layer across a baking sheet or jelly-roll pan. Place on the middle shelf of the preheated oven and toast until just lightly brown, 5 to 7 minutes, stirring once or twice with a wooden spoon or shaking the pan. Remove the nuts immediately from the oven as soon as you smell them baking or see signs of browning.

Spread the nuts on a kitchen towel and using your fingers, rub briskly with the towel to remove the skins. Or, cut away the skins with a small knife. Do this carefully, making sure that all bits of skin are removed. Set the nuts aside.

Have ready a wooden spoon to stir the candy, a metal spatula for spreading, and a pastry brush, a cup of hot water to brush down the sugar crystals from the sides of the pan, a candy thermometer, and a metal spatula for spreading (see Go Burn!, page 196).

Butter a 10 × 15-inch jelly-roll pan and set aside.

In a large, heavy 4-quart saucepan, combine the sugar, water, and corn syrup, and mix until well blended.

Place on medium-high heat and bring the syrup to a boil, stirring constantly with the wooden spoon, until the sugar is dissolved. Cover the pan and boil the syrup for 3 minutes.

Remove the lid. Dip the brush in the water and brush down the sides of the pan. Attach the candy thermometer to the side of the pan.

Continue cooking the syrup over high heat, swirling the pan but not stirring until it is golden brown and reaches the hard crack stage, or 300 to 310 degrees, frequently brushing down the sides of the pan. This should take about 10 minutes.

Remove the pan from the heat and remove the thermometer. Swirl in the butter, vanilla extract, and the toasted pistachio nuts, mixing well. Quickly pour the candy onto the jelly-roll pan. Using the metal spatula, spread the candy as evenly and as thinly as possible.

Let the candy set until it hardens, at least several hours or overnight, and then break into 2-inch pieces.

To serve with ice cream, wrap the candy in a towel, crush with a mallet or hammer, and then scatter over the ice cream.

Store the candy pieces in airtight containers.

Makes about 1 pound

Nut Brittle: In place of pistachio nuts, use 1 heaping cup coarsely chopped pecans or unsalted cashews, or lightly toasted almonds, peanuts, or sesame seeds. Or, use a combination of any of these nuts.

Brittle made with raw peanuts is very popular in the South. A favorite recipe comes from my running buddy, Lois LeBlanc, a commercial interior designer who lives in New York City, not far from me but on Central Park West. Lois hails from Hampton, Virginia, and says that her father made this candy frequently for family gatherings, always using, of course, Virginia peanuts, which literally "roast" in the hot syrup. Lois is just as theatrical as my Aunt Mary, and this delicious candy is delightful. Cook the candy to 270 degrees or the soft crack stage. Swirl in a generous cup of raw peanuts and continue cooking to 300 to 310 degrees or the hard crack stage, and proceed as directed above.

Coffee Caramels

Margie, my brother John's wife, and I tried our best to remember Aunt Mary's exact recipe for the little, chewy caramel morsels that she made for the Christmas holidays. She would twist the tiny sweet squares in wax paper, and pile them in a glass bowl that sat on a table near the front door, inviting nuggets for visitors.

"There is a lot to remember about your aunt," Margie said, and not knowing exactly what she meant, I left the statement alone.

Anyway, we both remember delightful plain caramels, chocolate caramels, and our favorite, aromatic coffee-laced caramels, which Margie insisted were made with bitter chicory-laced coffee blended in Louisiana.

I used instant espresso powder and the caramels were as delicious as Aunt Mary's. I prefer softer caramels, and stop the syrup at 240 degrees rather than let it burn until 245 degrees, which is the traditional temperature.

Remember, though, this candy is still quite chewy, so don't crack down if you have fragile teeth.

³⁄₄ cup heavy cream

2 to 3 tablespoons instant espresso powder, such as Medaglia D'Oro

1 cup light brown sugar, firmly packed

1 cup granulated sugar

½ cup light corn syrup

4 tablespoons unsalted butter

½ cup sweetened condensed milk

1 teaspoon vanilla extract

Have ready a pastry brush, a cup of hot water for brushing the sugar crystals from the sides of the pan, a candy thermometer, a long-handled wooden spoon, and a metal spatula (see Go Burn!, page 196).

Butter generously an 8- or 9-inch square metal baking pan and set aside. (Do not use glass; the piping hot candy may crack it.)

Combine the heavy cream and espresso powder in a 4-quart heavy saucepan. Place the pan on medium-low heat and heat the mixture, stirring with the wooden spoon, until the coffee dissolves. Add both sugars, corn syrup, butter, and condensed milk.

Raise the heat to medium-high and cook the mixture, stirring, until the sugar is dissolved and the butter is melted, for about 5 minutes.

Bring the syrup to a boil, cover the pan, and cook the syrup for 3 minutes. Remove the lid. Dip the brush in water and brush the sides of the pan. Attach the thermometer inside the pan.

Cook the syrup, without stirring, swirling the pan by the handle to cook evenly, until the candy reaches 240 to 245 degrees, frequently brushing the sides of the pan with the damp brush. This should take from 13 to 14 minutes.

Remove the thermometer. Sprinkle over the vanilla extract and swirl the pan to combine with the syrup.

Immediately pour the candy into the baking pan. Smooth evenly with the wooden spoon or a metal spatula. Set the pan on a wire rack to cool for 20 to 25 minutes, or until cool enough to touch.

Using a sharp knife, mark the top of the warm candy into 1-inch squares for easier cutting.

If the candy is still not firm, let cool for a few more minutes. Then, turn the candy out onto a chopping board, top side up. Using a large sharp, buttered knife, carefully cut into 1-inch pieces, using the marking on the top as a guide.

Spread the candy on a sheet of buttered foil or wax paper and cool completely on wire racks.

For storing, wrap each piece in a square of wax paper or a candy wrapper, or place between layers of wax paper in an airtight container.

Makes 50 to 60 caramels

Chocolate Raisin Bark

When I was growing up the women in my family cooked every day, but it seemed that each one had a special touch with certain dishes. My sister, Helen, who was the head cook at a café in Choctaw County and later was the personal cook for a rich family, made ethereal cakes, rich and luscious ice cream, and artisan chocolate desserts. Mama made delicious pies, Aunt Agnes (our maternal aunt) made scrumptious cookies, and of course, Aunt Mary made candy.

Occasionally Helen made chocolate candy, and my favorite was this bark—a crunchy layer of caramel topped with raisins, nuts, and chocolate.

2 cups slivered almonds	3 tablespoons light corn syrup
1 cup light or dark raisins	1/3 cup water
2 sticks unsalted butter (1 cup), softened	1 teaspoon vanilla extract
2 cups granulated sugar	6 to 8 ounces good-quality bittersweet or semisweet chocolate

Have ready a long-handled wooden spoon, a pastry brush, a cup of hot water for brushing sugar crystals from the sides of the pan, and a candy thermometer (see Go Burn!, page 196). Set aside a metal spatula to use for spreading the candy.

Preheat the oven to 350 degrees.

Scatter the nuts on a shallow baking dish, preferably a 10 × 15-inch jelly-roll pan. Set on the middle shelf of the preheated oven and toast for 5 to 7 minutes, stirring occasionally with a wooden spoon, until just lightly brown. Watch carefully and don't allow the nuts to burn.

Remove the pan from the oven and set on a wire rack. Remove half the nuts from the pan and set aside. Spread the remaining nuts and the raisins evenly on the pan and set aside.

Place the butter in a heavy 3-quart saucepan. Set the pan over low heat and stir the butter until it melts. Add the sugar, corn syrup, and water and mix well.

Raise the heat to medium-high and bring the syrup to a boil, stirring until the sugar is completely dissolved. Cover the pan and boil the syrup for 3 minutes more.

Remove the lid. Dip the brush in the water and wipe down the sides of the pan. Attach the candy thermometer inside the pan.

Cook the syrup, without stirring, but swirling the pan, until the thermometer reaches 290 to 300 degrees, and the syrup is deep golden. This should take about 10 minutes.

Remove the pan from the heat, remove the thermometer, and swirl in the vanilla extract. Immediately pour the hot syrup into the baking pan, covering the nuts and raisins. Using the metal spatula, spread the candy in a thin, even layer.

Carefully transfer the baking pan to a wire rack and allow the candy to cool completely, for several hours or until firm.

Then, coarsely chop the chocolate into 1-inch-size pieces. Put the chocolate in a heatproof bowl and set the bowl in a pan of hot water.

Stir the chocolate briskly until it melts and is smooth. Pour the chocolate over the cooled candy, spreading evenly with a metal spatula. Sprinkle the top with the remaining nuts.

Cool the candy completely and then chill for at least an hour or until the candy is firm and set.

Before serving, break the "bark" into 1¹/₂-inch pieces.

Makes about 40 pieces

Variation: Substitute 2 cups Brazil nuts for the almonds. Toast lightly and then chop rather finely but not until pulverized.

Go Burn! When sugar is cooked it caramelizes and develops a nutty, burnished flavor that adds an exquisite touch to desserts. Much-praised candies such as praline, brittle, and bark are variations of caramelized sugar, and so is caramel or burnt sugar sauce, which is delicious drizzled over a pudding, custard, ice cream, or cake.

When I was growing up the pièce de résistance at church gatherings and holiday celebrations was a Caramel Cake (page 94)—a moist yellow layer cake stacked and frosted with a slick, amber, glassy icing that at best, doesn't show one grain of sugar.

Not an easy task, for the bane of caramelized or burnt sugar is sugar crystals. One moment you are looking at a hot, smooth, glistening amber syrup and you blink an eye and it has congealed into a grainy mass, or mess.

A syrup "turns to sugar," as Aunt Mary used to say, when a few stray, undissolved sugar crystals fall into the boiling syrup and contaminate the liquid, setting in crystallization.

To combat this, dissolve the sugar before boiling, and frequently wash down the sides of the pan with a pastry brush dipped into hot water. But make sure that the pastry brush is in good condition; if it is ragged, you run the risk of bristles dropping into the hot liquid. I personally prefer using a piece of cloth or cheesecloth tied around a wooden spoon, and dipped in water. (Aunt Mary used a hickory stick tied with a wad of clean cloth for this delicate task.)

A pinch of cream of tartar or a few drops of an acid such as lemon juice added to the syrup also helps retard crystallization, but this isn't surefire. A tablespoon or so of light corn syrup does the same.

Have ready a candy thermometer, a large heavy saucepan or skillet, preferably enameled cast iron or heavy stainless steel, a long-handled wooden spoon—which doesn't transmit heat—and a heavy mitt, and of course, the pastry brush and water.

Caution: You've got to hang tight at the stove when burning sugar, so take the telephone off the hook and don't think about wandering away for 1 second.

Combine the sugar and a little water and a drop of lemon juice or a pinch of cream of tartar in the pan or skillet. Set over medium-high heat and cook, stirring constantly, until the sugar completely dissolves. Cover the pot with a lid, bring the mixture to a boil, and steam for about 3 minutes, so as to wash down any sugar crystals.

Remove the lid. Dip the pastry brush in a cup of hot water and brush down the sides of the pan. Attach the candy thermometer inside the pan, making sure that it does not touch the bottom of the pan.

Increase the heat a bit, but don't stir the syrup during the final boil. Instead, take the pan or skillet by the handle and swirl so as to move the hot liquid around. This way, you don't run the risk of scraping crystals, which, despite your best efforts, may have sneaked in and settled on the bottom of the pan. Pests!

Continue wiping down the sides of the pan with the wet brush, and boil the syrup to the stage specified in the recipe (see Hot and Syrupy Stages, page 207).

Don't panic; practice helps here. But even if a syrup does become grainy and hardens, simply remove the pan from the heat, stir in a couple tablespoons of milk or cream or water, and heat the syrup over low heat until the crystals dissolve.

Then, continue cooking the syrup until the desired stage. The candy or frosting may not turn out perfect, but it is tasty, too.

Most homemade candies can be stored just like cookies, in airtight jars or flat containers like those made by Rubbermaid and Tupperware, or in tight tin boxes. Place hard candy such as brittle and pralines between layers of waxed paper. The candy will keep for at least two weeks.

However, soft candy such as Chocolate Kisses (page 199), Chocolate Raisin Bark (page 194), and any fudge is best kept in the refrigerator. Store in a single layer in a container with a tight lid. These candies will also keep for two weeks. ❀

By my last year of high school Aunt Mary's savings were dwindling, and since she had made her living from a small beauty shop that she operated from her closed-in back porch, she was now making do with a Social Security check. Uncle John had long retired as a musician, and even though he was secretive and stingy, I think his finances were tight, too.

I don't know exactly when she decided to supplement her income with day work, and I don't know exactly whom she worked for, for she only referred to her employer, rather obliquely, as "Miss Lady."

And then airily, "Just a day or two every week dusting and keepin' company."

I remember my last visit with her before I left home for good; spring break, early 1960s. Her old house was rather stuffy, furnished with oversized chairs, a chunky sofa, numerous cluttered tables and lamps, scores of framed photographs, and stacks of 78 rpm records, some by her stepson, Lee Collins, a trumpet player like his father, whom she said was well-known in jazz circles. Her most prized possession was an old Victrola in a mahogany cabinet holding both a radio and a turntable that always resounded with music.

Lonely without her presence, I venture to the front porch to wait for her. The shimmering sea is less than a mile away. Breathing deeply, the saline air tickles my nose.

Soon the city bus rolls to a stop a block from her house. I watch her descend the bus, dressed in a simple black dress and wearing a little black hat with a veil, set at a rakish angle. She walks, gingerly at first, and then picks up her gait and falls into the same hip-hop bouncy steps that I see in my son, Roy, and my brother Joe, which must be a genetically transmitted movement.

She pushes open the front gate, looks up at me, bursts out into laughter, and says, "Look what the cats have dragged to my front porch."

Levity graced my thoughts. Soon we were scurrying about fixing supper, getting ready to tackle the crossword puzzle contest in the *New Orleans Picayune-Times,* our late afternoon ritual.

Late in the evening she would set out nibbles, and the dish varied from day to day. Sometimes pecans were tossed in butter, sprinkled with salt, and roasted. At other times they were caramelized or sugared. Apples were both baked and candied. Her favorite cookies were Pecan Sand Tarts (page 34), and from time to time she would crack and grate fresh coconut for fudge or brownies.

Here are favorite recipes:

Chocolate Kisses

I often give boxes of candy as gifts, and these melt-in-your-mouth kisses are always a big hit. They are a little too soft and mushy to mail out, but they are perfect for handing over, and on more than one occasion I saw Aunt Mary pass a box to a friend or neighbor. Any host or hostess would appreciate these.

Since these succulent candies are so easy to make, you may want to double the recipe and share with friends. But don't forget to save a few for yourself.

8 ounces good-quality semisweet chocolate

2 tablespoons unsalted butter

½ cup sweetened condensed milk

½ teaspoon vanilla or almond extract

2 to 4 tablespoons bourbon

FOR COATING:
½ cup unsweetened cocoa

Break the chocolate into pieces and set aside.

Combine in a heavy saucepan the butter, milk, vanilla, and bourbon. Place the pan on medium heat and stir the mixture until it is hot and bubbly, 3 to 4 minutes.

Remove the pan from the heat, immediately stir in the chocolate, and beat the mixture until it is smooth and creamy.

Place the pan on a wire rack and let the chocolate stand at room temperature until it is quite firm and holds a peak, about 40 minutes.

Line two baking sheets with wax paper. To shape the candies, drop a scant tablespoon of the chocolate onto the baking sheets. Using the tip and back of the spoon, gently nudge the mound into a cone-shape, forming "kisses." (You can also transfer the chocolate to a pastry bag fitted with a ½-inch plain tip, pipe the mixture onto the baking sheets, and shape into a cone with a spoon.) Chill the kisses until set, at least 2 hours or overnight.

To coat: Put the cocoa in a small strainer and sift the cocoa onto the kisses, coating all over. Let the candy warm to room temperature before serving.

Makes about 4 dozen kisses

Coconut Fudge

Florida Ingram Brown sent me a stack of family recipes from her childhood near Columbus, Georgia, along with a note about scratching her fingers grating fresh coconuts during the Christmas holidays.

My hands bear the same marks. Coconut desserts reigned supreme in the Old South, and our tables were set with coconut cake, coconut custard pies, coconut ice cream, and my favorite, coconut fudge.

In fact, Florida says that the first dessert she ever made was a pan of brownies at age ten or so. But I couldn't resist this creamy fudge, which brought back so many of my childhood memories.

Her fudge reminded me of Aunt Mary's confection.

1½ cups dark brown sugar
1 cup granulated sugar
½ cup unsweetened cocoa
⅛ teaspoon salt
¾ cup undiluted evaporated milk or
    half-and-half

2 tablespoons light corn syrup
4 tablespoons unsalted butter
1½ teaspoons vanilla extract
1 cup freshly grated coconut (see
    Cracking Coconuts, page 245) or 1
    cup unsweetened dried coconut

Have ready a long-handled wooden spoon, a pastry brush, a cup of hot water to brush sugar crystals from the sides of the pan, and a candy thermometer (see Go Burn!, page 196).

Lightly butter an 8- or 9-inch square metal cake or baking dish and set aside.

Combine both sugars, cocoa, and salt in a heavy, 4-quart saucepan. Using the wooden spoon, stir in the milk or half-and-half and corn syrup and mix until well combined.

Place the pan on medium-high heat, and cook, stirring, until the sugar is completely dissolved. Bring the syrup to a boil, cover the pan, and boil the syrup for 3 minutes.

Remove the lid. Dip the brush in the water and brush down the sides of the pan. Attach the candy thermometer inside the pan.

Cook the syrup, without stirring, but occasionally swirling the pan, about 10 to 12 minutes or until the thermometer reads 236 to 238 degrees, frequently brushing the sides of the pan with the damp brush.

Remove the thermometer. Turn the heat off from under the pan and swirl in the butter and vanilla extract. Remove the pan from the stove and set the pan on a wire rack.

Cool the fudge in the pan for 2 to 3 minutes. Stir in the coconut and immediately pour the fudge into the buttered pan, taking care not to scrape the bottom of the pan, which may be sugary.

Cool the candy completely, at least several hours, and then mark in 1-inch squares. Remove the candy from the pan, place on a chopping board, and cut into pieces.

Makes about 48 pieces

Candied Apples

Whenever Aunt Mary candied apples she would invite one or two of her "buddies" to help out, and soon the kitchen was so alive with the chatter and merriment of the women, I was afraid that they would forget this was suppose to be a treat for the children. They never did.

Neighbors' children and my brother John's six sons were the lucky recipients, although my dear aunt loved all children from a distance.

I absolutely love these candied apples, which have a sparkling, brittle coating that has a slight caramelized flavor. The syrup is cooked until it reaches 300 degrees, the hard crack stage. Children or seniors may prefer a softer coating, and the apples are fine when the syrup is cooked to 280 degrees or the soft crack stage.

Candied apples require fast work, and two pairs of hands are better than one for this recipe. Recently, Brenda Richardson and I got together and made a dozen candied apples for her teenage son's—Mark Junior's—Valentine's Day party.

And we had as much fun as Aunt Mary and her "buddies" did.

6 to 8 sweet apples, such as Red Delicious, McIntosh, or Empire (see A Is for Apples, page 243)

1½ cups nuts, such as walnuts or pecans, or lightly toasted peanuts

2 cups granulated sugar

¼ teaspoon cream of tartar

½ cup light corn syrup

⅓ cup unsweetened cranberry juice

½ teaspoon ground cinnamon or allspice or ginger

Have ready a pastry brush, a cup of hot water to brush sugar crystals from the sides of the pan, a candy thermometer, and a long-handled wooden spoon (see Go Burn!, page 196).

Clear the oven top of all pots and pans so that you have plenty of work space. Butter a baking sheet or jelly-roll pan and set near the stove.

Wash the apples and dry well. Insert a flat wooden skewer or popsicle stick into the stem ends of the apples, burying at least 1 inch deep. Place the apples on a plate or platter and set on an empty burner. Chop the nuts, scatter on a plate, and set on another burner.

Combine in a heavy 4-quart saucepan, the sugar, cream of tartar, corn syrup, cranberry juice, and cinnamon or allspice or ginger. Place over medium-high heat and cook, stirring, until the sugar is dissolved.

Bring the syrup to a boil, cover the pan, and boil the syrup for 3 minutes. Remove the lid. Dip the brush in water and brush down the sides of the pan. Attach the candy thermometer inside the pan.

Cook the syrup, without stirring, swirling the pan by the handle every now and then, until the candy thermometer reaches 280 to 300 degrees.

Immediately remove the syrup from the heat to an empty burner and remove the thermometer. Quickly dip the apples one at a time into the syrup and ladle over the syrup with the wooden spoon, covering the apples completely.

Quickly roll the apples in the chopped nuts. (If the syrup begins to harden, turn on the heat and quickly stir in a couple tablespoons of hot water; raise the heat and stir the syrup until it softens.)

Place the Candied Apples on the baking sheets, stick sides up, and let set until hard at room temperature for several hours.

Makes 6 servings

The last time I saw Aunt Mary was in the summer of 1969, and I remember the precise day because I was wearing a handkerchief-size pink and floral mini-skirt; sporting a bushy Afro, and was almost as thin as Twiggy.

"There is no modesty there," she greeted me, laughing, grabbing my hands and eyeing me. I wondered if she was just wittily playing on Gertrude Stein's words about Oakland, California, or if my appearance was really so startling.

I flinched. I felt then that my family was always "on" me—about my nappy hair and too-short clothes, about traveling to strange foreign countries, and most of all, about being insanely in love with a mad brother who was going to overthrow the government—tomorrow. Fighting back, I threw verbal salvos, too.

"But other than that you look absolutely fabulous," she quickly added.

I laughed, pleased at her finely executed reproach.

When I returned to the Gulf Coast in the summer of 1981 Aunt Mary was nearing the end of her life. Despite my brother John's urging, I decided against seeing her during her last days, a decision I now regret.

But I wanted sweet final memories, such as this:

When I close my eyes I can see her hunched over the *New Orleans Times-Picayune* newspaper, which is spread out on the dining room table. Her eyes are squinting, and she is alternately drawing on a cigarette and sipping a strong cup of chicory-laced coffee, while I riffle the dictionary at her behest.

Uncle John is in his room, morose and grouchy, listening to jazz. It is spring break, early 1960s.

Aunt Mary pushes a little bowl of aromatic Candied Pecans at me, and I try not to stuff myself. I am her aide-de-camp, and she is in the throes of her unending passion, the crossword puzzle contest. Stammering and talking to herself, she throws out a word to me. I look it up in her old Winston dictionary, and she tells me about *faux amis* and double entendres.

I wonder to myself how in the world could a woman who has been denied a formal education by a cruel apartheid school system know so much, but I am too much in awe to ask. I offer a suggestion and she gives me an appreciative look. When the word doesn't fit she chides me for my error.

Finally she is satisfied with her answers. I slip on my heavy blue car coat and she playfully pushes me toward the door. I rush to the post office, hoping to beat out the other contestants with an early postmark.

We never win.

The next day, undaunted, we begin our pursuit again, nibbling on crunchy, barely sweet candied nuts:

Candied Pecans

½ cup superfine sugar
2 tablespoons water
¼ teaspoon grated nutmeg or ground
　cinnamon

¼ teaspoon cream of tartar or ½
　teaspoon lemon juice
1½ cups pecan halves

Generously butter a shallow baking pan (preferably a 15 × 10-inch jelly-roll pan) and set aside (see Go Burn!, page 196). Have ready a long-handled wooden spoon, a pastry brush, and a cup of water.

Combine the sugar, water, nutmeg or cinnamon, and cream of tartar or lemon juice in a 1-quart heavy saucepan or skillet and mix well. Place on medium-high heat and cook, stirring with the wooden spoon, until the sugar dissolves.

Bring the syrup to a boil, cover the pan, and boil 3 minutes longer.

Uncover the pan. Dip the pastry brush in the water and wash down the sides of the pan.

Cook the syrup over high heat without stirring, but swirling the pan by the handle, for 2 to 3 minutes, or just until the syrup turns the color of lightly brewed tea.

Scatter the pecans over the syrup and stir quickly with the wooden spoon to cover the nuts with the liquid.

Cook the syrup 2 or 3 minutes longer or until it is golden brown and the nuts are just lightly toasted.

Immediately pour the nuts and syrup onto the baking pan. Working quickly, separate the pecans with a fork. Set the pan on a wire rack and cool the candy until hard, at least an hour. Or place the pan on a wire rack and let the candy set in one layer, at least an hour. Break into pieces.

Makes 1½ cups

Variation: Substitute shelled Brazil, walnuts, blanched almonds, or unsalted cashew nuts for the pecans, and proceed as directed above.

Brown Sugar Nut Candy

This candy has a dense fudgelike texture and is more robust and earthy than pralines. And like fudge, you pour it into a pan and cut into sweet, crunchy squares. I like this candy with Brazil nuts, which Daddy brought home from Mobile when he was working there on the docks. You can also use a mixture of nuts, such as walnuts, black walnuts, or pecans.

2 cups granulated sugar
1 cup firmly packed light brown sugar
1 tablespoon light corn syrup
½ cup half-and-half or undiluted
   evaporated milk

1½ cups coarsely chopped nuts, such
   as walnuts, black walnuts, Brazil
   nuts, or pecans, or a mixture
2 tablespoons unsalted butter
½ teaspoon vanilla extract

Have ready a long-handled wooden spoon, a pastry brush, and a cup of hot water to brush down sugar crystals from the sides of the pan, a candy thermometer, and a metal spatula (see Go Burn!, page 196).

Line a 9 × 2-inch metal baking pan with parchment paper or foil, extending the paper at least an inch over the ends of the pan. Butter the paper or foil generously and set aside.

Combine in a heavy 4-quart saucepan both sugars, the corn syrup, and the half-and-half or milk, stirring with the wooden spoon to dissolve the sugar. Place the pan on medium-high heat and bring the syrup to a boil, stirring until the sugar is completely dissolved, 3 or so minutes.

Cover the pan and cook the syrup without stirring, 3 minutes. Remove the cover. Dip the pastry brush in water and brush the sides of the pan. Attach the candy thermometer to the inside of the pan.

Boil the syrup, uncovered, without stirring, until it reaches 225 degrees, tilting and swirling the pan by the handle as the syrup turns brown, frequently brushing the sides of the pot with the damp brush.

Quickly scatter the nuts over the syrup and continue cooking, swirling the pan, until the syrup reaches 236 degrees or the soft ball stage and is deep amber brown in color.

Immediately remove the candy from the heat, remove the candy thermometer, and top with the butter and vanilla extract, swirling the pan to blend.

Set the candy on the wire rack and cool for exactly 3 minutes. Pour the candy into the lined pan, shaking the pan to level the mixture, or spread with a metal spatula.

Let the candy cool for 20 to 30 minutes. Then, using a sharp knife, with the candy still in the pan, mark the top of the candy for cutting into 1½-inch squares, or desired shapes.

Once the candy is completely hard, remove from the pan by lifting the paper or foil. Peel off the paper or foil and discard. Place the candy on a cutting board and finish cutting into pieces.

Makes 34 to 36 pieces

Hot and Syrupy Stages

Years ago Aunt Mary would stir up a batch of candy without giving a thought to a candy thermometer. She simply dropped a small amount of the hot syrup into a cup of cold water to see how it reacted. This method depends on "feel" and eye to determine whether the syrup has reached a certain consistency or stage.

For once I go with technology. I prefer a good-quality candy thermometer that has clearly marked stages, along with degrees in Fahrenheit. Metal-backed thermometers are best for candy making.

Attach the thermometer to the inside of the pan, making sure that it doesn't rest on the bottom of the pan, where the temperature is several degrees hotter than the syrup.

The candy stages and Fahrenheits are: thread—at 230 to 234, for syrups and icings; soft ball—at 234 to 240, for fondant, fudge, and pralines; and firm ball—at 242 to 248, for caramels and nougat candy. As the mercury rises you get hard ball—from 250 to 268, which is required for taffy, divinity, and pulled candies.

Soft crack—at 270 to 290, for toffee and butterscotch, and very hot hard crack—at 300 to 310, are necessary for brittle and candied apples. Caramel is 320 to 345. Beyond 350 degrees the syrup turns black and is used for coloring gravies and for "browning" in desserts such as the West Indian Christmas Cake (page 103). ❀

SIX

Cool
Ice Cream

Nobody remembers just what happened to the old hand-cranked ice cream freezer that years ago provided our family in Alabama with so many moments of pleasure on Sunday afternoons, but several of the ice cream dishes still remain.

Mama acquired most of the dishes with Octagon laundry soap coupons that she glued in a little book and redeemed at the general store. During the week they were displayed on a what-not stand, along with the other porcelain figurines and kitsch that she obsessively collected to pretty up our existence.

Most are pressed glass. Some are leaf-shaped, others are oblong, a few are oval-shaped and as graceful as a boat; others are round with knobbed bottoms, and the colors range from crystal clear to a delicate peach-apricot to a deep kelly green. As I finger them, I am rushed with memories.

For years Daddy operated the ice plant in the southern section of Choctaw County for a rich white owner, and perhaps that explains why homemade ice cream became a family ritual. Only moneyed families were serviced by REA (Rural Electric Association), so a big block of ice always rested in a shed in our backyard, wrapped in burlap and stored in a hole dug in the ground that was filled with sawdust. The "icebox" was covered with a sheet of tin, insulated against the torch of the summer Alabama sun.

We churned ice cream on late summer Sunday afternoons, after church, and the child lucky enough to be turning the freezer when it chugged to a stop would be rewarded the dasher. By the time I was twelve I had mastered the mechanics of ice cream churning, and I was forever pushing and shoving trying to get to the crank at the opportune moment, since I just had to have the first taste of the delicious concoction.

I have five older brothers and they suffered my antics with customary chauvinism, and generally let me have my way, laughing as I struggled to turn the freezer on its last leg, and laughing even more as I licked the dasher. Anyway, in an hour's time the ice cream was "ripen" and ready to serve and Mama would pass out the pretty dishes. Everybody would gather about, and the family would linger on the front porch until darkness fell, chasing away the summer heat with a cold dish of ice cream.

Vanilla ice cream was popular but we liked other flavors, too. Sometimes my only sister, Helen, would reward us with chocolate ice cream to go with her best-ever chocolate icing cake and I would pass the afternoon with my head buzzing. When the peaches and huckleberries were at peak ripeness, Mama would sprinkle the fruit with sugar, and fold into the ice cream before ripening, and Daddy said this was his favorite. Mama liked the tangy-sweet flavor of buttermilk ice cream, and often she would serve this with a sweet berry or plum sauce, or stir in peaches or figs, which were grown on two trees right at our back door.

Once, Aunt Mary, Daddy's sister, came up from the Gulf Coast to visit and she made a Burnt Sugar Ice Cream, which had a deep, burnished flavor. I sat devouring her lush, sophisticated creation, thinking of faraway places.

The recipe follows:

Burnt Sugar Ice Cream

1 cup granulated sugar
¼ teaspoon cream of tartar
3 tablespoons water
½ cup brewed hot coffee
2 cups milk
⅛ teaspoon salt
6 egg yolks

1½ cups light brown sugar, firmly
    packed (see Dark and Sweet, page
    25)
1 tablespoon vanilla extract
¼ cup bourbon, dark rum or brandy
3 cups heavy cream, chilled

Have ready a pastry brush, a cup of hot water to brush down sugar crystals from the sides of the pan, a candy thermometer, and a long-handled wooden spoon (see Go Burn!, page 196).

Combine the granulated sugar, cream of tartar, and 3 tablespoons water in a 6 cup heavy saucepan. Set the pan over medium-high heat and cook, stirring with the wooden spoon, until the sugar dissolves. Cover the pan and cook the syrup for 3 minutes.

Remove the cover. Dip the pastry brush into the water and brush down the sides of the pan. Attach the candy thermometer to the inside of the pot.

Cook the syrup until it turns deep, dark brown in color, has a reddish undertone, and reaches 320 to 325 degrees on the candy thermometer, swirling the pan to stir the liquid rather than using a spoon.

Remove the pan from the heat and allow to cool, 2 or 3 minutes. Then, pour a tablespoon of coffee at a time down the side of the pan into the syrup. The syrup will release steam and splatter, so do this carefully.

Once all the coffee is added, stir the syrup and set aside.

Combine the milk and salt in the top of a double boiler. Cook over— not in—hot water until the milk is hot and bubbly, for about 10 minutes.

Meanwhile, combine the egg yolks and brown sugar in a medium bowl. Using a handheld electric mixer set at medium-high speed, beat until pale and lemony, for about 2 minutes, scraping the bowl with a rubber spatula once or twice.

Add a few tablespoons of the hot milk to the egg yolk–sugar mixture and whisk briefly. Add another ladleful of hot milk to the egg yolks and whisk again. Now pour the warmed egg mixture into the double boiler and mix well.

Raise the heat a bit. Cook the custard, stirring frequently with a wooden spoon, for 10 to 12 minutes, or until it thickens and coats a spoon, and reaches 170 on a candy or instant read thermometer. (Don't let the custard boil; it can curdle.)

Stir in the caramelized syrup and coffee mixture, the vanilla extract, and the bourbon or rum or brandy and mix well.

Remove the custard from the heat and pour immediately through a strainer into a large clean bowl. Set the bowl of custard in an ice water

Freeze! The ice cream recipes in this book yield $2\frac{1}{2}$ to 3 quarts. If your ice cream freezer or maker doesn't hold this amount, freeze the ice cream in batches, empty into bowls or plastic containers, and place in the freezer compartment of the refrigerator. Ice cream makers that don't require ice range from 1- to 2-quart size.

When using a crank freezer, follow the manufacturer's directions and these tips:

Start Off Hot: Before using, wash the lid, can, and dasher (scraper) with hot soapy water and then rinse well and scald with boiling water. This step sterilizes all the equipment. Also make sure that the lid fits properly so that melted ice can't seep into the can during the freezing.

Keep It Neat: Place the freezer in a foot tub or basin to catch the brine that forms as the ice melts. The flowing salty water can get real messy.

Salt and Ice: You'll need at least 15 pounds of crushed ice and about 3 pounds of coarse crystal salt to crank-freeze 2 to 4 quarts of ice cream. But be generous and buy more than you need; salt and ice are relatively inexpensive.

bath (see On Ice, page 237) and chill completely, stirring occasionally to release steam.

Add the cream to the custard and mix well. Cover the bowl with plastic wrap or foil, set in the refrigerator, and chill at least 3 hours or overnight.

Pour the custard into a chilled ice cream freezer container, and stir to mix well. Freeze according to the manufacturer's direction.

Makes about 2½ quarts

Here's the freezing ratio: Use 1 cup coarse salt to every 8 cups (2 quarts) of crushed ice, which freezes quicker than ice cubes. Layer the salt and ice to the top of the freezer, but don't cover the lid with salt. It can seep into the canister and you end up with salty ice cream!

Churning: The delectable concoction is ready when the crank sputters and wheezes you have difficulty turning it, 15 to 25 minutes.

Packed: Remove the crank unit and carefully wipe off the lid of the freezer canister with a clean cloth. Remove the dasher. Scrape down the sides of the container, and if desired, stir in sugared berries or fruits or nuts at this time. Pack down the ice cream.

Cover the top of the container with a sheet of wax paper or foil and replace the lid. The ice cream will become harder during the ripening, which requires the addition of more salt and ice, about four parts ice to one part salt.

Ripe On: Repack the freezer bucket with ice and coarse salt according to manufacturer's direction, or harden the ice cream in the refrigerator freezer and set in a cool place. ❀

I remember seeing Jacqueline Corr for the first time as she is standing at the edge of her yard, swabbing a suckling pig that is roasting on a grill just a few feet away from a pitched tent, where at least sixty to seventy guests have gathered.

She is wearing a long blue dress printed with tiny flowers over a rose-colored polo shirt, and her heavy mane of hair is piled on her head; a few strands have gone awry and are hanging over her beautiful face, which is lightly beaded with perspiration.

A half-dozen long serving tables are crowded with food. A jazz trio or quartet is jamming—but oh so low key—right next to the bar, which is set up across the lawn near the rear entrance to Jackie's home in Bloomfield Hills, a Detroit suburb.

It is late August, a Saturday afternoon, and I am visiting with my dear friend Shirley Brown, and her wonderful husband, Brother Mel. I go to this party kicking and screaming, telling myself that I would rather be out on my friends' porch deck drinking gin and listening to Otis Redding.

But the French countryside setting in sepia right outside of Dee-troit is a little intoxicating. So I take a deep breath, enjoy the camaraderie, relax, but wonder if the hostess is going to continue cooking all evening. She does.

At that time I know little about Jackie

other than this: She is a chef at a private restaurant in Detroit; she was once married to a famous major league baseball player, and she and her mother, Rosemary, pitch this knock-down party every year.

I learned about Jackie's passion for ice cream later, and this information came from Jackie herself.

I am surprised; she is gregarious, has a tendency to make fun of herself, and as I scribble away—every encounter is always a potential story—she rattles off the twenty-one varieties of ice cream she makes, providing a capsule recipe as she talks.

I am intrigued by now, being an old ice cream maker myself, and I listen spellbound as she talks on with a sprinter's speed. She lists vanilla ice cream speckled with vanilla bean, peanut butter ice cream, a slew of fruit ice creams, such as pomegranate, persimmon, and mango; at least a half-dozen spice, brandy, and liqueur-infused ice creams such as peach schnapps and pina colada, and an equal number of ice creams flavored with nuts, candy, and cookies. And the kicker here is that she does this for pleasure and passion rather than profit—for family gatherings, as gifts for friends.

"I went crazy when I started making ice cream," Jackie recalls, laughing. "I used to go into the kitchen and turn into Frankenstein, making ice creams. Late at night, after the news, around 11:30 P.M., I would start on my creations. I like to work when it's quiet; no distractions. Many nights I wouldn't get to bed until 2:30 in the morning."

I shift nervously in my seat, trying to think of some tactful away to ask this woman, who is as fit as a marathon runner, about the wheels that put this pastime in motion, without sounding like some Freudian fool.

She laughs and tells me about how in the early 1970s she quit her job as an X-ray technician and decided to see the world as a flight attendant. One day, she recalls, she stopped for dinner at a little restaurant near the airport in Memphis, Tennessee. An older man was the chef and perhaps even the owner, and at the end of the meal the brother sidled up and asked the pretty woman if she wanted a little bowl of something sweet and cold.

Jackie remembers that he set before her a dish of watermelon ice cream—not sherbet—which slid down her throat like honey, releasing the unmistakable flavor of watermelon, but creamy and rich and fruity at the same time.

"Every time I flew into Memphis I went back to the restaurant and ate that ice cream," she says, her voice racing. "I begged the man for the recipe but he wouldn't give it to me. But I kept going back, and finally I figured out the recipe myself. Now my watermelon ice cream tastes just like his."

And so began her pursuit.

"I started off back in 1985 with an old hand-cranked freezer," she remembers. "I now use an electric crank freezer. But I can't tell you how many freezers I've been through over the past fifteen years. Once I was making peach ice cream and dumped in too many fresh peaches. The freezer's motor burned out on the spot."

But I can guess. By now I know that I am talking with a woman who tackles every project with passion and study.

Then, she stops talking, and as I wait for that last recipe, the watermelon ice cream recipe that she pursued for years, I am gripped with excitement. I can feel her arranging the list of ingredients in her head, and I have my pen at the ready.

"My watermelon ice cream recipe is a secret," she says finally. "You have to come up with your own recipe."

I gasp, and as I find her face, there is a mischievous glint in her eyes. Finally I sigh, audibly, at peace.

Vanilla Bean Ice Cream

Vanilla is indigenous to Mexico, and the best beans come from that country—and from Madagascar off the coast of East Africa. Always look for plump beans; if they are dry and shriveled, they lack flavor. A good brand is Nielsen-Massey.

And if you are visiting Mexico, don't forget to stock up on bottled pure vanilla extract, which is also excellent and moderately priced.

Jackie doesn't spare expenses when she makes ice cream and uses four vanilla beans in this recipe, and yes they are quite pricey. If your budget is a little tight, two vanilla beans will also provide you with delicious flavor and fragrant aroma.

2 to 4 whole vanilla beans	$\frac{1}{8}$ teaspoon salt
2 cups ranulated sugar	10 large eggs yolks
2 cups half-and-half	4 cups (1 quart) heavy cream, chilled

Chop the vanilla beans and place in a coffee grinder; pulverize as finely as possible.

Combine the pulverized vanilla beans and the sugar in a food processor or blender. Process or whirl the mixture until the vanilla beans and sugar are well blended, 2 to 3 minutes. Set aside.

Place the half-and-half and salt in the top of a double boiler. Heat the cream over hot water until hot and bubbly—but not boiling—about 10 minutes.

Meanwhile, place the egg yolks in a large mixing bowl and beat briskly with a whisk. Stir in the sugar-vanilla bean mixture.

Using a handheld electric mixer set at medium-high speed, beat the eggs and sugar 2 to 3 minutes, scraping the bowl with a rubber spatula once or twice.

Add a few tablespoons of the hot cream to the egg yolk–sugar mixture and whisk briefly. Add another ladle of hot cream to the egg yolks and whisk again. Pour the warmed egg mixture into mixture in the double boiler and mix well.

Raise the heat a bit. Cook the custard, stirring frequently with a wooden spoon, for 10 to 12 minutes, or until it thickens and coats a spoon, and reaches 170 degrees on a candy thermometer or instant read thermometer. (Don't let the custard boil; it can curdle.)

Remove the custard from the heat and pour into a large clean bowl. (Don't strain the custard yet; the vanilla beans will impart flavor during the chilling.) Set the bowl of custard in an ice water bath (see On Ice, page 237) and chill completely, stirring occasionally to release steam.

Add the heavy cream to the custard and mix well. Cover the bowl with plastic wrap or foil, set in the refrigerator, and chill at least 3 hours or overnight.

Pour the chilled custard through a strainer into a chilled freezer container, stirring to mix well. Freeze according to the manufacturer's direction.

Makes 3 generous quarts

The Scoops

A batch of vanilla custard ice cream is as basic as a simple black dress, and just as elegant. It can be dressed up with so many flavorings. Here are some of Jackie's favorite ice cream renditions. All are creative and delicious.

Spicy: Mix together in a small saucepan 3 tablespoons cognac or brandy, 3 tablespoons dark rum, 2 teaspoons ground cinnamon, 1 teaspoon ground or grated nutmeg, and 1 teaspoon ground cloves. Place the pan on low heat and cook, stirring, 3 or 4 minutes. Remove from the heat right away.

Stir the spice mixture into the hot custard before chilling, and proceed as directed in the recipe.

Crunchy: If desired, substitute 1 cup of maple syrup for 1 cup of the sugar in the custard. Then, before ripening the ice cream, stir in 1 generous cup of coarsely chopped black walnuts (or English walnuts) and 2 teaspoons black walnut or maple extract.

Salsa: Stir into the hot, cooked custard, 1 can (15 ounces) cream of coconut, such as Coco Lopez or Coco Goya, and $^3/_4$ cup shredded coconut, preferably freshly shredded. Stir in a couple tablespoons of lime or lemon juice, if desired.

Mix well and proceed as directed in the recipe.

Plummy: Rinse, drain, and remove the stems from 3 to 4 pounds fresh, ripe plums. Cut in half lengthwise. Remove the pits and discard. Don't peel. Set aside.

Combine in a heavy saucepan 1 cup sugar and 1 cup water. Bring to a boil and cook for about 2 minutes. Stir in the plums. (If you prefer the ice cream less sweet, use less sugar and an equal amount of water.)

Reduce the heat to low and cook for 10 to 12 minutes or until the plums are just tender and the syrup is thick. Remove from heat, cool thoroughly. Remove the plum skins and discard.

For a real smooth ice cream, puree the fruit mixture in a blender or food processor. If you desire tiny bits of fruit in the ice cream, crush or mash the plums into pieces with a potato masher or wooden spoon. Set aside.

Pour the custard into the ice cream canister and freeze for 10 to 12 minutes or until the ice cream is fluffy and almost firm. Unplug the freezer, remove the dasher, and carefully remove the lid. Stir into the partially frozen ice cream the pureed or mashed plums.

Close the freezer and continue freezing the ice cream until it hardens and the crank whirls to a stop.

Kiddie Delight: If it is a theme party, add 2 drops of food coloring to the ice cream custard and watch eyes light up.

Churn the ice cream for 10 minutes, turn off the freezer, remove the lid, and stir in $^1/_2$ cup colored sugar crystals (nonpareils) or $^1/_2$ cup cinnamon hots to the partially frozen mixture. Continue freezing until the ice cream is firm. ❀

Watermelon Ice Cream

Since my friend Jacqueline Corr guards the recipe for her watermelon ice cream as closely as my brother John does his barbecue sauce, I was left with the challenge of developing my "own" recipe. Jackie's ice cream is fruity, creamy and exquisite, and I went almost stir-crazy trying to match her creation, partly because I love watermelon in any form, and second, because her ice cream is so downright delicious.

I first made an egg-based custard and poured the mixture over watermelon chunks and pureed until smooth and creamy. I churned the ice cream, and although it was acceptable, the watermelon flavor was very subtle, almost fleeting, not intense in flavor like Jackie's.

Feeling a little frustrated, I called my sister, Helen, and she suggested that I use the traditional Philadelphia ice cream method, which is made without egg yolks, but with heavy cream and sugar and flavoring. This way, we decided, the fruit flavor would shine.

I went back to the drawing board and simply heated the sugar and heavy cream and flavoring and poured the hot mixture over the watermelon chunks and then pureed. I called in a half-dozen friends to test this ice cream, and three or four of them really liked it. Brenda Richardson and I were the holdouts.

"Too bad we have to think about this delicious ice cream," says Brenda, causing all of us to laugh. "I'd rather just enjoy it."

Brenda and I felt that although the ice cream was creamy and smooth, it still lacked "watermelon" flavor. So I went at it again. The next time I made a syrup out of half the watermelon chunks, and by doing this, evaporated some of the fruit's natural water and intensified its flavor. I poured the hot syrup over the watermelon chunks and pureed the mixture.

The results: a fresh and fruity and irresistible creamy watermelon ice cream, which I plan to make, freeze, pack in dry ice, and carry to Jackie during my next visit to Detroit and Bloomfield Hills. I know she will love it and may just claim it as her own.

½ of a whole real ripe watermelon, 5 to 6 pounds
2 cups granulated sugar, less if the watermelon is sugar sweet
¼ to ⅓ cup liqueur, such as crème de cassis (black currant-flavored) or sweet ruby port or sherry
2 teaspoons vanilla extract
3 cups heavy cream, well chilled

Cut the watermelon flesh into small pieces. Using a spoon, remove the seeds and discard. Measure out 6 cups of the watermelon (make sure that the cups are firmly packed with the fruit) and place in a large mixing bowl. (After you finish this recipe, cool out and eat the leftover watermelon; it is good for you.)

Place 3 cups of the watermelon in a blender or food processor and puree until smooth. Pour the pureed watermelon into a large stainless heavy saucepan. Stir in the sugar and mix well.

Set the pan on medium heat and cook the mixture, stirring, until the sugar dissolves and the syrup begins to bubble. Reduce the heat to low, and continue cooking the syrup 10 to 12 minutes, until it deepens in color and is slightly thickened. Don't let the syrup boil.

Immediately remove the pan from the heat. Stir in the liqueur or wine and vanilla extract. Pour the hot syrup over the remaining watermelon in the bowl and mix well.

Cool the watermelon mixture completely. Stir in the heavy cream. Cover the bowl with plastic wrap or foil, set in the refrigerator, and chill 2 to 3 hours.

Pour the watermelon-cream mixture into a blender or food processor and puree or pulse until very smooth. Do this in batches and pour the pureed mixture through a sieve or strainer into a chilled ice cream canister.

Stir the melon-cream mixture again, using a long spoon.

Freeze according to the manufacturer's directions.

Makes about 3 quarts

Star Anise Peach Ice Cream

When my son, Roy, was studying in Beijing, China, I wrote and told him to bring me back some "real" tea, not the kind exported for foreigners. And so he did, plus a packet of a delightful spice called star anise, which the merchant pressed on him and told him to "give to mother to use in cookies."

Star anise is native to China, and has a delicious licorice-like flavor. It is wonderful in cookies, but sublime in this tangy and spicy ice cream, which is a variation of the fruit-flavored buttermilk ice cream that Mama made years ago.

When I was testing recipes for this book, my friends Mark and Brenda Richardson graciously set aside their busy schedules—Mark is a professor of divinity—and tested batch after batch of ice cream with me. And when it was all done, Mark pronounced this star anise as his favorite.

"Thanks for twisting our arm and making us do this," he joked.

And I thank them—my wonderful friends and neighbors.

2 pounds medium-size ripe peaches, white or yellow (about 8 or 9)	3 cups heavy cream
	Pinch of salt
½ cup granulated sugar, plus 1½ cups	8 egg yolks
2 tablespoons water	1½ teaspoons cornstarch
2 tablespoons lemon juice	1 tablespoon vanilla extract
2 to 3 tablespoons star anise pieces	3 cups buttermilk, chilled

Rinse the peaches, remove the stems, peel, and cut into quarters lengthwise. Discard the pits.

Combine the peaches, ½ cup sugar, and 2 tablespoons water in a heavy saucepan. Cook over medium-low heat, stirring often, 12 to 18 minutes, or until the fruit is soft and tender and lightly caramelized in color.

Remove the peaches from the stove, stir in the lemon juice. Using a wooden spoon or potato masher, crush or mash the peaches into small bits, but don't puree. Cover and set in the refrigerator. (This can be done in advance and kept covered in the refrigerator.)

Finely crush the star anise and scatter it in a small heavy skillet (see Got a Crush, page 60). Set over low heat and toast for a few minutes, stirring. Remove from the heat.

In the top of a double boiler, combine the star anise, cream, and salt. Heat the mixture over hot water until hot and bubbly, about 10 minutes, but don't allow the cream to boil.

Meanwhile, combine the egg yolks, the remaining $1^{1}/_{2}$ cups sugar, and cornstarch in a medium bowl. Using a handheld electric mixer set at medium-high speed, beat the mixture about 2 minutes, scraping the bowl with a rubber spatula once or twice.

Add a few tablespoons of the warm cream to the egg yolk–sugar mixture and whisk briefly. Stir another ladle of hot cream into the egg yolks and whisk again. Now add the warmed egg yolk mixture to the mixture in the double boiler and mix well.

Raise the heat a bit. Cook the custard, stirring frequently with a wooden spoon, 10 to 12 minutes, or until it thickens and coats a spoon or reaches 170 degrees on a candy or instant read thermometer. (Don't let the custard boil; it may curdle.) Stir in the vanilla extract.

Remove the custard from the heat and let set for about an hour to meld flavors. Then pour through a fine strainer into a large clean bowl.

Set the bowl of custard in an ice water bath (see On Ice, page 237) and chill completely, stirring occasionally to release steam.

Stir the buttermilk into the chilled custard. Cover the bowl with foil or plastic wrap and chill several hours or overnight.

Pour the custard into the freezer container, and stir to mix well. Freeze according to the manufacturer's directions, 10 to 12 minutes, or until the custard is partially frozen and has turned into soft ice cream.

Unplug the freezer, remove the dasher, and wipe the top of the canister with a clean cloth. Remove the canister lid and stir in the peaches with a long-handled spoon, mixing well.

Close the freezer again and continue freezing the ice cream until firm.

Makes 2 ½ to 3 quarts

Variation: Rinse 3 cups blueberries or blackberries, remove the stems, and drain. Combine the berries and $^{1}/_{2}$ cup sugar in a heavy saucepan. Bring to a quick boil.

Immediately reduce the heat to medium-low and cook, stirring, for about 5 minutes, just until the sugar dissolves and the berries are softened. Remove the pan from heat and set aside. Chill the fruit. Freeze the custard 10 to 12 minutes or until it turns to soft ice cream. Stir in the fruit, mixing well with a long-handled spoon. Continue freezing the ice cream until it is firm.

Chocolate Cinnamon Ice Cream

I added cinnamon to my sister Helen's chocolate ice cream recipe, and even she said it was delicious.

Cinnamon is often combined with chocolate in Mexican cooking, and it adds a bracing and aromatic note to this luscious ice cream. Both cocoa and semisweet chocolate are used, and the ice cream has a rich, deep, dense flavor.

2 cinnamon sticks or 1½ to 2 tablespoons ground cinnamon
½ cup unsweetened cocoa
⅛ teaspoon salt
2 cups milk
2 cups granulated sugar (see Note below)

8 large egg yolks
1 tablespoon vanilla extract
4 ounces semisweet chocolate
4 cups (1 quart) heavy cream, chilled

Break the cinnamon sticks into small pieces and pulverize into tiny bits in a coffee grinder. (If using ground cinnamon, omit the cinnamon sticks.)

Place the cinnamon bits or the ground cinnamon, cocoa, and salt in the top of a double boiler. Stir in the milk and mix well. Cook over hot water for about 10 minutes, stirring occasionally, or until the mixture is hot and bubbly.

Meanwhile, combine the sugar and egg yolks in a medium bowl. Using a handheld electric mixer set at medium-high speed, beat the mixture for 2 minutes, scraping the bowl with a rubber spatula once or twice.

Add a few tablespoons of the warm milk to the egg yolk–sugar mixture and whisk briefly. Stir in another ladle of hot milk to the egg yolks and whisk again. Now add the warmed egg yolk mixture to the double boiler and mix well.

Raise the heat a bit. Cook the custard, stirring frequently, with a wooden spoon, 10 to 12 minutes, or until it thickens and coats a spoon or reaches 170 degrees on a candy or instant read thermometer. (Don't let boil; the custard can curdle.) Stir in the vanilla extract.

Remove the custard from the heat. Coarsely chop the chocolate, stir into the hot custard, and beat briskly until well blended.

Pour the custard through a fine strainer into a large bowl. Set the bowl of custard in an ice water bath (see On Ice, page 237) and chill completely, stirring occasionally to release steam.

Add the heavy cream to the custard, stir, and cover the bowl with plastic wrap or foil. Set the custard in the refrigerator and chill for at least 3 hours or overnight.

Pour the custard into the freezer container, stirring to mix well. Freeze according to the manufacturer's directions.

Makes about 2½ quarts

Note: For an intense earthy flavor, substitute 1 cup of dark muscovado sugar for 1 cup of the 2 cups of granulated sugar used in the recipe.

My family's Sunday ice cream ritual began to decline during the early 1980s, as a glistening refrigerator now stood in every household, stocked with frozen produce, including store-bought ice cream, a convenient pleasure. By that time barbecue grills and smokers were the focus at family gatherings, and our old hand-crank ice cream freezer was swept away with technology and change.

So I turn to photographs for memories. The one I am holding now is dated July 1967, and my beautiful sister, Helen, is standing in our backyard in Alabama, smiling broadly, holding a crystal bowl filled with just-churned vanilla ice cream topped with hot fudge sauce, and scattered with crushed pecan brittle. Mama is seated in a chair near the freezer, as if on guard, and at the edge of the yard, framed by tall pine trees in the distance, are Helen's two youngest boys, Tyrone and Ceola Junior, and her husband, Ceola. I am home visiting from a frightening place called New York City.

It is late afternoon, and other family members have not yet arrived, but I am sure that they are on their way. Word of freshly churned ice cream travels fast, and before sundown, we are scraping the bottom of the canister for the last, delicious, sweet scoop.

The quickest way to enjoy homemade ice cream is to dip and enjoy, or scrape it off the dasher as I still like to do. But top it with fresh fruits and nuts, or spoon it over plain cake or cookies, or layer in a glass with fruit and sauce and simple ice cream becomes a sophisticated dessert.

Fruits such as fresh berries, peaches, figs, and plums are sublime with ice cream. Grated coconut, chopped nuts, or a sprinkling of grated chocolate add pizzazz. A cup of sugar can be caramelized in minutes flat for a delectable sauce, or hardened for brittle, which adds a flavorful bite to mellow ice cream.

Split a banana, top it with a couple scoops of ice cream, drizzle over a heady chocolate sauce, and watch the adults nudge the children out of the way. Or, place a scoop or two of ice cream in a tall glass, add fresh fruit and champagne or club soda, and please the young at heart.

The creations are limitless. Homemade ice cream is a show—impressive and memorable. Here are favored recipes for ice cream sundaes, parfaits, floats, shakes, and sauces:

Banana Peanut Caramel Sundae

This rather sophisticated version of an old ice cream pleasure, the banana split, offers a "burned" flavor in the ice cream, caramel sauce, and molasses cookies.

You can cool off this sundae with a generous dab of whipped cream.

Burnt Sugar Ice Cream (page 211)
Caramel or Burnt Sugar Sauce (page 234)

Molasses Lace Cookies (page 15)
3 fully ripe medium bananas
1½ cups lightly toasted peanuts

Prepare the ice cream, sauce, and cookies according to recipe directions. Peel the bananas and cut crosswise on the bias or slant into ¼-inch-thick slices.

To assemble the sundae, spoon a couple tablespoons of the sauce into 6 tall glasses or sundae dishes. Top with a scoop of ice cream. Add a few banana slices and scatter with peanuts. Spoon over a little more sauce and add another scoop of ice cream. Add a couple more banana slices, and top with more sauce.

Sprinkle each serving generously with the toasted peanuts, and stick two rolled Molasses Lace Cookies in the top of each serving. Serve immediately.

Makes 6 servings

Fruit Sundae

I like vanilla ice cream in this sundae but Watermelon Ice Cream (page 219) is also delightful, especially if you make the fruit sauce using a combination of berries.

Vanilla Bean Ice Cream (page 216)   Cinnamon Nut Cookies (page 21)
Fresh Fruit Sauce (page 54)

Prepare the ice cream, fruit sauce, and cookies according to recipe directions.

To assemble the sundaes, arrange two or more cookies in six shallow ice cream dishes, overlapping the cookies if necessary. Top each serving with two or three scoops of ice cream.

Generously spoon over the fruit sauce and serve immediately.

Makes 6 servings

Pecan Brittle Cherry Sundae

This sundae is a delicious combination of "old" flavors: vanilla ice cream, chocolate sauce, Pecan Brittle, and a heaping of glazed cherries—a retro classic of the 1960s. Glazed blueberries can be prepared in the same way and are equally delicious. Follow the recipe for Nut Brittle to make the candy, using pecans.

Vanilla Bean Ice Cream (on page 216)
Chocolate Fudge Sauce (page 236)
Nut Brittle (page 191)
2 cups fresh Bing cherries (1 pint)

2 or 3 tablespoons sugar, or to taste
1 tablespoon cornstarch
2 tablespoons fruit liqueur or cherry fruit brandy

Prepare the ice cream, fudge sauce, and brittle according to recipe directions. If desired, set the fudge sauce on low heat and keep warm.

Rinse the cherries, remove the stems and discard. To pit the cherries, cut in half with a small knife. Insert the point of the knife into the cut, and cut around the pit, loosening from the fruit. Discard the pits.

Combine in a medium saucepan the sugar, cornstarch, and liqueur or fruit brandy. Set the pan on medium-high heat and bring to a boil, stirring constantly. Cook until the sugar dissolves and the liquid is quite thick, 3 to 4 minutes.

Stir in the cherries and mix well. Reduce the heat to low and cook 2 minutes. Immediately remove the pan from the heat, stir gently, and set aside. Once cooled, chill the cherries, if desired.

Break the brittle into six pieces, about 2-inch size. Wrap the candy in a tea towel, and using a rolling pin or hammer, crush it into pea-size pieces.

Place two or three scoops of ice cream into six ice cream coupes or other glass serving dishes. Top with the fudge sauce. Spoon over the cherries and sprinkle on the crushed Pecan Brittle.

Serve immediately and shout with joy.

Makes six servings

Double Chocolate Pistachio Sundae

I am not quite a chocoholic, but I do have to pinch myself and say "stop" when I sit down to this sundae. The pistachio nuts, which are lightly toasted, add a pretty sparkle and contrasting flavor. Divine.

1 cup unshelled pistachios, more if
    desired
Chocolate Fudge Sauce (page 236)
Chocolate Cinnamon Ice Cream (page
    224)

1 cup chilled heavy cream, whipped
    (see Perfectly Whipped Cream, page
    74)

Preheat the oven to 350 degrees. Shell the pistachio nuts and scatter on a large, shallow roasting pan.

Toast in the oven for 5 to 7 minutes, or until lightly browned, shaking the pan to move the nuts around midway through the baking or stirring with a wooden spoon.

Remove the nuts from the oven. Scatter on a tea towel. Using the towel, briskly rub the nuts with your fingertips and remove the skins, or cut away with a small knife. Set aside.

Assemble the sundaes: Place a tablespoon or so of the fudge sauce in the bottom of six sundae dishes or tall glasses. Top with two scoops of ice cream and sprinkle each serving with a couple tablespoons of the pistachio nuts.

Spoon over more fudge sauce, and top generously with the remaining pistachio nuts. Add a dollop of whipped cream and serve immediately.

Makes 6 servings

Liqueur Parfait

Perhaps the best and simplest way to adorn a bowl or glass of ice cream is with a generous pouring of liqueur. So heady and creamy and delicious, and the dessert literally melts in your mouth. And that's not surprising, since the word *liqueur* means "to melt" in Latin.

There are many varieties of this elixir, which is a sweet alcoholic beverage made from an infusion of flavoring ingredients such as seeds, fruits, herbs, flowers, nuts, or spices, and generally a neutral or plain grain alcohol, but it can be made with brandy, rum, or whiskey. Many today are flavored with the extracts of essential oils.

Liqueurs are real popular, ranging from Amaretto (almonds and apricot pits) to Triple Sec (oranges). I particularly like Benedictine and B&B, the orange-flavored liqueurs such as Cointreau and Grand Marnier; crème de cassis (black currants), the coffee-flavored liqueurs such as Kahlúa and Tia Maria, and Southern Comfort, a bourbon-based American-made liqueur. And there are scores of other delicious liqueurs crowding liquor stores.

Just a splash of any of these liqueurs adds an elegant note to ice cream, and if you top with fresh fruit or a fruit sauce, you have a fabulous dessert in minutes.

Vanilla Bean Ice Cream (page 216) or Burnt Sugar Ice Cream (page 211)

6 ounces liqueur of choice, or more if desired

Fresh Fruit Sauce (page 55)

Fill four tall chilled glasses with alternate layers of ice cream and liqueur. Top with the fresh fruit sauce and serve immediately.

Makes 4 servings

Brandied Peach Float

The first time I made this float, Norma Boucher and her friend, James (Jimmy) Fonsville, were coming to dinner. Jimmy loves elegant wines and I knew he would love this concoction, which is made with brandied peaches and champagne.

He did. He even took tasting notes and asked for the recipe.

³/₄ cup sliced Brandied Peaches (page 265)

1½ cups Vanilla Bean Ice Cream, slightly softened (page 216)

½ cup club soda or champagne, or more, if desired

Mint leaves

Whirl the peaches in the blender or pulse in a food processor until smooth and thick. Pour the peach puree into two large, stemmed chilled glasses. Top with scoops of the ice cream, dividing evenly between the glasses.

Add the club soda or champagne and garnish with the mint leaves. Serve immediately.

Makes 2 servings

Variation: Substitute ³/₄ cup sliced fresh peaches for the Brandied Peaches. Puree with ¹/₄ cup (2 ounces) peach schnapps or brandy, or to taste. Proceed as directed in above recipe.

Banana Milk Shake

The late Lillie Sherfield of Rochester, New York, sent me this recipe several years ago, enclosing a note that said it was her children's favorite summer treat.

I can understand that. My son, Roy, is now a young man, but he loves this milk shake.

Vanilla ice cream is traditional, but Burnt Sugar Ice Cream is a good bet, too. And don't forget to make enough for the grown folks.

4 ripe medium bananas
2 cups milk
½ teaspoon vanilla extract

Vanilla Bean Ice Cream (page 216) or
Burnt Sugar Ice Cream (page 211)
½ teaspoon ground cinnamon

Chill four tall, 10- to 12-ounce glasses.

Peel the bananas and break into small pieces. Place in a blender or food processor and whirl or pulse until smooth. Add the milk and vanilla extract and whirl again until smooth.

Pour into the chilled glasses. Top each glass with a scoop or two of ice cream and sprinkle each serving with a little cinnamon. Serve immediately.

Makes 4 servings

Caramel or Burnt Sugar Sauce

The key to making this delectable sauce is to caramelize the sugar until it is deep brown with a reddish undertone.

But you must pay close attention, for the sugar is cooking at a high temperature and will burn and turn acrid in a flash.

On the other hand, if you don't "burn" the sauce enough, it will end up tasteless and weak in flavor. If this happens, start all over again.

As with most challenges, practice make perfect, and don't forget to turn off the phone while you are making this sauce (see Go Burn!, page 196).

1 cup sugar, preferably superfine
1 tablespoon light corn syrup
3 tablespoons hot water
¾ cup heavy cream or half-and-half

2 tablespoons unsalted butter
2 tablespoons brandy or bourbon or
   dark rum

Have available a long-handled wooden spoon, a pastry brush, a cup of hot water, and a candy thermometer.

Combine in a 1½-quart heavy stainless steel or enameled cast-iron pot, the sugar, corn syrup, and hot water. Stir with the wooden spoon until the sugar dissolves.

Bring the mixture to a boil over medium-high heat, stirring until the sugar dissolves. Cover the pan and cook the syrup, without stirring, for 3 minutes.

Remove the lid. Dip the brush in water and brush down the sugar crystals from the sides of the pan. Attach a candy thermometer inside the pan, making sure that it does not touch the bottom of the pan.

Cook the syrup, without stirring, but swirling the pan by the handle, until it turns deep reddish brown and the thermometer reads 320 to 345 degrees or the caramel stage, frequently brushing the pan with the damp brush.

Immediately remove the pan from the heat and set on a wire rack. Let the syrup cool for 2 or 3 minutes, and then carefully pour the heavy cream down the side of the pan, a tablespoon or so at a time. The mixture will boil and release steam so do this carefully; it may look curdled but will smooth out when beaten.

Set the pan on medium-low heat, and heat for about 10 minutes, beating briskly with a wire whisk until it is smooth.

Remove the pan from the heat, stir in the butter and brandy or bourbon or rum. The sauce can be used right away. If using later, pour into a jar with a tight-fitting lid, cool and then refrigerate.

The sauce will keep for a couple of weeks in the refrigerato., For long-term use, pour the sauce into a canning jar, leave at least an inch of head space, cap with the lid, and freeze. The sauce will keep in the freezer for several months; a delectable treat to always have on hand.

Makes about 1 cup

Chocolate Fudge Sauce

My sister, Helen, gave me this recipe years ago, and it is strong, deep in flavor, but quite sweet, the way we like it. It's the perfect topping for ice cream sundaes, parfaits, and splits, and for drizzling over plain cake topped with whipped cream or ice cream.

2 ounces good-quality unsweetened chocolate

1/4 cup unsweetened cocoa

1 1/4 cups granulated sugar

1 1/2 cups undiluted evaporated milk or heavy cream

1/2 cup brewed coffee

4 tablespoons (1/2 stick) unsalted butter

2 tablespoons light or dark corn syrup

1 teaspoon vanilla extract

Chop the chocolate into small pieces and set aside.

Combine in a heavy stainless steel pan the cocoa and sugar and mix well. Stir in the milk or heavy cream, coffee, butter, and corn syrup, and mix until well blended.

Place the pan on medium-high heat and bring the mixture to a gentle boil. Cook, swirling the pan instead of stirring the mixture, 10 to 12 minutes, or until the sauce thickens.

Add the vanilla extract and chocolate pieces and cook a few minutes longer over low heat, stirring briskly until the chocolate melts. Remove the pan from the heat and beat again.

Let the sauce set for a few moments to thicken and then beat briskly. If the sauce becomes too thick, stir in a tablespoon or so of milk or cream and reheat over low heat, stirring gently.

If serving over ice cream, serve warm. The sauce will keep in the refrigerator for two or three months in a canning jar with a tight lid. Reheat in the top of a double boiler or set the jar of sauce in a skillet filled with hot water. Place the skillet over medium heat and reheat the sauce.

Makes 2 generous cups

On Ice An ice water bath cools down hot custard real fast and stops it from cooking in minutes. Just pour the custard through a strainer into a large bowl and then set in a larger bowl—or kitchen sink—filled with ice and water. Let stand for 15 to 20 minutes, stirring occasionally.

Once thoroughly cooled, chill the custard in the refrigerator for several more hours or overnight, so that the flavors can meld.

An ice cream freezer works more efficiently and freezes faster when everything is real cold, so if using a crank freezer, chill the freezer container and the dasher. ❧

SEVEN

Simple and Sweet: Fruit Desserts

Two fig trees still stand at our family house down South, and if I return home during the hot summer months, I am rewarded with sappy, seedy, deep brown, honeyed figs that I sit and eat by the handfuls, lulled by their nectar. And just a few feet away, stands a duet of plum trees, fragrant and heavy bearing, offering red-golden sweet juicy plums, no bigger than marbles.

Years ago Mama made delicious cakes, pies, ice cream, and cobblers with the fruit, and before the season's end, they were canned into preserves and jellies for long winter days ahead.

Our house was on a hilltop, and the fruit trees were at the northern edge of her garden, which sloped gently toward a thicket of pine trees, row after row of tended vegetables. Near the bottom of the hill was a little patch of mint that flavored iced tea all the time, bourbon quite often, but was equally appreciated for the delightful aroma that it sent to our porch on summer evenings.

One day, when I was into my imitative Lena Horne period and things sophisticated, I gathered a bowl of the figs and plums and a few mint leaves. I sprinkled on sugar and topped the dessert with a spoonful of sweet condensed milk. When I showed my creation to Aunt Agnes she said it was as pretty as the pictures she saw in the books in the rich white folks' kitchens.

That was years ago and I know now that my dear aunt was being kind and encouraging, but even today my sweet finale is often just as simple, and delicious.

The simplest dessert, of course, is simply a piece or dish of fresh fruit. But with just a little bit of effort the same fruit can be stretched into a variety of other mouthwatering desserts.

Just think of syrupy fresh fruit compotes, a spicy bouquet of poached dried fruits on a winter evening, a pan of caramelized bananas inviting a dab of whipped cream, a baked meringue shell or tart crust showcasing a mélange of liqueur-flavored fresh fruit, the simple elegance of baked plums or apples shimmering with a coating of honey or jelly.

They are just desserts—simple and wholesome—but as seductive as the Garden of Eden.

Here's a rendition of my favorite childhood fruit dessert, followed by a guide for Pickin' Fruit (page 243) and after that, favorite recipes from family and friends.

Fresh Fig and Plum Compote with Honey Cream

Fresh figs arrive in New York in late summer and early fall, and when I put together this combination, I regret the too-short season. I serve the compote on a wedge of melon, but it is also delicious with a few sugar or butter cookies. Top with whipped Honey Cream (page 242) if you like.

1 pound ripe fresh black figs

6 to 7 ripe red or black plums, about 1½ pounds

2 tablespoons lemon juice

⅓ cup honey

2 to 3 tablespoons finely chopped fresh mint

½ cup water

1 tablespoon good-quality bourbon, if desired

1 medium ripe cantaloupe or honeydew melon

Honey Cream (recipe follows) (see Note below)

Rinse the figs and plums and remove the stems and discard. Cut the figs in half. Cut the plums into eighths and discard the pits. Place the fruit in a glass bowl and toss with the lemon juice. Set aside.

Combine the honey, mint, and ½ cup water in a large saucepan. Place the pan on medium-high heat and bring to a boil, stirring. Cook for 2 minutes.

Stir in the reserved figs and plums. Immediately reduce the heat to medium-low and stir in the bourbon. Cook the fruit for 10 to 12 minutes or until it is softened but not falling apart, occasionally ladling the syrup over the fruit as it poaches.

Remove the pan from the heat and cool on a wire rack. Using a slotted spoon, transfer the fruit to a serving bowl. Pour the syrup in the pan through a fine strainer over the fruit. Chill, if desired.

Rinse the melon, cut into six wedges, discarding the seeds and fiber.

At serving, spoon the fruit and syrup over the melon wedges and top with a dollop of Honey Cream.

Makes 6 servings

Note: If desired, you can use yogurt instead of Honey Cream.

Honey Cream

¼ cup honey, such as clover or
    wildflower
1 cup heavy cream, chilled

1 tablespoon honey liqueur or ¼
    teaspoon vanilla or almond extract

Pour the honey into a medium bowl. Gradually whisk in the heavy cream, mixing only until well blended. Add the liqueur or extract and mix again.

Chill the cream mixture and the beaters from a handheld electric mixer in the freezer for about 10 minutes or in the refrigerator for at least 20 minutes.

Beat the chilled cream on medium-high speed until it is smooth and fluffy and forms soft peaks. Don't overbeat.

Use as a topping for fruit compotes, fruit pies, or cakes. The cream can be made at least two days in advance. Cover the bowl tightly with plastic wrap or foil and set in the coldest part of the refrigerator.

Makes about 1½ cups

It was the first week of August and at my local farmers' market was a bin of Empire apples duly announced in bold letters. Pleased but surprised, I yelled to the vendor, "New crop or left over from last year?"

Before he could answer, a middle-aged woman holding an apple in her hand called out, "Take one bite of these babies and you'll answer your own question."

New crop. She was right; locally grown fresh fruit in season is a mouth-watering delight—juicy, sweet, flavorful, succulent, distinctive. And thanks to the growing number of urban-based farmers' markets, road stands, and the country's superb transportation network, fruit in season is now available nationwide, in big cities and hamlets alike.

In the Northeast the peak local apple season runs from August to December; pears and cranberries come in the fall, oranges, coconuts, and pineapples in the dead of winter, strawberries in the late spring, blueberries and melons in early summer, peaches in mid-summer, figs in late summer.

Other fruits, such as plums, nectarines, mangoes, and papayas, come twixt and between, just as ripe for the picking. All are perfectly simple for dessert.

Here is a handy guide:

A IS FOR APPLES: This fruit deserves to rise to the top of the class. A crisp apple offers a mouthful of juicy nutrients with every bite. No wonder that old adage about "one a day" keeps the good doc at bay.

Topping this goodness is the fact that most apples are naturally sweet, needing only a dusting of sugar when added to a fruit bowl or compote, or baked for a warming treat.

Commonly available eating apples are Empire, Macoun, McIntosh, Gala, Fuji, Braeburn, and Red and Golden Delicious. Cortland, Rome, Granny Smith, Ida Red, and yes, Golden Delicious, make boss baked apples.

The best tart cooking apples are Jonathan, Jonagold (a cross between tart Jonathan and mellow Golden Delicious), Granny Smith, and Greening. Sweetly tart varieties include Ida Red, Rome Beauty, and Cortland. Mutsu (also known as Crispin), McIntosh, Newton Pippin, and Golden Delicious offer a sweet flavor and cook well.

But there is also texture variation with all of these apples. For example, Mutsu or Crispin is sweet but very crispy, while Cortland has a sweet edge but is rather soft and tender, and Ida Red is tart and firm-fleshed.

When picking, whether for eating out of hand or for a fruit dessert, look for small, firm, crisp apples that are free from bruises and blemishes. Large apples can be overripe and mealy.

Handle gently to prevent bruising, and

Simple and Sweet: Fruit Desserts

243

refrigerate in the crisper section, away from strong-flavored foods. Apples stored at room temperature deteriorate quickly.

TOP BANANAS AND PLANTAINS: Give me a few ripe bananas with well-speckled brown peels, and I can have a delightful fruit dessert on the tables in minutes. Bananas combine well with other fruits such as berries, peaches, and plums, and the compote is absolutely delicious when tossed with a little rum or cream of coconut, such as Coco Lopez or Coco Goya. You can also turn bananas into a quick fruit sundae: sprinkle with brown crystallized sugar, top with ice cream or yogurt, and spoon over chocolate syrup and a sprinkling of nuts.

A banana known as the Cavendish is the main commercial variety, favored for exportation by growers because it doesn't bruise easily and is quite resistant to diseases. But there are many other varieties worth searching for in Latin and Asian markets, since they generally are full of flavor.

I particularly like the full-flavored red-peel bananas imported from Ecuador and Mexico. The dull red skin turns reddish purple or maroon when the banana is fully ripe, and the flesh is pinkish-orange and tasty.

I also like the finger-size succulent bananas imported from Mexico known as the Manzano or apple banana. They have both an apple-like and strawberry flavor, and although usually quite pricey, are truly delightful. These tiny bananas are best when the pale yellow skin is speckled with black, signaling peak ripeness.

Plantains are a starchy member of the banana family, often referred to as "potatoes of the air," or "cooking bananas," because they must be cooked before being eaten. You don't eat plantains raw.

Plantains are a staple crop in Africa and the Caribbean and in many Latin countries; in recent years they have become quite chichi in New York restaurants. They are delicious when sautéed in butter and sprinkled with a little sugar. A real simple dessert.

When buying, avoid mushy or bruised bananas or plantains, and store at room temperature in a cool place.

BERRY FINE: Strawberries start appearing at curbside markets in New York City in late spring, and I know then that the winter hawk has finally flown and summer is right around the corner. In a matter of weeks as the days lengthen and warm up, the fruit stands, farmers' markets and supermarkets also become crowded with little boxes of raspberries and blueberries, and occasionally, blackberries.

I love these sparkling jewels; they make luscious sweet treats, and often I will buy a box and eat the whole container out of hand, reveling in the fact that they are so low in calories and high in nutrients.

But berries can be quite fragile, so pay attention when you go picking. When buying, pick a clean, unstained box, and be sure to look at the bottom and the sides. If the box is juice-stained and moist, the berries inside are probably crushed and spoiled and moldy.

Berries are best eaten right way. Simply rinse off with cold water, drain, and enjoy. If you are using them later, store in the refrigerator but don't wash before putting in the fridge. Moisture causes most berries, especially blackberries and raspberries, to turn mushy and gather mold quickly.

If they are dry and clean, blueberries and strawberries should keep for 2 or 3 days; raspberries and blackberries for a day or two. But no berries ever linger uneaten in my refrigerator that long.

SWEET CITRUS: A while back, during the middle of July, I went into a local gourmet supermarket and found several bins of oranges imported from Australia. I bought a few, grated the peel to use in a buttermilk pie, and downed the juice and pulp on the spot. Real delicious. Then it occurred to me that it was the middle of winter in Australia. No wonder.

Although oranges grown in this country are available year-round, they are at their best during the winter when picked and shipped from Florida, Texas, and California, full of juice and sugar, promising sunshine and light.

There are many varieties: Temple, navel, Valencia, Thompson, and tangelo, actually a cross between a tangerine and a grapefruit; and increasingly popular, blood oranges, which have a dull red pulp and real sweet juice.

Another variety, the sour orange or Seville orange, was introduced into Spain by the Moors, and it is a bitter fruit that can't be eaten raw. It is delicious in pies, sorbet, and for making jelly or marmalade.

Citrus fruits are as indispensable in my kitchen as sugar. Orange and grapefruit sections add a bracing flavor to a fruit bowl. The peel of oranges, lemons, limes, tangerines, and grapefruit can be grated or candied, and the juice provide sour sweetness and a fragrant aroma.

When buying, look for plump, round citrus fruit that feel juicy and heavy. Avoid shriveled, blemished fruit since they are often dry and seedy and without flavor.

Once home, rinse the fruit and store in the refrigerator.

CRACKING COCONUTS: When I was a young child my father worked for years on the docks in Mobile, and he would often bring home on Friday evenings a bag of Brazil nuts and several coconuts, which I remember as a chore to crack, but so delightful when simply eaten out of hand, or turned into coconut cakes and pies—favorites in the Old South.

Years later during visits to Jamaica and elsewhere in the Caribbean, I learned that young coconuts have an emerald green, spongy covering that looks like a soccer ball, and not the identifying nubby, hard brown shell that I had seen all of my life. The flesh of young coconuts is soft and sweet, with a

Simple
and
Sweet:
Fruit
Desserts

245

gelatin-like texture, and is prized by local cooks for its exquisite flavor.

But coconuts don't ship well when young, and so they are sent to the United States when ripened: after a tough brown shell has formed and the interior meat has hardened into a thick white layer. Inside the coconut is a half cup of so of thin, sticky, sweet water or juice, which is often mistaken for coconut milk.

Actually, coconut milk is made from grated coconut pulp steeped in hot water, and strained to extract its essence and liquid. Both coconut milk and grated coconut add flavor and richness to a variety of desserts.

When buying a coconut, look for those without cracks or mold around the eyes—there are three—on the rounded end of the fruit.

To soften the coconut for easy cracking, place the whole coconut in a large metal bowl or pan and pour over a kettle of boiling water. Let sit for about 10 minutes.

Remove the coconut from the water, drain and dry, and wrap in a large kitchen towel. Sharply strike the coconut all over with a hammer or mallet. Keep doing this until the shell cracks, and hopefully, you can catch the water and pour it into a cup.

Discard the coconut water if desired, or drink on the spot as a tonic. My Jamaican friend, Norma Boucher, swears by the curative power of coconut water.

When I ask, "Cures what?" she responds: "Everything."

Once cracked, cut away both the woody coconut shell and the leathery brown layer covering the coconut meat with a small sharp knife.

To make the milk: Grate the coconut with a hand grater or cut into pieces and grate in a food processor. Then, using 1 cup of grated meat per 1 cup of boiling water for each cup of coconut milk, place the coconut and water in a blender (or food processor) and whirl for about 1 minute or process until the coconut is pulverized.

Allow the mixture to sit for about an hour and then strain through a large layer of cheesecloth, squeezing the pulp to extract all the milk. The milk will keep for a few days in the refrigerator in a tightly covered jar, or you can freeze it in a plastic container to use later.

Note: A good substitute for freshly grated coconut is dried unsweetened coconut, which is sold at health food stores, and increasingly, at supermarkets.

SEDUCTIVE FIGS: Legend has it that the asp that ended Sister Cleopatra's life was brought to her in a basket of figs—her favorite fruit. There was a fig tree in the biblical Garden of Eden, and it is said that the prophet Mohammed once exclaimed: "If I should wish a fruit brought to Paradise it would certainly be the fig."

I understand this hyperbolic passion: Figs are absolutely divine. When fully ripe and soft, they possess a nutty, syrupy sweetness and a creamy lush texture that is completely unlike any other fruit. But maybe I love this fruit because I was lucky enough to grow up with two fig trees right in my backyard.

Commercially available varieties range in color from pale green to amber to dark purple to black, each with its own nuanced flavor. The Calimyrna fig (the California version of the Smyrna fig—an import from Turkey) has a golden tender skin and a nutlike flavor. Mission figs run from deep purple to black and are great for eating out of hand. Green-skinned figs include both the Kadota, which has a creamy amber flesh when ripe, and the Adriatic, which turns golden when dried.

And in the South there are numerous other varieties, including the dark-skinned and delicious Brown Celeste and Beall figs, which may have been the pedigree of the trees in our backyard.

The largest crop of figs come to market in late summer and fall, produced primarily in California and Texas and with a smaller amount commercially available in Southern states.

Much of the Texas crop is canned, and in California, much of the fruit is dried and sent to market, offering another delectable natural dessert.

Try to buy fresh figs as ripe as possible. They may soften a little bit if spread out and held at room temperature for a few days, but not much.

MORE MANGOES: Back in the mid-1970s when I visited the Caribbean quite often, I would stuff myself with mangoes, hoping to get fully satiated with this delightful tropical fruit until my next visit. At peak ripeness a mango is rich and luscious, a lovely mélange of peach, apricot, and slightly pungent pineapple flavors. It is delicious eaten out of hand, mixed with other fruits in a compote, especially with grated coconut, or pureed with a little sugar and liqueur for an elegant fruit sauce.

But regardless of how much mango I ate during my Caribbean visit, soon after returning to New York City I would find myself yearning for more. So I would jump on the train and make the long trip out to Brooklyn in search of West Indian markets selling mangoes.

No more. Today, during the peak season from May to late fall, mangoes are sold across the country. When I was home in Choctaw County in Alabama last June, the fruit was piled up right next to the peaches and watermelons at the local Piggly Wiggly supermarket— unheard of during my childhood.

A madness for mangoes has developed in this country over the past twenty years, as consumers pursue the fruit with hot passion. The consumption has more than quadrupled over the past two decades, and growers in tropical countries such as Mexico, Haiti, Brazil, Ecuador, and the Philippines, have raced to meet the demand. Mangoes are also grown in Florida and California.

There are many varieties, such as Glenns, Hayden, Kent, and Tommy Atkins, but only the trained eye will know the difference. When choosing, look for orange-yellow skins that are well blushed with red, and as soft and ripe as possible.

But be on the lookout for mushy mangoes damaged in transit, which is quite common; these go off quickly. Underripe mangoes do ripen at room temperature, but once soft, refrigerate for safekeeping.

Mango, like a peach, is a clingstone fruit, meaning the flesh clings to the seed and must be cut away with a small sharp knife.

MARVELOUS MELONS: For years I thought the only way to eat watermelon was to cut off a hefty chilled wedge and sit on a front porch or stoop and enjoy. That was a favorite pastime during my childhood and I have vivid memories of the stories passed down during this summer ritual.

But I've learned to enjoy watermelon in other ways. Norma Boucher makes a delicious fruit cup of watermelon, mango, and fresh berries, which she tosses with a sprinkling of sugar and mint. And watermelon ice, sorbet, and ice cream are thirst quenching and delicious on a hot summer day.

Watermelon is an indigenous fruit of Southwest Africa and the Kalahari Desert. Sanskrit and early Egyptian records indicate that our ancestors were cultivating the fruit more than four thousand years ago. Botanically speaking, all melons, including watermelons, cantaloupes and honeydews, are gourds, members of the same family as cucumbers and squash. And for this reason, some botanists quibble and call them vegetables.

No matter; melons are simply perfect for fruit desserts. Cantaloupe and honeydew melons have a faint musky, fragrant aroma, and the rind runs from rough and netted to silky smooth. The flesh of cantaloupe is peach-salmon in color, while the honeydew has a pale green flesh. Combined chunks of cantaloupe, honeydew, and watermelon will give you a palette of colors and textures that pleases both the eyes and the taste buds.

When buying cantaloupe and honeydew melons look for heavy-feeling melons that are round and free of dents and blemishes. Then pick up the melon and smell it; the more fragrant, the sweeter it will be. These melons ripen at room temperature but will turn mushy if not refrigerated once fully ripe.

There are many varieties of watermelon on the market with enchanting names such as Sugar Baby, Crimson Sweet, Jubilee, and Charleston Gray— the most popular varieties.

Whenever possible, buy a whole melon, or ask the friendly grocer to cut a whole melon and sell you half. Wedges of watermelon left sitting in ice and water lose flavor and nutrients quickly. Watermelon is full of vitamins and you'll finish a half melon in a couple of days.

But if you have no choice in the matter and must buy pre-cut melon, avoid mealy, water-soaked wedges and look for crisp, red flesh instead.

When buying a whole watermelon, inspect it closely. Choose a firm, symmetrical, unblemished melon that has a heavy feel. Watermelon is 92 percent water and you should feel the weight; if not, the watermelon is probably dry and mealy.

Then check and make sure the watermelon is fully ripe, for it doesn't improve much in flavor and texture once picked. To determine ripeness, lift up the watermelon and look for the yellow belly, the spot where it rests on the ground. When a melon is fully ripe, the belly is no longer white but is actually butterscotch yellow. If the area is still white, pass up that melon.

You can also test a watermelon's ripeness by what my father used to call the old thump test. When you drum a melon with your fingers, like a thump to the chest, a fully ripe melon will have a hollow, resonant "punk" sound rather than "pink" or "pank."

You got that tune? Rap on!

PLUM CRAZY: By mid-August so many varieties of plums come to market in New York City that it is hard to keep track of names. I do know that most are juicy, sweet, and delicious, sporting a rainbow of colors, from green, yellow, and red to purple, deep blue, and black. And the sizes are just as varied: from as small as a cherry to as large as a tennis ball.

Dozens of varieties of plums were grown in the United States by Native Americans, and undoubtedly the trees at my family home in south Alabama in Choctaw County are an example. They were standing on a tract of wooded land that my father bought in the early 1950s,

weighted down with marble-size juicy red-streaked plums.

However, most of the cultivated plums grown in the country fall into three broad types: European, Damson, and Japanese, and each category provides ripe picking for both the fruit bowl and for cooking.

European plums were probably brought to the country by the Pilgrims, and one of the best known varieties is the greengage, which is also known as Reine Claude in France, its native country. The greengage is a green-yellow fruit with amber flesh and deep flavor; it is very juicy. It is an excellent dessert fruit and is also good for canning.

Another popular European variety is the Italian and French prune plum, which has a rather high sugar content and is ideal for drying into, well, prunes. But prune plums are equally delicious eaten fresh. They are oval in shape, with red-blue-purple skin, yellow-green flesh, and a distinctive rich flavor. They are also excellent for canning.

Damson plums are also known as mirabelles, and the best-known varieties in this category, surprisingly, bear the same names. Both the Damson and mirabelle are small tart plums that are best cooked with sugar and turned into jam or jelly.

Most of the plums grown in the United States today were developed from varieties brought to America in the 1880s from Japan, by the plant breeder Luther Burbank. And the most popular variety is the Santa Rosa, a large, round wine-red fruit with orange-yellow flesh. The Santa Rosa is excellent fresh or canned.

Other Japanese plums include the Elephant Heart, red-skinned plums that have watermelon-red flesh, and are especially good in tarts and compotes. The Shiro plum has thin yellow skin and is almost translucent, revealing the delightful flesh within. This plum is also delicious in compotes and sorbet.

Buy plump, juicy fresh plums that yield slightly when pressed gently. Avoid shriveled and blemished plums, a sure sign that their characteristic juice is long gone. And yes, plums do ripen off the vine. Let them sit at room temperature until soft to the touch and then refrigerate until ready to eat.

JUST PEACHY: Good-quality peaches start arriving at the city's farmers' markets in New York in mid-August, but that's a long wait from early May, when the season begins. Until that time I have to make do with thick-skinned, mealy supermarket peaches, which don't measure up to their moniker, the "queen" of fruit.

But at its best, this fruit is regal and just plain peachy: juicy, honey sweet; thin skin brushed with a little down, and a deep rich flavor with a subtle almond undertone.

At peak ripeness, the best way to enjoy peaches is to cut up and serve in a pretty glass bowl with a helping of berries, and if desired, a sprinkling of crystallized brown sugar—a perfect fruit dessert. And leave the skins on.

But of course, the "queen" is also famous for its pies and cobblers and shortcakes, and that old African-American favorite, peach ice cream. Peaches also make fine jam, jelly, and preserves, and when canned with brandy, a delightful topping for cakes or ice cream, or both (see recipe for Brandied Peaches, page 265).

Genetically, the only difference between peaches and nectarines is the lack of fuzz on nectarine skin. And like peaches, nectarines are often picked and shipped unripe, missing their characteristic mellow, syrupy flavor. But nectarines have a firmer flesh than peaches, and they do pick up flavor when baked (see Baked Nectarines in Tea Caramel, page 262).

Fragile, delicate, white-fleshed peaches are appearing more and more on the market, and they are exquisite. White peaches have a strawberry winelike flavor mingled with almond undertones. Serve a dish topped with slightly sweetened pureed raspberries or strawberries, and rejoice.

Peaches fall into two categories: clingstones, which have firm flesh clinging to the pit and are used primarily for canning, and freestones, a soft-textured fruit that separates easily from the pit.

There are hundreds of varieties, including such whimsical names as Georgia Belle, Crimson Lady, a stunning purplered peach from California, and Flamecrest, a large, firm, smooth-textured red and yellow fruit that is almost without fuzz. Peaches such as these are found at farmers' markets and road stands.

(California is the leading peach grower, followed by Georgia, the Peach State.)

But the peach that most of us pick at the supermarket is the old standby—Elberta, a sturdy, red-blushed freestone peach that has been cultivated for more than a hundred years. This peach travels well.

Peaches are best picked real ripe, since, unlike apples and pears and plums, they don't develop any sugar once plucked from the tree. They'll soften a little bit if left at room temperature for a day or so, but they won't develop flavor. And after more than a day sitting out, the peaches can turn mealy and mushy.

Color won't tell you much about the ripeness of a peach, but avoid those with even a hint of greenness. Remember also that a gorgeous-looking red or pink blushed peach can be hard as a rock, and unripened.

So look for peaches that are slightly soft at the stem end, and give off a floral aroma when you pick up and smell. They should smell ripe, sweet, and peachy.

Peaches are quite fragile and bruise easily; so handle gently and if they are fully ripe, refrigerate immediately.

PEAR-FECTION!: Like the apple, this shapely fruit is a member of the rose family, and at peak ripeness has a honeyed aroma that can bewitch your senses.

But unlike apples, pears are one of the unique fruits that ripen best off the tree. If allowed to ripen before they are har- vested, their smooth, delicate flesh often becomes hard and gritty and granular. And now I know why Mama would wrapp pear after pear in newspaper and stored them in the bottom of an old Empire Credenza, where they remained until juicy, sweet, and succulent—perfectly ripe.

Numerous varieties and extended growing seasons mean pears of all sizes and colors are available year-round today. But the season actually begins in late summer with the arrival of the Bartlett pear, a bell-shaped green pear that turns yellow, sweet, and fragrant when ripe. There is also a Red Bartlett that deepens in color when fully ripe.

But don't expect any other pear to change color; the Bartletts are the only variety that make this chameleon appearance.

The fall season brings sweet but firm Comice pears, russet-colored Bosc pears, and later on, spicy and firm-fleshed Anjou pears come to market.

My favorite pear is the delicious little bell-shaped Seckel, which at peak ripeness is sugar sweet—a fruit dessert in itself. I also like the small, yellow, crimson "freckled" Forelle pear that appears from time to time at local markets, but not often enough. It is sweet, juicy, and fragrant—a perfect slurping pear.

When buying, select pears that are free from bruises and cuts. If you plan to bake or cook the pears, select ones that are fairly firm; they'll hold shape better.

Don't shortchange a pear and eat it before it is fully ripe. Place in a paper bag at room temperature for a couple of days or store in a cool, dark place.

A ripe pear will yield when pressed gently at the stem end, and emit a sweet, roselike aroma.

PRINCELY PINEAPPLES: In many colonial houses and old Southern mansions you can still find gateposts, doorways, and tableware in the whimsical shape of the pineapple. And even today in the Caribbean a pineapple dangling in the doorway is a sign of welcome and hospitality.

In fact, no other fruit over the years has been more revered than this sweet, pungent fruit, which botantists believe is a native of what is now Brazil. Columbus stumbled upon the fruit in the Caribbean in 1493, took it back to Europe, and the pursuit for the visually stunning fruit that resembled a pine cone became the rage.

The pineapple is delectable when fully ripe; juicy and honeyed, with a firm-textured flesh that is often tangy, heady, and sweet at the same time. Peel, core, slice into rounds and grill with a sprinkling of sugar and rum, and you have a delightful dessert in minutes. When cut into chunks, it adds pizzazz to a fruit bowl or compote. And once crushed and cooked with sugar, it turns into the filling for the Pineapple Iced Cake (page 98) of the Old South.

To be fully appreciated, a pineapple must be savored when fully ripe. But for maximum sugar content, the fruit must be picked ripe. Once a pineapple is harvested, it doesn't ripen anymore. If left standing at room temperature for a few days the fruit will gradually turn yellow, but it won't increase in sugar content.

So choose carefully when buying. Look for a top (crown) with crisp, deep green leaves. Pick up the fruit; it should be heavy and plump. The larger the fruit, the greater the proportion of edible flesh.

Gently squeeze the pineapple; it should be slightly soft but not soft and mushy with rotten spots. Now sniff the fruit at the base. It should have a sweet, fragrant smell.

Avoid fruit that is bruised, discolored, has soft spots, a crown of dry leaves, is moldy, and has a fermented odor.

Pineapples harvested during the winter months from December to April are less sweet than the spring and summer harvests, even when picked fully ripe.

SIMPLE BOWLS OF FRUIT: DAZZLING DESSERTS

A very simple compote is simply one fruit simmered in an aromatic liquid, such as a pan of syrupy poached pears. But if you spoon the pears into a bowl, reduce the poaching liquid, and stir in chocolate, pears in chocolate sauce become Pears Noires, a showstopper. And if you cut up chunks of watermelon, honeydew, and cantaloupe, stir in a bowl with a generous dash of black currant liqueur, it's hard not to get all starry-eyed and think of the heavens.

Simple compotes can be made from one fruit or from a combination, and sometimes the fruit is gently cooked, but often it is not. And the fruits can be dried or fresh.

Typical example: Baked Nectarines in Tea Caramel (page 262) are poached gently in the oven. On the other hand, Norma Boucher mixes a sublime tropical fresh fruit mélange literally at table side.

Her home in Rochdale Village in Queens, New York, is a pretty setting: sleek floors, wraparound sofa, lovely mirrors, lots of plants, and living room walls lined with an art gallery's collection of photographs, all impeccably framed, starring you know who. There is Norma as a child in Jamaica in the West Indies, a cigarette between her fingers in a showbiz pose as a beautiful young woman in London, Norma on college graduation day, and most of all, as a reigning tennis player on the senior circuit in New York City: buffed, smiling, holding trophy after trophy.

A large dining table that easily seats ten is off the kitchen, and it is here that Norma sets out dish after dish of scrumptious down-home Jamaican food: shrimp or salmon laced with garlic, herbs, and hot peppers; rice and peas, jerk chicken, stewed oxtail, boiled yams, avocado and chayote salad. And all the while she is talking in a singsong voice that now has almost as much "American" accent as West Indian.

"I learned to cook just like I learned to play tennis," she says, laughing, "and I didn't start both until late in life. *Sports Illustrated* magazine referred to me as 'Grandma's on the varsity team.' I love that description. I played the number-one spot on the tennis team, and beat girls who weren't even half my age."

She clears the table; I offer to help, eyeing rum raisin ice cream, caramelized plantains, and a fruit compote bursting with sunshine and goodness, made with mango, pineapple, and ginger—staple ingredients in her native country.

"Every day I eat mangoes, papayas, or pineapples," she says, holding court, barefoot, dressed in a black dress with spaghetti strap top and a flaring skirt that is barely longer than one of Venus Williams's tennis outfits. "They are good for you. And I always cook with ginger, allspice, lemon or lime, and honey."

Gingered Tropical Fruits

This dessert is nourishing and delicious and dazzling, just like Norma.

3 large ripe mangoes	$1/2$ cup water
1 large ripe fresh pineapple	1 teaspoon vanilla extract
2 tablespoons lemon juice	Sugar-Crusted Cocoa Cookies (page
1 3-inch piece fresh ginger	30)
$1/4$ cup dark rum	Vanilla yogurt or whipped cream
$1/3$ to $1/2$ cup sugar	

Using a large sharp knife, peel the mangoes, stand them on a chopping board, cut into thick slices, and then dice, discarding the pit. Do this carefully; mangoes can be slippery. Place the fruit in a large, glass heatproof bowl.

Place the pineapple on the board and cut off the crown and a slice off the bottom crosswise. Stand the pineapple upright on the board and cut off the peel lengthwise. Remove the eyes with a small knife or a vegetable peeler.

Lay the fruit on the board, cut in half lengthwise, and cut out the core and discard. Cut each half crosswise into $1/2$-inch slices and then into 1-inch chunks.

Combine the pineapple chunks with the mango. Sprinkle over the lemon juice, mix well, and set aside. Peel the ginger and chop finely.

Combine in a medium saucepan the ginger, rum, sugar, and $1/2$ cup water. Bring to a boil, reduce the heat to medium, and cook the syrup for 8 to 10 minutes, or until thick and syrupy. Stir in the vanilla extract.

Pour the hot syrup over the fruit and mix well with a large spoon.

Chill and serve with Sugar-Crusted Cocoa Cookies. Or if desired, serve with vanilla yogurt or whipped cream.

Makes 6 servings

Variation: I also love this dessert with either watermelon and honey-dew melon. Substitute 1 small honeydew melon or $^1/_4$ of a whole water-melon for the pineapple. Cut the melon into 1-inch-square pieces and combine with the mangoes and the lemon juice and set aside. Combine the ginger, rum, sugar, and $^1/_2$ cup water. Follow the recipe directions for cooking. Add the vanilla extract. Cool the syrup and then pour over the fruit and mix well. Chill and serve.

Pears Noires (Chocolate Pears)

My beautiful niece Renee, who lives in Pacific Palisades near Los Angeles, sent me this elegant recipe that quickly became a favorite. Fresh pears are poached in a spicy, orange-infused sauce, and then topped with a silky chocolate sauce. So divine.

1 orange
1 cup granulated sugar
4 or 5 whole cloves or allspice berries
3 cups water
6 firm but ripe large pears with stems,
    preferably Anjou, Comice, or Bosc
    variety

2 tablespoons unsweetened cocoa
4 ounces bittersweet chocolate
½ teaspoon vanilla extract
2 tablespoons unsalted butter
Aunt Ella's Butter Cookies (page 27), if
    desired

Using a vegetable peeler, cut the peel from the orange in strips, avoiding the white pith, which is bitter. Then cut the peel into matchstick 1-inch strips.

In a large stainless steel saucepan or Dutch oven, combine the orange peel strips, sugar, cloves or allspice berries, and 3 cups water. Bring to a boil, stirring to dissolve the sugar.

Reduce the heat, cover, and simmer for 10 to 12 minutes.

Meanwhile, rinse the pears and cut away any blemishes. Leaving the stems intact, start at the top and peel the pears about three-fourths down. Cut a thin slice off the bottom of each pear so that they stand upright without tilting over.

Set the pears upright in the pot. Using a large spoon, ladle over the poaching liquid. Cover the pot.

Poach the pears for 15 to 20 minutes, or until tender throughout when pierced with a skewer, occasionally, ladling over the poaching syrup. (This can be done a couple days in advance and the pears can remain in the poaching liquid, in the refrigerator. For more flavor, lay the pears on their sides in the liquid and occasionally ladle over the poaching liquid.)

Remove the pears from the pan with a slotted spoon and set upright on a serving dish. Chill the pears.

Place the pan on medium-high heat and simmer the poaching liquid until it is reduced about one-half in volume and is thick and syrupy. You should have about $1^1/_2$ cups of cooking liquid; if you have more, boil it a little longer.

Remove the pan from the heat. Whisk in the cocoa and chocolate, beating until the mixture is smooth.

Set the pan over medium-low heat and whisk in the vanilla extract and butter. Cook 4 or 5 minutes, stirring, or until the sauce is heated through.

Pour the syrup through a fine strainer into a serving bowl. Cool the sauce to room temperature. The sauce should thicken to a honeylike consistency.

At serving, spoon the chocolate sauce over the chilled pears. If desired, serve with the cookies.

Makes 6 servings

Fresh Berry Compote

I made this dessert for Rubye Taylor-Drake when she flew into New York recently from Chicago for a board meeting of the United Negro College Fund.

Rubye wears many hats: trustee at Freedom Baptist Church in Chicago, college professor, UNCF volunteer, business owner, and hostess superb.

She and her handsome husband, Tommy, live in a beautiful home in Lockport, Illinois, that is a collector's delight. Rubye collects elephants—ceramic, porcelain, bronze, wood, name it and she has it—and Tommy collects crystal decanters for his beloved cognac.

When I was on the road with my first cookbook, Rubye, an old college pal, took time off from her busy schedule to shuttle me around the Windy City.

Rubye is also a fitness maven, but she had a second helping of this fruit compote, which brims with healthy fresh berries.

4 cups fresh berries, such as strawberries, blueberries, raspberries, or a mixture of berries
$1/3$ to $1/2$ cup honey
2 tablespoons fruit or honey liqueur

$1/2$ teaspoon ground allspice
1 cup nonfat vanilla yogurt
2 to 3 tablespoons granulated sugar or brown crystallized sugar (see Dark and Sweet, page 25)

Rinse the berries, discarding the stems and leaves. Reserve 1 cup of the berries to use as a sauce. Drain the remaining berries and place in a glass bowl. Chill, if desired.

In a medium saucepan, combine the reserved berries and the honey. Use a wooden spoon to crush the berries. Stir in the liqueur and allspice.

Place the pan on medium-high heat and bring to a gentle boil, stirring. Immediately reduce the heat to low and cook the mixture for 10 minutes, or until the sauce is thick and smooth, stirring often.

Remove the sauce from the heat. Pour the sauce through a strainer into the bowl of berries, pressing hard to extract all of the juice. Mix the berries and sauce, and chill for an hour, if desired. Top each serving with some vanilla yogurt; sprinkle with the sugar.

Makes 4 servings

Fruit Parfait

A dozen years ago Patricia Smith Prather, who lives in Houston, became concerned about preserving the important legacy of the African-American presence in Texas and set out to do something about it.

She scraped together modest funding from various sources, and before long she was writing and designing a monthly newsletter, the *Texas TrailBlazer,* which features the life and work of unsung African-Americans: schoolteachers, preachers, businessmen and -women, laborers, leaders. Fifty of the newsletters have been collated into a book, and it sits on a shelf in her office at her neat and orderly home in Houston, next to a book she wrote about Joshua Houston, an African-American who was a servant to the legendary Sam Houston.

Visiting with her is invigorating: good conversation, good friendship, and food that has the flavor of yesteryear.

"You can serve this fruit dessert with vanilla ice cream," she said to me over a delicious fruit cup, "but only if the ice cream is homemade."

You bet.

2 cups blueberries or blackberries
2 cups strawberries
3 large fresh peaches
2 or 3 ripe medium bananas
Juice of ½ large lemon
⅓ cup granulated or brown crystallized
   sugar, such as Sugar in the Raw
   (see Dark and Sweet, page 25)

½ teaspoon ground cinnamon or
   grated nutmeg or mace
½ cup water
2 tablespoons orange-flavored
   liqueur, such as Triple Sec or
   Grand Marnier
Vanilla Bean Ice Cream (page 216)

Rinse the fruit and drain. Remove the stems and leaves from the berries and discard. Peel the peaches and slice, discarding the pits and stems. Peel the bananas and cut into slanted crosswise slices. Place the fruit in a large glass bowl and set aside. Squeeze the lemon juice over the fruit and mix well. Set aside.

Meanwhile, in a small saucepan combine the sugar, cinnamon, nutmeg or mace, and ½ cup water. Bring to a boil, stirring, and cook over high heat 4 or 5 minutes or until the syrup thickens. Stir in the liqueur.

Remove the syrup from the heat and pour over the fruit, mixing well. Cool and then chill for 1 hour or longer.

At serving, fill six chilled large red wineglasses about one-fourth full with the chilled fruit. Top with a scoop of ice cream, and then ladle over more fruit and syrup.

Makes 6 servings

Dried Fruit Compote

I asked Ernest McCaleb, who owns and produces the aromatic, ambrosia-like honey wine, Sheba Te'j, to contribute a recipe for this book, and he came up with a fruit dessert. A perfect match. And since Ernest is a fine tennis player and part of Norma Boucher's network, I expected nothing less.

This bracing dried fruit compote is especially delightful on a cold winter evening. A plain butter cookie makes a nice partner.

1½ pounds dried fruits, a mixture of peaches, pears, apricots, and cherries, or your choice
1 large lemon or orange
1 teaspoon whole cloves or allspice berries
1 teaspoon grated nutmeg

⅓ cup honey
1½ cups honey wine, such as Sheba Te'j, or sweet sherry
1½ cups water
1 cup almonds, lightly toasted, if desired

Cut the dried peaches and pears in quarters and set aside with the apricots and cherries.

Using a vegetable peeler, cut the peel from the lemon or orange in strips, avoiding the white pith, which is bitter. Cut the peel into 1-inch strips.

Combine the citrus peel, cloves or allspice, nutmeg, honey, wine, and 1½ cups water in a large saucepan. Bring to a boil, stirring to dissolve the honey.

Add the dried fruit and simmer, covered, 15 to 20 minutes, or until just tender, stirring occasionally. Remove the fruit from the liquid with a slotted spoon and place in a serving dish.

Bring the liquid in the pot to a boil and cook over medium-high heat until it is thick and syrupy, about 5 to 7 minutes.

Pour the syrup through a strainer—over the fruit. Serve warm or at room temperature. Top with the nuts, if desired.

Makes 4 to 6 servings

Baked Nectarines in Tea Caramel

My nephew Joe, and his wife, Renee, live in Pacific Palisades, just a stone's throw from the ocean, and they are California physically fit and sophisticated.

Joe, a former professional football quarterback, is now a stockbroker, and gorgeous Renee is a real estate broker, and their young preteen son, Jalon, is a joy. They are loving and family-devoted, and I don't mind too much when they make me feel old and call me "Auntie Joyce."

So California cool, and so is this delicious recipe for baked nectarines, which are simmered in a caramel sauce made with black tea and ginger. If nectarines are unavailable, use the same amount of either fresh peaches or plums. Both are delectable.

1 cup boiling water
2 to 3 tablespoons black tea, such as Darjeeling, Ceylon, or Assam
1 teaspoon ground ginger
2 pounds ripe but firm nectarines (6 to 8)

1/3 cup light brown sugar, firmly packed
2 tablespoons unsalted butter
2 tablespoons brandy
Perfectly Whipped Cream (page 74)
Lemon Vanilla Wafers (page 13), if desired

Preheat the oven to 400 degrees.

Combine the boiling water, tea, and ginger in a teapot. Let sit to brew for at least 5 minutes.

Rinse the nectarines, drain and remove the stems. Don't peel the fruit. Cut into quarters, and discard the pits.

Generously butter a 1½-quart baking dish or a 10-inch skillet. Arrange the nectarines snugly in the pan, overlapping the fruit if necessary.

Pour the brewed tea through a strainer over the nectarines. Sprinkle on the sugar.

Cut the butter into small pieces and spread over the fruit.

Set the pan on the lower oven rack and bake the nectarines for 40 to 45 minutes or until they are lightly browned and tender when pierced with a fork, occasionally basting the fruit with the sauce.

Remove the pan from the oven and set on a wire rack. Using a slotted spoon, transfer the nectarines to a serving dish, pressing the fruit to remove as much liquid as possible.

Pour the sauce into a small saucepan and place on medium-high heat. Bring to a boil and cook rapidly for about 5 minutes, or until the sauce is as thick as honey, swirling the pan as the sauce cooks.

Stir in the brandy and pour the sauce over the nectarines.

Cool the nectarines and serve at room temperature or chill and serve.

Top each serving with a dab of whipped cream, and serve with Lemon Vanilla Wafers, if desired.

Makes 4 to 6 servings

I first met Frances Gordon more than two decades ago when I was a reporter for the *New York Daily News,* working in a suburban bureau. Frances was employed by a city agency in an adjacent office. We became friends; I was eventually transferred from that bureau, Frances changed jobs too and we lost contact.

Then one day, several years ago, I was crossing the street a few blocks from my apartment when Frances and I almost simultaneously faced off. We both started screaming, and I am sure passersby were wondering what in the world was wrong with those two women.

Frances has her own business now, makes dazzling designer T-shirts and jewelry, leads walking tours in Harlem, where she now lives, and after we stumbled into each other she came to visit, bringing vivid memories from long ago.

I cherish our reunion: It is mid-afternoon, summer. In short order I offer tea, cookies, light salad, bottled water.

She accepts only the water, sips daintily, and says, "Oh I am fine."

She is wearing a form-fitting black leotard, top and bottom, gold slippers, matching loop earrings, and her hair, which is a cross between an old-style afro and new-style twigs, is tinted the exact rose-purple color as her well-manicured nails, forming a bouffant circle around her unlined face—all zany and elegant at the same time.

I gaze at her, remembering that her daughter, Pearl, an only child, was in college when we first met. I try to do a little mental calculation but come up with zero, and finally decide that the gods have simply been kind to her.

We chat; about family, childhood, future plans. She tells me about her daily regimen and I am no longer baffled as to why she simply hasn't aged a day: daily walks, five to ten miles; early morning aerobics, lifts weights three times weekly; eats mostly steamed vegetables with garlic, a little fish and tofu, nuts for nibbling, especially almonds, which she loves, and fruits for dessert.

"But I do like to unwind at night with a glass of Lillet with a little twist of lemon," she says, referring to the French imported aperitif wine. "I am kind of picky about food but I like things French."

A light goes off in my head. I set out a bowl of Brandied Peaches (page 265) that I can every year when the fruit is in peak season—my summer passion. I sprinkle on toasted almonds, and offer a spoonful of ice cream, which she politely declines.

"My family is from Georgia," Frances says again, "and years ago my grandmother used to send us jars and jars of canned peaches and preserves during the summer. These peaches are delicious."

I exhale, pleased.

Brandied Peaches

I love these peaches mixed with fresh raspberries or blueberries and topped with vanilla ice cream, but they are a heady treat on their own.

They are pungent and full of spices, which add wonderful flavor to canned fruit, jams, and preserves, but after several months of storage they do impart a dark coloring to the produce. If you want canned fruit and preserves to remain crystal clear and jewel-like, place the spices in the center of a square of cheesecloth or thin white cotton and tie into a knot, making a spice bag. A 4- to 6-inch square of cloth is fine.

Cook the fruit with the spice bag and then remove the bag and discard before you pack the fruit in the canning jars.

The jars of peaches in this recipe are processed in boiling water to prevent spoilage during storage. And since it is easier to can fruit in small batches, do half of the recipe at a time.

5 pounds firm but ripe medium freestone peaches	1 teaspoon whole cloves
5 cups water	1 teaspoon ground ginger
5 cups granulated sugar, or to taste (see How Sweet It Is, page 277)	2 teaspoons cinnamon bark pieces (see Note, page 267)
	1 to 1¼ cups good-quality brandy

Select medium-size firm but fully ripe unblemished peaches that are free of bruises. Assemble at least 5 pint-size canning jars and sterilize the jars and all the canning utensils. Set aside a 4- or 5-quart heavy stainless steel pot (see Hot Stuff, page 274).

Place the peaches in the kitchen sink or basin. Bring a kettle of water to boil and pour over the peaches. Let the fruit remain in the hot water and then bring another kettle of water to boil. Drain the peaches, and pour over the second kettle of water. Drain the peaches right away.

Peel half the fruit, cutting way any blemishes. (The skin should pull off easily.) Remove the stems and discard.

Cut the fruit in half lengthwise and remove the pits. Save six pits to boil with the syrup and discard the rest. The pits impart an almond-like flavor to the syrup. Place the peaches in a glass bowl and set aside.

Make the syrup in two batches, using half the ingredients at a time: Combine in the large pot, 2½ cups water and 2½ cups sugar (or less if desired). Add three of the peach pits, $^1/_2$ teaspoon cloves, $^1/_2$ teaspoon ginger of the cloves, and 1 teaspoon cinnamon bark pieces. If desired, tie the peach pits and spices in a cheesecloth bag.

Bring the mixture to a boil, stirring with a wooden spoon until the sugar dissolves. Reduce the heat and simmer the syrup, uncovered, for 10 to 12 minutes or until slightly thickened.

Using the wooden spoon, add the peaches to the hot syrup, and stir to coat well. Raise the heat under the peaches and bring the syrup to a gentle boil, carefully turning over the fruit with the spoon.

Cook the peaches, turning occasionally, for 5 to 7 minutes or until tender but not too soft when pierced with a fork. Watch the fruit carefully and don't let it scorch.

Remove the peach pits; if using a spice bag, discard it. Then, spoon the peaches into the sterilized jars, using a funnel, filling about $^3/_4$ full. Press down the fruit lightly with the back of the spoon to release air bubbles and to make sure the peaches are packed quite tightly. The fruit will fill two pints jars. Spoon any remaining fruit into a third jar.

Place the slotted spoon over the mouth of the jars and drain the syrup back into the pot. Do this a couple of times.

Return the syrup to the heat and boil, stirring, until it is as thick as honey, for about 10 minutes. Remove from the heat and stir in half of the brandy.

Pour the syrup over the peaches, dividing evenly between the jars, leaving a generous $^1/_2$-inch headspace in each jar.

Insert a sterilized butter knife between the fruit and the jar to eliminate air bubbles, then gently stir the peaches to disperse the syrup. If more than $^1/_2$ inch headspace remains, add more syrup or brandy, but don't fill the jars to the top. (The headspace keeps the jars from cracking during the final processing.)

Prepare and can the remaining peaches in the same way. Wipe the mouth of the jars with a clean cloth dipped in hot water. Seal at once and screw or clamp on the bands and set aside. Process all the fruit for 20 minutes according to the directions on page 279.

Cool the fruit on a wire rack and then store the cooled peaches in a dark place. Refrigerate after opening.

Makes 4 to 5 pints

Note: If cinnamon bark is not available, use a generous teaspoonful of ground cinnamon

Variation: Nectarines, plums, pears, apricots, cherries, and cranberries can be canned in the same way as peaches, and good-quality bourbon can replace the brandy.

Berry Preserves Dessert Topping

The inspiration for this delicious fruit topping, and the rest of the canned fruit recipes, came from my friend Jeanne Lesem, a cookbook author, retired pioneering newspaper woman, and canning expert.

I met Jeanne almost three decades ago when she was the food editor at UPI, and I was an assistant food editor at the *New York Daily News.* And she was the one I reached out to—and still do—for canning tips and best procedures.

Her book on canning, *Preserving in Today's Kitchen* (Henry Holt), is a classic.

Now an octogenarian, Jeanne is as bouncy, feisty, and full of advice as ever.

"You can do so much with fruit preserves and jams and jellies," she says, still with an eastern Kansas twang after a half-century in New York City. "You can spoon it on ice cream for an instant dessert, or brush it on grilled fruits, such as pineapple or bananas, or on baked pears and apples and quince.

"Fruit preserves are delicious thinned with a little liqueur and used as a topping. And in the middle of the winter you can replace half of the sugar in a sorbet or sherbet recipe with homemade preserves or jelly or jam and have an instant summer flavor."

Talking breathlessly, as always, Jeanne was busy at work, making marmalade from fresh fruit she had frozen during the past summer.

"I'll thaw the fruit, can it up, and put up a couple jars to give as a Christmas gift," she says. "I am getting older now and have to do things in stages; the simple way."

This topping is simply delicious, and it does make a nice gift.

1 quart fresh strawberries (4 cups)	3 cups granulated sugar, or to taste
1 pint blueberries or raspberries (2 cups)	1 cup fresh orange juice
	1 teaspoon cardamom seeds, crushed

Assemble 5 half-pint canning jars and sterilize the jars and all the canning utensils. Set aside a 4- or 5-quart heavy stainless steel pot (see Hot Stuff, page 274).

Rinse the fruit and discard the stems and the leaves from the strawberries. Cut the strawberries into $1/4$-inch slices. Place the fruit in a glass bowl and set aside.

Combine the sugar and orange juice in the canning pot. Crush the cardamom seeds in a coffee grinder or with a rolling pin. Place in the center of a 4-inch square of cheesecloth or other thin white cloth. Tie tightly into a knot, making a bag. Add the bag of spice to the canning pot.

Place the pot on the heat and bring the mixture to a boil, stirring constantly until the sugar dissolves. Boil the syrup for 2 minutes, stirring frequently.

Stir in the berries and boil for 3 more minutes. Reduce the heat to medium and cook the berries and syrup, stirring often, 15 to 20 minutes, or until the syrup is as thick as honey and shows resistance when stirred.

Remove the pot from the heat. Discard the spice bag. Carefully ladle the fruit into the hot jars, using a funnel if available, leaving 1/2-inch headspace in each jar. Wipe the rim of the jars with a clean damp cloth. Seal the jars at once and place on the screw bands.

Process for 10 minutes (see directions, page 279).

For best flavor, allow the preserve topping to remain in the jars for two or three weeks to develop flavor.

Makes 5 half-pints

Apple-Pear Preserves

Take a pan of baked apples or pears out of the oven and brush with this preserve and you have deep flavor right away, and a delectable fruit dessert. Or, spread on bananas or fresh pineapple slices and broil until caramelized and delicious. Spoon on a waffle, add a dab of whipped cream, and you have another delicious dessert.

Hint: Quick-cooking apples with a firm but not hard flesh are best for making preserves. Good choices are Jonagold, Golden Delicious, or Ida Red. Save the hard-textured apples, such as Greening and Granny Smith, for apple pie.

Fresh figs are also delectable in this recipe. They can replace the pears, or you can make the recipe using all figs.

2½ pounds firm apples (6 to 8) (see A Is for Apples, page 243)

1½ pounds ripe but firm pears, (3 to 4) preferably the Bosc variety

½ large lemon

1½ cups water

3½ cups granulated sugar, or to taste

½ cup mild-flavored honey, such as clover or tupelo

1 to 1½ teaspoons ground allspice or cinnamon

2 teaspoons grated lemon or orange peel

Assemble 6 half-pint canning jars and sterilize the jars and all the canning utensils. Set aside a 4- or 5-quart heavy stainless steel pot (see Hot Stuff, page 274).

Wash the apples and pears and discard the stems. Using a stainless steel knife, peel the fruit, core and coarsely dice. Place in a large glass bowl. Squeeze over the lemon, mix well, and set aside.

Combine in the pot 1½ cups of water, the sugar, honey, allspice or cinnamon, and grated lemon or orange peel. Bring to a boil and cook the syrup for 3 minutes, stirring to dissolve the sugar.

Stir in the apples and pears. Reduce the heat and cook the fruit over medium heat for 20 to 30 minutes, stirring often, or until the fruit is tender, clear, and translucent, and the syrup is the consistency of very thick honey. The fruit and syrup mixture should show resistance when stirred.

Pack the cooked fruit into the hot sterilized canning jars, using a funnel if available. Wipe the rim of the jars with a clean damp cloth. Seal the jars at once and place on the screw bands.

Process the fruit for 10 minutes according to directions, page 279.

Makes 5 to 6 half-pints

Peach or Plum Preserves

Every summer I send a couple jars of these preserves to my friend Shirley Brown out in Farmington Hills, Michigan, and as soon as she receives my care package she calls and says: "Girl, these are too pretty to eat. When are you coming out so that I can have an excuse to open them up."

I don't need an excuse to open a jar of these preserves, especially during the winter when summer is a distant memory. They are delightful spread on a baked apple or pear or quince tart, providing shine and shimmer as bright as sunlight.

In the fall of the year I brush fresh figs with the preserves and set the pan under a hot broiler for a few minutes, for a simple dessert in no time.

And during the holidays when I go into my marathon baking mode, I always pray that I have a jar or two of these preserves left to use as a filling in an old down-home favorite: Coconut-Peach Cake (page 85).

$2\frac{1}{2}$ pounds fresh peaches or plums
4 or 5 whole cloves or allspice berries
$2\frac{1}{2}$ to 3 cups granulated sugar
1 cup water

$\frac{1}{2}$ teaspoon almond or vanilla extract
2 tablespoons almond liqueur, such as
   Amaretto

Assemble 4 half-pint canning jars and sterilize the jars and all the canning utensils. Set aside a 4- or 5-quart heavy stainless steel pot (see Hot Stuff, page 274).

Select medium-size firm but fully ripe unblemished peaches or plums that are free of bruises. Place the fruit in the kitchen sink or basin. Bring a kettle of water to boil and pour over the fruit. Let the fruit remain in the hot water and then bring another kettle of water to boil. Drain the fruit and pour over the second kettle of water. Drain the fruit right away.

Peel the fruit with a stainless steel knife, cutting away any blemishes. (The skin should pull off easily.) Remove the stems and discard.

Cut the fruit in half lengthwise and remove the pits. If using peaches, save 3 of the pits to boil with the syrup and discard the rest. The pits impart an almond-like flavor to the syrup.

If desired, tie the cloves or allspice berries and the pits into a 5- or 6-inch square of cheesecloth or other thin white cloth and tie into a knot, making a spice bag for easy removal.

Coarsely chop the fruit and set aside in a large glass mixing bowl. You should have at least 5 cups peaches or plums.

Combine the sugar, cloves or allspice berries, and $1^1/_2$ cups water in the large pot. Bring to a rolling boil, stirring with a wooden spoon. Boil for 2 minutes.

Add the peaches or plums and cook over high heat for 15 to 20 minutes, or until the fruit is clear and translucent and tender, and the syrup is thick and honey-like. Stir in the almond or vanilla extract and liqueur and mix well.

If using the spice bag, remove and discard. If using peaches, remove the pits.

Using a funnel, pack the fruit into the hot sterilized jars, leaving a $^1/_2$-inch headspace in all jars.

Seal the jars at once and place on the screw rings.

Process the preserves for 10 minutes, according to directions on page 279.

Makes about 4 half-pints

Hot Stuff Use canning jars that are free of cracks, nicks, and chips to prevent air from seeping into the jar and spoiling the canned fruit. Always sterilize an extra canning jar because the yield will vary with the sugar and juice content of the fruit. You will also need a large, deep canning pot for sterilizing all the equipment, preferably made of enamel.

There are many canning pots on the market, but any large pot fitted with a metal rack or steaming rack that holds the jars at least $1/2$ inch above the bottom of the vessel so that they don't crack is fine. A round cake cooling rack is ideal. Years ago canners simply folded a heavy towel two or three times, placed it on the bottom of the canning pot, and set the jars on the towel. A canning funnel is sold in most hardware and housewares stores, and this is handy for filling the jars with the fruit.

Also have available a large wooden spoon, a stainless steel paring knife, a slotted spoon, a butter knife, a pair of tongs, and a heavy 4- or 5-quart stainless steel pot to cook the fruit and a pair of heavy mittens to use to transport the canned fruit from the canning pot to the cooling rack.

First, scrub the cooking pot with hot soapy water, then with baking soda, rinse well, and then scald with boiling water. Rinse a large mixing bowl and the canning funnel with boiling water.

Then, wash the jars, lids, and screw bands in hot soapy water and rinse well. Place the jars upright on the rack in the pot, along with the wooden spoon, paring knife, slotted spoon, butter knife, and tongs.

Fill the jars and the pan with water and cover the pot. Set the pot on high heat, bring to a boil, and sterilize the utensils on medium-high for 10 to 15 minutes. Reduce the heat to low and leave the jars and other equipment in the hot water until you are ready to fill them with the fruit.

Place the lids inside the screw bands and set in a large skillet, rings upward. Cover with water, insert an instant read thermometer, and bring the water to 180 to 190 degrees. Remove the skillet from the heat, with the screw bands and lids inside the pan. (If you boil the lids, you run the risk of destroying the gumlike sealant.)

Avoid touching the mouths of the jars—or any of the equipment—when removing from the hot water, and do not invert the jars to drain. Use the tongs to transport the lids and screw bands. ❧

Pear and Plum Crisp

A while back I scooted in to say hello to Louise McCrae, and on my way out she pushed at me several tomatoes, a head of lettuce, a couple cucumbers, and a handful of mint, all of which she had grown in her urban garden in a city park in Harlem.

Louise is a retired dietitian, but it seems to me that she is busy as ever. Besides tending a garden, she quilts, makes exquisite calendars and all kinds of decorative mobiles, using "junk" such as wood skewers, rings from a six-pack of beer or soda, plastic credit cards.

She glues and sprays her found objects with paint, and carries many to the Friendship Baptist Church in Harlem, where she teaches an arts and crafts class.

She is also a meticulous cook, and watches calories so closely that I had to call and ask if I could sprinkle a couple tablespoons of sugar on her delectable fruit crisp.

"Ever since I was a little girl I have been careful about what I eat," says Louise, who is age seventy-five plus. "When I go back home (Nathalie, Virginia, near Lynchburg) for my high school reunion, my classmates say I haven't gained a pound over the years."

No wonder. I made this healthy crisp with plums and pears, but a combination of blueberries and nectarines is also delicious.

3 large plums, either red or black	$\frac{1}{2}$ teaspoon ground cinnamon
3 large pears, preferably the Bosc or Comice variety	$\frac{1}{2}$ teaspoon ground allspice
	1 tablespoon lemon juice
4 tablespoons unsalted butter	$1\frac{1}{2}$ cups fresh bread crumbs, made from firm white bread
$\frac{1}{3}$ cup maple syrup or honey, such as wildflower	1 to 2 tablespoons sugar

Preheat the oven to 350 degrees.

Rinse and drain the fruit but don't peel. Remove the stems and cut the fruit into halves. Remove the pits and seeds, core the pears, and then cut the fruit into $\frac{1}{4}$-inch-thick slices lengthwise.

With some of the butter, generously grease a $1\frac{1}{2}$-quart baking dish. Arrange the fruit slices over the bottom of the dish, beginning with the pears, overlapping pieces if necessary.

Combine in a small bowl the syrup or honey, cinnamon, allspice, and lemon juice. Mix well, spoon the syrup mixture over the fruit, and spread evenly with a spatula. Cut 1 tablespoon of the butter into small pieces and scatter over the fruit. Set the dish aside.

Place the remaining butter in a small saucepan. Melt the butter over low heat and remove from the heat right away. Stir in the bread crumbs and toss lightly with a fork.

Scatter the buttered crumbs over the fruit. Sprinkle on the sugar.

Set the dish on the lower oven rack and bake 40 to 50 minutes, or until the fruit is tender and the topping is lightly browned.

Remove the dish from the oven and cool on a wire rack until warm, or cool completely and chill.

Serve either warm or chilled with whipped cream or ice cream, if desired.

Makes 6 servings

How Sweet It Is

A primary ingredient in canning sweet things is the canning syrup, which is made when you mix sugar and water or some other liquid, such as juice or wine.

The ratio of sugar to liquid determines whether the canned fruit is light and delectable, or candy-sweet and delicious, and how much you use is really up to you. The syrup itself is delightful for spooning over bread pudding, ice cream, rice pudding, melon wedges, or grilled fruits, such as bananas or pineapples.

The canning syrup is also the basis of jellies, jams, and preserves. And again, the amount of sugar to use depends on the sweetness of the fresh fruit and your personal taste. I allow $^1/_2$ to $^3/_4$ cup sugar for every cup of fruit when I make preserves and jams, varying the amount according to the condition of the fruit at hand.

Fruit that is sugar sweet, free of blemishes, in peak season, and full of juice requires less sugar than fruit that is not at its best.

Note: Since I prefer preserves and jams that are soft and slurpy rather than solidly jelled, none of the recipes here uses commercial pectin, a thickener extracted from fruit. But you can add pectin, if you like, following the package directions.

In the Brandied Peaches recipe I used a heavy syrup, mixing 1 cup of sugar and 1 cup of water for every pound of fruit. Actually, I prefer a medium sauce, which would have required half that amount of sugar, but Norma Boucher was standing over my shoulder saying, "I want my peaches real sweet and full of liquor."

Make your own sweet choice. Here is a guideline:

LIGHT . . . 1 cup sugar to 3 cups liquid

MEDIUM . . . 1 cup sugar to 2 cups liquid

HEAVY . . . 1 cup sugar to 1 cup liquid

EXTRA-HEAVY . . . 2 cups sugar to 1 cup liquid ❀

Sugared Plantains

I love plantains in any form or fashion, but when they are sautéed until golden and then sprinkled with sugar, rum, and allspice, this member of the banana family is really tops.

Norma Boucher makes these caramelized plantains because she knows that her best friend, James (Jimmy) Fonsville, loves the dish. And so do I. So succulent and delicious.

4 large ripe plantains, with black-speckled skin, about 2½ pounds
¼ cup granulated or light brown sugar, firmly packed
1 teaspoon allspice, or to taste

4 to 6 tablespoons unsalted butter
¼ cup pineapple or orange juice
2 tablespoons dark rum
Perfectly Whipped Cream (page 74)

Trim off the ends of the plantains and then cut a thin strip from the tip of each fruit to the bottom. Insert your fingers into the slit and loosen the fruit from the peel, rotating the plantain as you move from top to bottom.

Lift each fruit from the peel and cut crosswise but on the bias or slant, into ¼-inch-thick slices.

Mix together the sugar and allspice and set aside.

Heat half of the butter in a large, heavy skillet, preferably cast iron. Add half of the plantains and sauté over medium-low heat until lightly brown, about 5 to 7 minutes, turning often with a metal spatula. (Watch carefully; they can burn quickly.)

Remove the browned plantains from the pan, and sauté the remaining plantains in the same way.

Return all the plantains to the pan. Pour over the juice. Sprinkle with the sugar-spice mixture and the rum. Reduce the heat to low and cook the fruit 5 minutes, or until the sugar is melted and caramelized, turning the plantains often and shaking the pan.

Serve warm or at room temperature, topped with whipped cream.

Makes 6 servings

Processed Fruits canned in syrup have a high water content and should be processed in boiling water to prevent spoilage. But it is not absolutely necessary to process preserves, marmalades, and jams, since they aren't made with very much water, and have such a high sugar content that spoilage is rare.

But I always do, especially when sending through the mail as gifts. I envision mailrooms, chutes, and transporting trucks with soaring temperatures, and thoughts that these precious jewels could "go off" during transit have me saying, "Better safe than sorry."

Here's how to process: Place a rack in a large canning pot and set the pot on a burner. Spread a tea towel over the rack so that the jars don't tilt over or bump into each other. Set the canned jars of fruit in the pot on the rack, making sure they don't touch each other or the sides of the container.

Add enough water to cover the jars by 2 inches or more. Caution: The water must cover the jars to keep them from cracking or exploding during the processing.

Cover the pot with a lid and bring the water to a full boil. As soon as you see the pot steaming, start counting and boil the canned fruit for 20 minutes more for pint jars or 10 minutes for half-pints.

Spread a towel under a wire rack. Remove the jars from the hot water with tongs and a pot holder and set on the rack. Allow to cool. The lid of a sealed jar will appear slightly sunken in the middle.

Remove the screw bands and try to open the lids with your fingertips. If you can't, a jar is properly sealed. If not, reprocess the jar or store it in the refrigerator for immediate use. ❀

Index

lemon juice:

    in angel pie, 130–32

    in orange tea cake variation, 71–73

lemon liqueur, in lemon meringue pie, 111–12

lemon vanilla wafers, 13–14

    in baked nectarines in tea caramel, 262–63

    in new banana pudding, 159–60

lime juice, in lemon meringue pie variation, 111–12

Limoncello, in lemon meringue pie, 111–12

liqueur parfait, 231

Liquori di Limoni, in lemon meringue pie, 111–12

mace, in spicy molasses pecan pie, 148–49

McIntosh apples, in candied apples, 202–3

mangoes:

    in fresh fruit sauce, 55

    in gingered tropical fruits, 254–55

    selecting of, 247–48

maple syrup:

in crunchy vanilla bean ice cream, 216–17

in pear and plum crisp, 275–76

marmalade:

    canning and processing of, 274, 279

    orange, in strawberry-apricot topping, 175

measuring cups and spoons, 3

meringue pie, lemon, 111–12

milk shake, banana, 233

mint:

    in brandied peach float, 232

    in fresh fig and plum compote with honey cream, 241–42

mixers, 1

molasses, dark, in gingersnaps, 36–37

molasses, light:

    in butternut squash pie, 146–47

    in spicy molasses pecan pie, 148–49

molasses lace cookies, 15–16

    in banana peanut caramel sundae, 227

mortars and pestles, 4

muscovado sugar, 25

    in chocolate cinnamon ice cream, 224–25

nectarines:

    baked, in tea caramel, 262–63

    in brandied peaches variation, 265–67

    in fresh fruit sauce, 55

    selecting of, 250–51

    in summer peach pie and cobbler variation, 136–38

new banana pudding, 159–60

nonpareils:

    cake decorating with, 91

    in kiddie delight vanilla bean ice cream, 216–18

    nut brittle, 190–91

    in pecan brittle cherry sundae, 229

nut(s), nutty:

    brittle, 190–91

    butter cookies, 29

    candy, brown sugar, 206–7

    chopped, decorating cakes with, 91

    chopping of, 1

    cinnamon cookies, 21–22

    storing of, 5

    toasting of, 49

    see also specific nuts

nut brown glaze, 70

    in short'nin' bread cookies variation, 40–41

nutmeg:

    in apple-cranberry pie, 139–40

nutmeg: *(cont.)*
  in buttermilk ginger cake with fresh fruit
    sauce, 53–55
  in dried fruit compote, 261
  grating of, 4
  in raisin-rice pudding with caramel
    threads, 170–71
  in spicy molasses pecan pie, 148–49
  in spicy vanilla bean ice cream, 216–17
  in summer peach pie, 136–37

oatmeal cookies, rum raisin, 17–18
one-pan cakes, 56–81
orange(s):
  buttermilk pie, 122–23
  in dried fruit compote, 261
  in pears noires (chocolate pears), 256–57
  peel, candied, *see* candied orange peel
  selecting of, 245
  tea cake, 71–73
orange-flavored liqueur, 231
  in fruit parfait, 259–60
  in orange tea cake, 71–73
  in strawberry-apricot topping, 175
  see also Cointreau; Grand Marnier;
    Triple Sec
orange juice:
  in berry preserves dessert topping,
    268–69
  in orange buttermilk pie, 122–23
  in orange tea cake, 71–73
  sour, *see* sour orange juice
  in sugared plantains, 278
  in sweet potato praline pie variation,
    143–45
orange marmalade, in strawberry-apricot
  topping, 175
Oreo spiced sugar, 45
oven thermometers, 2–3

pans, baking, 1–2
papayas, in fresh fruit sauce, 55
parchment paper, 5
parfait:
  fruit, 259–60
  liqueur, 230
partially or fully baked single pie or tart
    crust, 117–18
pastry:
  bags and tubes, 5
  brushes, 5
  clothes, 5
peach(es):
  brandied, *see* brandied peach(es)
  cobbler, 137–38
  -coconut cake, 85–88
  in fresh fruit sauce, 55
  in fruit parfait, 259–60
  pie, summer, 136–37
  selecting of, 250–51
  star anise ice cream, 221–23
peaches, dried:
  in dried fruit compote, 261
  in fruity butter cookies, 29
  in pineapple iced cake, 98–101
peach preserves, 272–73
  in coconut-peach cake, 85–88
peach schnapps:
  in brandied peach float variation, 232
  in coconut-peach cake, 85–88
peanut(s):
  banana caramel sundae, 227
  brittle, 190–91
  in candied apples, 202–3
  -chocolate cookies, Kwanza, 19–20
  in devil's food cake pie, 152–53
pear(s):
  -apple preserves, 270–71
  in brandied peaches variation, 264–65